RETIREMENT ISSUES, PLANS AND LIFESTYLES

RETIREMENT SAVINGS AND SECURITY

SELECTED ELEMENTS AND CONSIDERATIONS

RETIREMENT ISSUES, PLANS AND LIFESTYLES

Additional books in this series can be found on Nova's website under the Series tab.

Additional E-books in this series can be found on Nova's website under the E-book tab.

RETIREMENT ISSUES, PLANS AND LIFESTYLES

RETIREMENT SAVINGS AND SECURITY

SELECTED ELEMENTS AND CONSIDERATIONS

LINDA A. EISTERHOLD
EDITOR

nova publishers
New York

For permission to use material from this book please contact us:
Telephone 631-231-7269; Fax 631-231-8175
Web Site: http://www.novapublishers.com

Library of Congress Cataloging-in-Publication Data

ISBN: 978-1-62948-132-6

Published by Nova Science Publishers, Inc. † New York

CONTENTS

PREFACE

This book provides an overview of select elements and considerations of retirement savings and security with a focus on Social Security financing and benefits under current law; eligibility requirements, contribution limits, tax deductibility of contributions, and rules for withdrawing funds from traditional and Roth Individual Retirement accounts (IRAs); 401(k) plans and retirement savings; Federal Employees' Retirement System benefits and financing and the role of the Thrift Savings Plan; and the benefits, risks and regulations of annuities with guaranteed lifetime withdrawals.

Chapter 1 - The Social Security program began in the 1930s and has been modified by Congress many times over the past seven decades. Today, Social Security provides monthly cash benefits to retired or disabled workers and their family members, and to the family members of deceased workers. Among the beneficiary population, approximately 80% are retired or disabled workers, and 20% are the family members of retired, disabled, or deceased workers. In April 2013, 57.3 million Social Security beneficiaries received a total of $66 billion in benefit payments for the month.

Workers become eligible for Social Security benefits for themselves and their family members by working in Social Security-covered employment. An estimated 94% of workers in paid employment or self-employment are covered, and their earnings are subject to the Social Security payroll tax. In 2013, employers and employees each pay 6.2% of covered earnings, up to the annual limit on taxable earnings ($113,700 in 2013).

To be eligible for a Social Security retired-worker benefit, a person generally needs at least 40 earnings credits, or 10 years of Social Security-covered employment (among other requirements). Fewer earnings credits are needed for a disabled-worker benefit, depending on the worker's age. A worker's initial monthly benefit is based on his or her career-average earnings in covered employment. Social Security retired-worker benefits are first payable at the age of 62, subject to a permanent reduction for early retirement. Full (or unreduced) retirement benefits are first payable at the full retirement age (FRA), which is increasing gradually from 65 to 67 under a law enacted by Congress in 1983. The FRA will reach 67 for persons born in 1960 or later (i.e., persons who become eligible for retirement benefits at the age of 62 in 2022 or later). In addition to payroll taxes, Social Security is financed by federal income taxes that some beneficiaries pay on a portion of their benefits and by interest income that is earned on the Treasury securities held by the Social Security trust funds. In 2012, the Social Security trust funds had receipts totaling \$840 billion, expenditures totaling \$786 billion, and accumulated assets (in the form of Treasury securities) totaling \$2.7 trillion. Projections by the Social Security Board of Trustees show that, based on the program's current financing and benefit structure, benefits scheduled under current law can be paid in full and on time until 2033. The projections also show that Social Security expenditures will exceed income by about 20% on average over the next 75 years. Restoring long-range trust fund solvency and other policy objectives have made Social Security reform an issue of ongoing congressional interest and debate.

This report is designed to provide an overview of Social Security financing and benefits under current law. Specifically, the report covers the origins and a brief history of the program; Social Security financing and the status of the trust funds; how Social Security benefits are computed; the types of Social Security benefits available to workers and their family members; the basic eligibility requirements for each type of benefit; the scheduled increase in the Social Security retirement age enacted in 1983; and the federal income taxation of Social Security benefits.

Chapter 2 - In response to concerns over the adequacy of retirement savings, Congress has created incentives to encourage individuals to save more for retirement through a variety of retirement plans. Some retirement plans are employer-sponsored, such as 401(k) plans, and others are established by individual employees, such as Individual Retirement Accounts (IRAs).

This report describes the primary features of two common retirement savings accounts that are available to individuals. Although the accounts have many features in common, they differ in some very important aspects. Both traditional and Roth IRAs offer tax incentives to encourage individuals to save for retirement. Contributions to traditional IRAs may be tax-deductible for taxpayers who (1) are not covered by a retirement plan at their place of employment or (2) have income below specified limits. Contributions to Roth

IRAs are not tax-deductible and eligibility is limited to those with incomes under specified limits. The tax treatment of distributions from traditional and Roth IRAs differs. Distributions from traditional IRAs are generally included in taxable income whereas distributions from Roth IRAs are not included in taxable income. Some distributions may be subject to an additional 10% tax penalty, unless the distribution is for a reason specified in the Internal Revenue Code (for example, distributions from IRAs after the individual is age 59 1/2 or older are not subject to the early withdrawal penalty). Individuals may rollover eligible distributions from other retirement accounts (such as an account balance from a 401(k) plans upon leaving an employer) into IRAs. Rollovers preserve retirement savings by allowing investment earnings on the funds in the retirement accounts to accrue on a tax-deferred, in the case of traditional IRAs, or a tax-free basis, in the case of Roth IRAs.

The Retirement Savings Contribution Credit (also known as the Saver's Credit) is a nonrefundable tax credit of up to $1,000. It was authorized in 2001 to encourage retirement savings among individuals with income under specified limits. The report explains the eligibility requirements, contribution limits, tax deductibility of contributions, and rules for withdrawing funds from the accounts. It also describes the Saver's Credit and provisions enacted after the Gulf of Mexico hurricanes in 2005 and the Midwestern storms in 2008 to exempt distributions to those affected by the disasters from the 10% early withdrawal penalty.

Chapter 3 - Current law provides many incentives to promote saving. The goal of these provisions is to increase saving for special purposes such as education or retirement, and to increase national saving. Increased national saving can lead to faster wealth and capital accumulation, which can boost future national income. An increasingly important retirement saving vehicle is the individual retirement account (IRA). IRA savings is encouraged by two mechanisms—a carrot approach and a stick approach. First, tax provisions allow individuals to defer taxes on IRA contributions and investment earnings or to accumulate investment earnings tax free. Second, withdrawals before the age of 591/2 are generally subject to a 10% penalty tax in addition to regular taxes.

There are two types of IRAs: the traditional IRA and the Roth IRA. The traditional IRA allows for the tax-deferred accumulation of investment earnings, and some individuals are eligible to make tax-deductible contributions to their traditional IRAs while other individuals are not. Some or all distributions from traditional IRAs are taxed at retirement. In contrast, contributions to Roth IRAs are not tax deductible, but distributions from Roth

IRAs are not taxed on withdrawal in retirement. Expanded contribution limits were adopted in 2001, but were scheduled to expire after 2010; the Pension Protection Act of 2006 made those increases permanent.

In November 2005, President Bush's Advisory Panel on Federal Tax Reform proposed changes to IRAs. The panel's plan would have created Save for Retirement Accounts (SRAs) to replace traditional and Roth IRAs. Additionally, President Bush proposed consolidating IRAs into a Roth-style retirement savings account. The Obama Administration appears to be taking a different tack by proposing additional incentives to increase saving by low- and moderate-income workers in existing retirement saving accounts that have proven effective in evaluations. Neither conventional economic theory nor the empirical evidence on savings effects tends to support the argument that increased IRA contributions are primarily new savings—often increased retirement saving comes at the expense of reduced nonretirement saving. Roth-style accounts are less likely to induce new private savings than are traditional ones. Furthermore, these proposals would predominantly benefit higher-income individuals and families, who are the ones most likely to save without the added incentive. Proposals that increase retirement saving among low- and moderate-income workers could be effective in increasing new saving because these workers typically have little or no nonretirement saving to reduce.

Chapter 4 - Over the past 25 years, defined contribution (DC) plans—including 401(k) plans—have become the most prevalent form of employer-sponsored retirement plan in the United States. The majority of assets held in these plans are invested in stocks and stock mutual funds, and the decline in the major stock market indices in 2008 greatly reduced the value of many families' retirement savings. The effect of stock market volatility on families' retirement savings is just one issue of concern to Congress with respect to defined contribution retirement plans.

This report describes seven major policy issues with respect to defined contribution plans:

1. *Access to employer-sponsored retirement plans.* In 2007, only 61% of employees in the private sector were offered a retirement plan of any kind at work. Fifty-five percent were offered a DC plan. Only 45% of workers at establishments with fewer than 100 employees were offered a retirement plan of any kind in 2007. Forty-two percent were offered a defined contribution plan.

2. *Participation in employer-sponsored plans.* Between 20% and 25% of workers whose employer offers a DC plan do not participate. Workers under age 35 are less likely than older workers to participate.
3. *Contribution rates.* On average, participants in DC plans contributed 6% of pay to the plan in 2007. The median contribution by household heads who participated in a DC plan in 2007 was $3,360. This was just 22% of the maximum allowable contribution of $15,500 in that year.
4. *Investment choices.* At year-end 2007, 78% of all DC plan assets were invested in stocks and stock mutual funds. This ratio varied little by age, indicating that many workers nearing retirement were heavily invested in stocks and risked substantial losses in a market downturn like that in 2008. Investment education and target date funds could help workers make better investment decisions.
5. *Fee disclosure.* Retirement plans contract with service providers to provide investment management, record-keeping, and other services. There can be many service providers, each charging a fee that is ultimately paid by participants in 401(k) plans. The arrangements through which service providers are compensated can be very complicated and fees are often not clearly disclosed.
6. *Leakage from retirement savings.* Pre-retirement withdrawals from retirement accounts are sometimes called "leakages." Current law represents a compromise between limiting leakages from retirement accounts and allowing people to have access to their retirement funds in times of great need. In general, borrowing from a 401(k) plan poses less risk to retirement security than a withdrawal. Pre-retirement withdrawals can have adverse long-term effects on retirement income.
7. *Converting retirement savings into income.* Retirees face many financial risks, including living longer than they expected, investment losses, inflation, and possible large expenses for medical care and long-term care. Annuities can protect retirees from some of these risks, but few retirees purchase them. Developing polices that motivate retirees to convert assets into a reliable source of income will be a continuing challenge for Congress and other policymakers.

Chapter 5 - Most civilian federal employees who were hired before 1984 are covered by the Civil Service Retirement System (CSRS). Federal employees hired in 1984 or later are covered by the Federal Employees' Retirement System (FERS). Both CSRS and FERS require participants to contribute toward the cost of their pensions through a payroll tax. Employees who are covered by CSRS contribute 7.0% of pay to the Civil Service Retirement and Disability Fund (CSRDF). They do not pay Social Security taxes or earn Social Security benefits. Employees enrolled in FERS and first hired before 2013 contribute 0.8% of their pay to the CSRDF. Employees enrolled in FERS and first hired in 2013 or later contribute 3.1% of pay to the CSRDF. All employees enrolled in FERS contribute 6.2% of wages up to the Social Security taxable wage base ($113,700 in 2013) to the Social Security trust fund.

The minimum retirement age (MRA) under CSRS is 55 for workers who have at least 30 years of service. The FERS MRA was 55 for employees born before 1948. The MRA for employees born between 1953 and 1964 is 56, increasing to the age of 57 for those born in 1970 or later. Both FERS and CSRS allow retirement with an unreduced pension at the age of 60 for employees with 20 or more years of service and at the age of 62 for employees with at least 5 years of service.

The Thrift Savings Plan (TSP) is a retirement savings plan similar to the 401(k) plans provided by many employers in the private sector. In 2013, employees covered under either CSRS or FERS can contribute up to $17,500 to the TSP. Employees aged 50 and older can contribute an additional $5,500 to the TSP. Employees under FERS receive employer matching contributions of up to 5% of pay from the federal agency by which they are employed. Federal workers covered by CSRS also can contribute to the TSP, but they receive no matching contributions from their employing agencies.

The Office of Personnel Management (OPM) estimates the cost of CSRS to be an amount equal to 26.0% of employee pay. The federal government pays 19.0% of this amount and the other 7.0% is paid by employees. OPM estimates the cost of the FERS basic annuity at an amount equal to 12.7% of pay. For FERS employees first hired before 2013, the federal government contributes 11.9% of this amount and the other 0.8% is paid by employees. For FERS employees first hired in 2013 or later, the federal government contributes 9.6% of this amount and employees pay the remaining 3.1%. There are three other employer costs for employees under FERS. Both the employer and employee pay Social Security taxes equal to 6.2% of pay up to the maximum taxable amount; agencies automatically contribute an amount equal to 1% of employee pay to the TSP; and agencies make matching contributions to the TSP equal to up to 4% of pay.

At the start of FY2011, the CSRDF had an unfunded liability of $622.3 billion, consisting of a $634.5 billion deficit for CSRS and a $12.2 billion surplus for FERS. Although the civil service trust fund has an unfunded liability, it is not in danger of becoming insolvent. OPM projects that the balance of the CSRDF will continue to grow through at least 2080, at which point it will hold assets equal to more than 4.7 times total payroll and about 20 times total annual benefit payments.

Chapter 6 - Federal employees participate in one of two retirement systems. The Civil Service Retirement System (CSRS) was established in 1920 and covers only employees hired before 1984. Participants in the CSRS do not pay Social Security payroll taxes and they do not earn Social Security benefits. For a worker retiring after 30 years of federal service, a CSRS annuity will be equal to 56.25% of the average of his or her highest three consecutive years of basic pay. The Social Security Amendments of 1983 (P.L. 98-21) required federal employees hired after 1983 to participate in Social Security. Because the CSRS was not designed to coordinate with Social Security, Congress directed the development of a new retirement plan for federal workers hired after 1983. The result was the Federal Employees' Retirement System (FERS) Act of 1986 (P.L. 99-335). The FERS has three elements: (1) Social Security, (2) the FERS basic retirement annuity and FERS supplement, and (3) the Thrift Savings Plan (TSP). The amount of the FERS basic retirement annuity is determined by three factors: (1) the salary base, (2) the accrual rate, and (3) years of service. The salary base is the average of the worker's highest three consecutive years of pay. Under FERS, the benefit accrual rate is 1.0% per year of service, or 1.1% for workers retiring at the age of 62 or later with 20 or more years of service. A worker with 30 years of service retiring at the age of 62 will receive a FERS pension equal to 33% of the average of his or her highest three consecutive years of pay, or about 32% of final annual salary. The TSP is a defined contribution retirement plan similar to the 401(k) plans provided by many employers in the private sector. The income that a retired worker receives from the TSP will depend on the balance in his or her account. In 2013, employees covered by FERS or CSRS can contribute up to $17,500 to the TSP. Employees aged 50 or older can contribute an additional $5,500. Contributions of up to 5% of pay made by workers under FERS are matched by the federal government. Workers covered by CSRS can contribute to the TSP, but they receive no matching contributions.

The TSP is a key element of the FERS, especially for workers at the upper ranges of the federal pay scale. The Social Security benefit formula is designed to replace a greater share of income for low-wage workers than for high-wage workers. The FERS basic annuity will replace about 32% of final salary for an employee retiring at the age of 62 with 30 years of service. Higher-wage federal workers need to contribute a greater percentage of pay to the TSP to reach the same level of income replacement as lower-paid workers can achieve from just the FERS retirement annuity and Social Security. At an annual rate of return of 6.0%, income from the TSP can replace about 33% of final pay for a federal employee who contributes 10% of pay over 30 years.

Chapter 7 - Report of The United States Government Accountability Office on Retirement Security: Annuities with Guaranteed Lifetime Withdrawals Have Both Benefits and Risks, but Regulation Varies across States, dated December 2012.

In: Retirement Savings and Security
Editor: Linda A. Eisterhold ISBN: 978-1-62948-132-6

Chapter 1

SOCIAL SECURITY PRIMER*

Dawn Nuschler

SUMMARY

The Social Security program began in the 1930s and has been modified by Congress many times over the past seven decades. Today, Social Security provides monthly cash benefits to retired or disabled workers and their family members, and to the family members of deceased workers. Among the beneficiary population, approximately 80% are retired or disabled workers, and 20% are the family members of retired, disabled, or deceased workers. In April 2013, 57.3 million Social Security beneficiaries received a total of $66 billion in benefit payments for the month.

Workers become eligible for Social Security benefits for themselves and their family members by working in Social Security-covered employment. An estimated 94% of workers in paid employment or self-employment are covered, and their earnings are subject to the Social Security payroll tax. In 2013, employers and employees each pay 6.2% of covered earnings, up to the annual limit on taxable earnings ($113,700 in 2013).

To be eligible for a Social Security retired-worker benefit, a person generally needs at least 40 earnings credits, or 10 years of Social Security-covered employment (among other requirements). Fewer

* This is an edited, reformatted and augmented version of a Congressional Research Service publication, CRS Report for Congress R42035, prepared for Members and Committees of Congress, from www.crs.gov, dated June 17, 2013.

earnings credits are needed for a disabled-worker benefit, depending on the worker's age. A worker's initial monthly benefit is based on his or her career-average earnings in covered employment. Social Security retired-worker benefits are first payable at the age of 62, subject to a permanent reduction for early retirement. Full (or unreduced) retirement benefits are first payable at the full retirement age (FRA), which is increasing gradually from 65 to 67 under a law enacted by Congress in 1983. The FRA will reach 67 for persons born in 1960 or later (i.e., persons who become eligible for retirement benefits at the age of 62 in 2022 or later).

In addition to payroll taxes, Social Security is financed by federal income taxes that some beneficiaries pay on a portion of their benefits and by interest income that is earned on the Treasury securities held by the Social Security trust funds. In 2012, the Social Security trust funds had receipts totaling $840 billion, expenditures totaling $786 billion, and accumulated assets (in the form of Treasury securities) totaling $2.7 trillion. Projections by the Social Security Board of Trustees show that, based on the program's current financing and benefit structure, benefits scheduled under current law can be paid in full and on time until 2033. The projections also show that Social Security expenditures will exceed income by about 20% on average over the next 75 years. Restoring long-range trust fund solvency and other policy objectives have made Social Security reform an issue of ongoing congressional interest and debate.

This report is designed to provide an overview of Social Security financing and benefits under current law. Specifically, the report covers the origins and a brief history of the program; Social Security financing and the status of the trust funds; how Social Security benefits are computed; the types of Social Security benefits available to workers and their family members; the basic eligibility requirements for each type of benefit; the scheduled increase in the Social Security retirement age enacted in 1983; and the federal income taxation of Social Security benefits.

INTRODUCTION

Social Security is a self-financed program that provides monthly cash benefits to retired or disabled workers and their family members and to the family members of deceased workers. As of April 2013, there were 57.3 million Social Security beneficiaries. Of those, 40.1 million (70.0%) were retired workers and family members, 11.0 million (19.1%) were disabled workers and family members, and 6.3 million (10.9%) were survivors of deceased workers.[1]

Social Security is financed by payroll taxes paid by covered workers and their employers. An estimated 160.6 million workers are covered by Social Security.[2] In 2013, employers and employees each pay 6.2% of covered earnings, up to the annual limit on taxable earnings ($113,700 in 2013);[3] self-employed individuals pay 12.4% of net self-employment income, up to the annual limit ($113,700 in 2013).[4] Social Security is also credited with tax revenues from the federal income taxes paid by some beneficiaries on a portion of their benefits. In addition, Social Security receives interest income from Social Security trust fund investments. Social Security income and outgo are accounted for in two separate trust funds authorized under Title II of the Social Security Act: the Federal Old-Age and Survivors Insurance (OASI) trust fund and the Federal Disability Insurance (DI) trust fund.[5] In 2012, the combined Social Security trust funds (OASDI) had total receipts of $840 billion, total expenditures of $786 billion, and accumulated holdings (assets) of $2.7 trillion.[6]

ORIGINS AND BRIEF HISTORY OF SOCIAL SECURITY

Title II of the original Social Security Act of 1935[7] established a national plan designed to provide economic security for the nation's workers. The system of Old-Age Insurance it created provided benefits to individuals who were aged 65 or older and who had "earned" retirement benefits through work in jobs covered by the system. Benefits were to be financed by a payroll tax paid by employees and their employers on wages up to a base amount ($3,000 per year at the time). Monthly benefits were to be based on cumulative wages in covered jobs. The law related the amount of the benefit to the amount of a worker's wages covered by the program, but the formula was progressive. That is, the formula was weighted to replace a larger share of the earnings of low-wage workers compared with those of higher-wage workers. Before the Old-Age Insurance program was in full operation, the Social Security Amendments of 1939[8] shifted the emphasis of Social Security from protection of the individual worker to protection of the family by extending monthly cash benefits to the dependents and survivors of workers. The program now provided Old-Age and Survivors Insurance (OASI).

During the decades that followed, changes to the Social Security program were mainly ones of expansion. Coverage of workers became nearly universal (the largest groups remaining outside the system are state and local government employees who have not chosen to join the system and federal employees who were hired before 1984). In 1956, Congress established the Disability Insurance (DI) program.[9] Over the years, there were increases in the payroll tax rate, which increased from 2.0% of pay (1.0% each for employees and employers) in the 1937-1949 period to its current level of 12.4%.[10] In addition, there were increases in the amount of wages subject to the payroll tax (the taxable wage base), which increased from $3,000 in the 1937-1950 period to its current level of $113,700.[11] The types of individuals eligible for benefits were expanded over the years,[12] and benefit levels were increased periodically. In 1972, legislation provided for automatic cost-of-living adjustments, starting in 1975, indexed to the change in consumer prices as measured by the Consumer Price Index for Urban Wage Earners and Clerical Workers (CPI-W) published by the Department of Labor's Bureau of Labor Statistics.[13]

Beginning in the late 1970s, legislative action regarding Social Security became more concentrated on solving persistent financing problems. Legislation enacted in 1977 raised taxes and curtailed future benefit growth in an effort to shore up the system's finances.[14] Still, in 1982, the OASI trust fund needed to borrow assets from the DI trust fund and the Medicare Hospital Insurance (HI) trust fund (borrowed amounts were fully repaid by 1986). In 1983, Congress passed additional major legislation that was projected to restore solvency to the Social Security system *on average* over the 75-year projection period at that time.[15]

Current projections by the Social Security Board of Trustees show that the Social Security system has a long-range funding shortfall and that the system will operate with annual cash-flow deficits each year through the end of the 75-year projection period (2087). These projections, and other factors, have focused attention on potential Social Security program changes.[16]

SOCIAL SECURITY FINANCING

The Social Security program is financed primarily by revenues from Federal Insurance Contributions Act (FICA) taxes and Self Employment Contributions Act (SECA) taxes. FICA taxes are paid by both employers and employees, but it is employers who remit the taxes to the U.S. Treasury. Employers remit FICA taxes on a regular basis throughout the year (e.g., weekly, monthly, quarterly, or annually), depending on the employer's level of total employment taxes (Social Security, Medicare, and federal individual income tax withholding).

The FICA tax rate of 7.65% each for employers and employees has two components: 6.2% for Social Security and 1.45% for Medicare HI.[17] Under current law, employers and employees each pay 6.2% of covered wages, up to the taxable wage base, in Social Security payroll taxes. The SECA tax rate is 15.3% for self-employed individuals, with 12.4% for Social Security and 2.9% for Medicare HI. Self-employed individuals pay 12.4% of net self-employment income, up to the taxable wage base, in Social Security payroll taxes. One-half of the SECA taxes are allowed as a deduction for federal income tax purposes.[18] SECA taxes are normally paid once a year as part of filing an annual individual income tax return.[19]

In addition to Social Security payroll taxes, the Social Security program has two other sources of income. First, certain Social Security beneficiaries must include a portion of Social Security benefits in taxable income for the federal income tax, and the Social Security program receives part of those taxes.[20] Second, the Social Security program receives interest from the U.S. Treasury on its investments in special U.S. government obligations.

As the Managing Trustee of the Social Security trust funds, the Secretary of the Treasury is required by law to invest Social Security revenues in interest-bearing federal government securities held by the trust funds.[21] The revenues exchanged for the federal government securities are deposited into the general fund of the U.S. Treasury and are indistinguishable from revenues in the general fund that come from other sources. Because the assets held by the trust funds are federal government securities, the trust fund balance represents the amount of money owed to the Social Security trust funds by the general fund of the U.S. Treasury. Funds needed to pay Social Security benefits and administrative expenses come from the redemption of federal government securities held by the trust funds.[22]

Taxation of Social Security Benefits

Since 1984, Social Security benefits have been subject to the federal income tax. First, as part of the Social Security Amendments of 1983 (P.L. 98-21), Congress made up to 50% of a person's Social Security benefits subject to the federal income tax if he or she has modified adjusted gross income (AGI) above a specified threshold ($25,000 for an individual tax filer and $32,000 for a married couple filing jointly). Modified AGI is defined as the total income from all sources recognized for tax purposes plus certain otherwise tax-exempt income, including half of Social Security benefits. Tax revenues from this "first tier" of taxation are credited to the Social Security trust funds. In 2012, the trust funds received $27.3 billion (3.2% of total trust fund income) from this provision.[23]

Second, as part of the Omnibus Budget Reconciliation Act of 1993 (P.L. 103-66), Congress made up to 85% of a person's Social Security benefits subject to the federal income tax if he or she has modified AGI above a second higher threshold ($34,000 for an individual tax filer and $44,000 for a married couple filing jointly). Tax revenues from this "second tier" of taxation are credited to the Medicare HI trust fund. In 2012, the HI trust fund received $18.6 billion (7.7% of total trust fund income) from this provision.[24]

The income thresholds are fixed under current law (i.e., they are not adjusted for inflation or wage growth), so that over time an increasing number of beneficiaries will be subject to the federal income tax on benefits. According to the Congressional Budget Office, in 2005, 16.9 million Social Security beneficiaries (39%) were affected by the income taxation of Social Security benefits.[25]

STATUS OF THE SOCIAL SECURITY TRUST FUNDS

Projections by the Social Security Board of Trustees (the trustees) show that Social Security expenditures will exceed *tax revenues* each year through the end of the 75-year valuation period (2087).[26] That is, Social Security will operate with annual *cash-flow deficits*. When interest income to the trust funds is taken into account, Social Security is projected to have a *total surplus* (tax revenues plus interest income will exceed expenditures) each year through 2020. The trustees project that the trust funds will have a positive balance until 2033, and Social Security benefits scheduled under current law can be paid in full and on time until then (until the accumulated assets held by the trust funds are exhausted). Although the trust funds are projected to have a positive balance until 2033 on a *combined basis*, the OASI trust fund is projected to be exhausted in 2035, and the DI trust fund is projected to be exhausted in 2016. Under current law, DI benefits could not be paid in full and on time following DI trust fund exhaustion in 2016. The trustees state, "the DI Trust Fund reserves become depleted in 2016, at which time continuing income to the DI Trust Fund would be sufficient to pay 80 percent of DI benefits. Therefore, legislative action is needed as soon as possible to address the DI program's financial imbalance. In the absence of a long-term solution, lawmakers could choose to reallocate a portion of the payroll tax rate between OASI and DI, as they did in 1994."[27]

Over the long run, the trustees project that Social Security expenditures will exceed income by about 20% *on average* over the next 75 years. Social Security's projected long-range funding shortfall is attributed primarily to demographic factors (such as lower fertility rates and increasing life expectancy) and program design features (such as a wage-indexed benefit formula and annual COLAs).[28]

At the end of 2012, the trust funds were credited with accumulated assets of $2.7 trillion. The trustees project that the trust fund balance will continue to grow over the next several years due to interest income, peaking at $2.9 trillion in current dollars ($2.4 trillion in constant 2013 dollars) at the end of 2020. Beginning in 2021, Social Security expenditures will exceed total income (tax revenues plus interest income) and the trust fund balance will begin to decline, until the accumulated trust fund assets are exhausted in 2033.

After trust fund exhaustion, the program would continue to operate with incoming Social Security receipts that are projected to be sufficient to pay 77% of benefits scheduled under current law in 2033 and 72% of scheduled benefits in 2087. Social Security does not have authority to borrow from the general fund of the Treasury. Therefore, the program cannot simply draw upon general revenues to make up the difference between incoming receipts and benefit payments when the program no longer has accumulated assets to draw upon. The Social Security Act does not state what would happen to the payment of benefits scheduled under current law in the event of Social Security trust fund exhaustion. Two possible scenarios are (1) the payment of full monthly benefits on a delayed schedule, or (2) the payment of partial (reduced) monthly benefits on time.[29]

Social Security Cash-Flow Surpluses and Deficits

From 1984 to 2009, Social Security generated surplus tax revenues (i.e., the program operated with annual cash-flow surpluses). Surplus tax revenues and interest income credited to the trust funds in the form of federal government securities contributed to a growing trust fund balance. Surplus Social Security tax revenues totaled $1.21 trillion (in current dollars) from 1984 to 2009. Beginning in 2010, however, the program began operating with annual cash-flow deficits, and the trustees project that Social Security tax revenues will remain below program expenditures each year throughout the 75-year projection period (2013-2087).

When Social Security operates with a cash-flow deficit, the trust funds redeem more federal securities than the amount of current Social Security tax revenues, relying in part on accumulated trust fund assets to pay benefits and administrative expenses. Because the federal securities held by the trust funds are redeemed with general revenues, this results in increased spending for Social Security from the general fund. When there are no surplus governmental receipts, the federal government must raise the necessary funds by increasing taxes or other income; reducing other spending; borrowing from the public; or some combination of these measures.

With respect to the program's reliance on general revenues, it is important to note that the program is relying on revenues collected for Social Security purposes in previous years that were used by the federal government at the time for other (non-Social Security) spending needs and interest income earned on trust fund investments. The program draws on those previously collected Social Security tax revenues and interest income when current Social Security tax revenues fall below current program expenditures.

SOCIAL SECURITY REFORM DEBATE

Social Security reform is an issue of ongoing interest to policymakers. For some advocates of reform, the focus is on restoring long-range solvency to the trust funds. For others, the focus is on constraining the projected growth in spending for entitlement programs—including Social Security, Medicare, and Medicaid—in the context of broader efforts to reduce growing federal budget deficits. The Social Security reform debate reflects other policy objectives as well, such as improving the adequacy and equity of benefits, and different philosophical views about the role of the Social Security program and the federal government in providing retirement income. The debate reflects two fundamentally different approaches to reform. The *traditional approach* would maintain the current structure of the program (i.e., a defined benefit system funded on a pay-as-you-go basis) by making relatively modest changes, such as an increase in the retirement age or an increase in the taxable wage base. Generally, the goal of this approach is to preserve the social insurance nature of the program. In contrast, the *personal savings and investment approach* would redesign the 1930s-era program to create a pre-funded system in which benefits would be based partially or entirely on personal savings and investments.[30]

Social Security Benefit Rules

Social Security provides monthly cash benefits to retired or disabled workers and to the family members of retired, disabled, or deceased workers. The computation of a worker's primary insurance amount (PIA) is based on his or her earnings record in Social Security-covered employment. The worker's PIA is the initial monthly benefit amount payable at the full retirement age (i.e., before any adjustments for early or delayed retirement). Benefits paid to the family members of a worker are based on a percentage of the worker's PIA. The eligibility requirements for each category of benefits differ, as described below.

Full Retirement Age

Social Security retirement benefits are first payable to retired workers at the age of 62, subject to a permanent reduction for early retirement. The age at which full (or unreduced) retirement benefits are first payable is the full retirement age (FRA).[31] For most of the program's history, the FRA was 65. As part of the Social Security Amendments of 1983 (P.L. 98-21), Congress raised the FRA from 65 to 67. The 1983 law established a gradual phase-in from 65 to 67 over a 22-year period (2000 to 2022).

Specifically, persons born in 1938 or later are affected by the increase in the FRA (i.e., persons who become eligible for retirement benefits at age 62 in 2000 or later). The increase in the FRA will be fully phased-in for persons born in 1960 or later (i.e., persons who become eligible for retirement benefits at age 62 in 2022 or later). *Table 1* shows the scheduled increase in the FRA being phased-in under current law.[32]

Computation of a Social Security Retired-Worker Benefit

To be eligible for a Social Security retired-worker benefit, a person generally needs a minimum of 40 earnings credits, or 10 years of Social Security-covered employment (among other requirements).[33]

Table 1. Increase in the Full Retirement Age Scheduled Under Current Law

Year of Birth	Full Retirement Age
1938	65 and 2 months
1939	65 and 4 months
1940	65 and 6 months
1941	65 and 8 months
1942	65 and 10 months
1943 to 1954	66
1955	66 and 2 months
1956	66 and 4 months
1957	66 and 6 months
1958	66 and 8 months
1959	66 and 10 months
1960 or later	67

Source: SSA, 2013 Social Security/SSI/Medicare Information, February 28, 2013, available at http://www.socialsecurity.gov/legislation/2013factsheet.pdf.

A worker's initial monthly benefit is based on his or her 35 highest years of earnings, which are indexed to historical wage growth (earnings through age 60 are indexed; earnings thereafter are counted at nominal value). The 35 highest years of indexed earnings are divided by 35 to determine the worker's career-average annual earnings. The resulting amount is divided by 12 to determine the worker's average indexed monthly earnings (AIME). If a worker has fewer than 35 years of earnings in covered employment, years of no earnings are entered as zeros in the computation, resulting in a lower AIME and therefore a lower monthly benefit.

The worker's PIA is determined by applying a formula to the AIME as shown in *Table 2*. First, the AIME is sectioned into three brackets (or segments) of earnings, which are divided by dollar amounts known as bend points. In 2013, the bend points are $791 and $4,768.[34] Three progressive replacement factors—90%, 32%, and 15%—are applied to the three brackets of AIME.[35] The three products derived from multiplying each replacement factor and bracket of AIME are added together. For workers who become eligible for retirement benefits (i.e., those who attain age 62), become disabled, or die in 2013, the PIA is determined as shown in the example in *Table 2*.

Table 2. Computation of a Worker's Primary Insurance Amount (PIA) in 2013 Based on an Illustrative AIME of $5,000

		PIA for Worker with an
Factors	Three Brackets of AIME	Illustrative AIME of $5,000
90%	first $791 of AIME, plus	$711.90
32%	AIME over $791 and through $4,768, plus	$1,272.60
15%	AIME over $4,768	$34.80
Total: Worker's PIA		$2,019.30

Source: Congressional Research Service.

A worker's PIA increases each year from the year of eligibility (at age 62) to the year of benefit receipt based on the Social Security COLA. In addition, Social Security benefits already in payment increase each year based on the COLA.[36]

Adjustments to Benefits Claimed Before or After the FRA

A worker's initial monthly benefit is equal to his or her PIA if he or she begins receiving benefits at the FRA. A worker's initial monthly benefit will be *less* than his or her PIA if he or she begins receiving benefits *before* the FRA, and it will be *greater* than his or her PIA if he or she begins receiving benefits *after* the FRA.

A retired-worker benefit is payable as early as the age of 62, however, the benefit will be permanently reduced to reflect the longer expected period of benefit receipt. Retirement benefits are reduced by five-ninths of 1% (or 0.0056) of the worker's PIA for each month of entitlement before the FRA up to 36 months, for a reduction of about 6.7% a year. For each month of benefit entitlement before the FRA in excess of 36 months, retirement benefits are reduced by five-twelfths of 1% (or 0.0042), for a reduction of 5% a year.

Workers who delay filing for benefits until after the FRA receive a delayed retirement credit (DRC). The DRC applies beginning with the month the worker attains the FRA and ending with the month before he or she attains the age of 70. Starting in 1990, the DRC increased until it reached 8% per year for workers born in 1943 or later (i.e., starting with those who attained age 62 in 2005 or age 66 in 2009).

The actuarial adjustment to benefits claimed before or after the FRA is intended to provide the worker with roughly the same total lifetime benefits, regardless of the age at which he or she begins receiving benefits. Therefore, if a worker claims benefits before the FRA, his or her monthly benefit is reduced to take into account the longer expected period of benefit receipt. For a worker whose FRA is 66, the decision to claim benefits at the age of 62 results in a 25% reduction in his or her PIA. For a worker whose FRA is 67, the decision to claim benefits at the age of 62 results in a 30% reduction in his or her PIA. Similarly, if a worker claims benefits after the FRA, his or her monthly benefit is increased to take into account the shorter expected period of benefit receipt.

Other Adjustments to Benefits (Including GPO and WEP)

Other adjustments to benefits may apply, such as those related to simultaneous entitlement to more than one type of Social Security benefit. Under the dual entitlement rule, a Social Security spousal benefit is reduced if the person is receiving a Social Security retired-worker benefit. Under the government pension offset (GPO), a Social Security spousal benefit is reduced if the spousal beneficiary is receiving a pension from work that was not covered by Social Security (a non-covered pension).[37] Under the windfall elimination provision (WEP), the Social Security benefit formula is modified to reduce benefits for a worker beneficiary who has a pension from non-covered employment in federal, state, or local governments.[38] Under the retirement earnings test (RET), the monthly Social Security benefit is reduced for a person who is below the FRA and has wage or salary income above an annual dollar threshold (an annual exempt amount).[39] Under the Social Security maximum family benefit provision (discussed below), the benefits of individual family members may be reduced to keep the total benefits payable to a family based on the worker's record within a specified limit.

Disabled-Worker Benefit

For Social Security disability benefits, "disability" is defined as the inability to engage in substantial gainful activity (SGA) by reason of a medically determinable physical or mental impairment expected to result in death or last at least 12 months. Generally, the worker must be unable to do any kind of work that exists in the national economy, taking into account age, education, and work experience. As noted above, a worker generally needs a minimum of 40 quarters of coverage for a Social Security retired-worker benefit. A worker may qualify for Social Security disabled-worker benefits with fewer quarters of coverage, depending on the age at which the worker became disabled. However, a minimum of six quarters of coverage is needed. Similarly, while the worker's 35 highest years of earnings are used to compute a retired-worker benefit, fewer years of earnings may be used to compute a disabled-worker benefit. Because a disabled worker's benefit is not reduced for entitlement before the FRA, a disabled worker's benefit is equal to his or her PIA.[40]

Benefits for the Worker's Family Members

Social Security is often viewed as a program that provides benefits to retired or disabled workers; however, approximately 20% of current Social Security beneficiaries are the dependents and survivors of retired, disabled, or deceased workers.[41]

Social Security benefits are payable to the spouse, divorced spouse, or child of a retired or disabled worker. Social Security benefits are also payable to the widow(er), divorced widow(er), child, or parent of a deceased worker. In addition, in the case of a deceased worker, benefits are payable to the mother or father of a deceased worker's child when the child is under the age of 16 or disabled and entitled to a Social Security child's benefit based on the worker's record.[42] Benefits payable to family members are equal to a specified percentage of the worker's PIA, subject to a maximum family benefit amount. For example, the spouse of a retired worker may receive up to 50% of the retired worker's PIA, and the widow(er) of a deceased worker may receive up to 100% of the deceased worker's PIA. Benefits paid to family members may be subject to adjustments based on the person's age at entitlement, receipt of his or her own Social Security retired-worker benefit, and other factors, as described above.

Table 3 provides a summary of Social Security benefits payable to family members of a retired, disabled, or deceased worker, including basic eligibility requirements and basic benefit amounts before any applicable adjustments are made (such as for the maximum family benefit amount).[43]

Maximum Family Benefit Amount

The total amount of Social Security benefits payable to a family based on a retired or deceased worker's record is capped by the maximum family benefit amount. The maximum family benefit varies from 150% to 188% of the retired or deceased worker's PIA. It cannot be exceeded regardless of the number of beneficiaries entitled to benefits on the worker's record.[44] If the sum of all benefits based on the worker's record exceeds the maximum family benefit amount, each dependent's or survivor's benefit is reduced in equal proportion to bring the total amount of benefits within the family maximum. For the family of a worker who attains the age of 62 in 2013, or dies in 2013 before attaining the age of 62, the total amount of benefits payable is limited to

- 150% of the first $1,011 of the worker's PIA, plus
- 272% of the worker's PIA over $1,011 and through $1,459, plus
- 134% of the worker's PIA over $1,459 and through $1,903, plus
- 175% of the worker's PIA over $1,903.

The dollar amounts in the maximum family benefit formula ($1,011, $1,459, and $1,903 in 2013) are indexed to average wage growth, as in the regular benefit formula. A different family maximum applies in the case of a disabled worker. For the family of a worker who is entitled to disability benefits, the maximum family benefit is the lesser of 85% of the worker's AIME or 150% of the worker's PIA. In no case, however, can the family benefit be less than 100% of the worker's PIA.[45]

Table 3. Social Security Benefits for the Worker's Family Members

Basis for Entitlement	Basic Eligibility Requirements	Basic Benefit Amount Before Any Applicable Adjustments
Spouse	At least age 62, or Any age if caring for the child of a retired or disabled worker. The child must be under the age of 16 or disabled and entitled to a child's benefit based on the worker's record. The worker on whose record benefits are based must be receiving benefits.	50% of worker's PIA
Divorced Spouse	At least age 62	50% of worker's PIA
(if divorced individual was married to the worker for at least 10 years before the divorce became final and is currently unmarried)	Generally, the worker on whose record benefits are based must be receiving benefits. However, a divorced spouse may receive benefits on the worker's record if the worker is eligible for (but not receiving) benefits and the divorce has been final for at least two years.	
	(Note: A divorced spouse who is	

Basis for Entitlement	Basic Eligibility Requirements	Basic Benefit Amount Before Any Applicable Adjustments
	under the age of 62 is not eligible for spousal benefits even if he or she is caring for the child of a retired or disabled worker and the child is entitled to benefits based on the worker's record.)	
Widow(er) & Divorced Widow(er)	At least age 60	100% of worker's PIA
(if divorced individual was married to the worker for at least 10 years before the divorce became final and did not remarry before age 60)		
Disabled Widow(er) & Divorced Disabled Widow(er) (if divorced individual was married to the worker for at least 10 years before the divorce became final and did not remarry before age 50)	At least age 50 The qualifying disability must have occurred: (1) before or within seven years of the worker's death;	100% of worker's PIA
	(2) within seven years of having been previously entitled to benefits on the worker's record as a widow(er) with a child in his or her care; or (3) within seven years of having been previously entitled to benefits as a disabled widow(er) that ended because the qualifying disability ended (whichever is later).	
Mothers and Fathers	Surviving parent of any age who cares for the deceased worker's child, when the child is either under age 16 or disabled and entitled to a child's benefit based on the deceased worker's record. To receive mother's or father's benefits, the person must be unmarried and not entitled to widow(er)'s benefits.	75% of deceased worker's PIA (subject to the maximum family benefit amount)

Table 3. (Continued)

Basis for Entitlement	Basic Eligibility Requirements	Basic Benefit Amount Before Any Applicable Adjustments
Parents	At least age 62 and has not married since the worker's death. The parent must have been receiving at least one-half of his or her support from the worker at the time of the worker's death or, if the worker had a period of disability which continued until death, at the beginning of the period of disability.	If one parent is entitled to benefits: 82.5% of deceased worker's PIA If two parents are entitled to benefits: 75% of deceased worker's PIA (for each) (subject to the maximum family benefit amount)
Child	A child (including a dependent, unmarried biological child, adopted child, stepchild, and, in some cases, grandchild) of a retired, disabled, or deceased worker who was fully or currently insured at the time of death. The child must be (1) under age 18; (2) a full-time elementary or secondary student under age 19; or (3) a disabled person aged 18 or older whose disability began before age 22.	50% of worker's PIA for child of a retired or disabled worker 75% of deceased worker's PIA for child of a deceased worker (subject to the maximum family benefit amount)

Source: Congressional Research Service.

Notes: The table shows the minimum eligibility age for each type of benefit (i.e., the age at which benefits are first payable on a reduced basis). The maximum family benefit may apply, reducing the benefit received by each family member on a proportional basis. The maximum family benefit varies from 150% to 188% of a retired or deceased worker's PIA. For the family of a worker who is entitled to disability benefits, the maximum family benefit is the lesser of 85% of the worker's AIME or 150% of the worker's PIA, but no less than 100% of the worker's PIA. Other benefit adjustments may apply.

Social Security Beneficiaries

In April 2013, there were 57.3 million Social Security beneficiaries. As shown in *Table 4*, retired-worker and disabled-worker beneficiaries accounted for 80.4% of the beneficiary population. The largest category of beneficiaries was retired workers (64.9% of the total), with an average monthly benefit of $1,266.81. The second-largest category was disabled workers (15.5% of the total), with an average monthly benefit of $1,129.63. Family members of retired, disabled, or deceased workers accounted for the remainder of the beneficiary population (approximately 20% of the total). *Table 4* provides a detailed breakdown of the Social Security beneficiary population in April 2013.

Table 4. Social Security Beneficiaries, by Type, April 2013

Type of Beneficiary	Number of Beneficiaries (in thousands)	Percentage of Beneficiaries	Total Monthly Benefits ($ in millions)	Average Monthly Benefit (in dollars)
All beneficiaries	57,332	100.0%	$66,312	$1,156.63
Old-Age and Survivors	46,372	80.9	55,598	1,198.97
Insurance				
Retirement benefits	40,112	70.0	48,954	1,220.44
- Retired workers	37,199	64.9	47,124	1,266.81
- Spouses of retired workers	2,279	4.0	1,437	630.42
- Children of retired workers	634	1.1	393	620.68
Survivor benefits	6,260	10.9	6,644	1,061.38
- Children of deceased workers	1,942	3.4	1,557	801.78
- Widowed mothers and fathers	148	0.3	132	891.78
- Nondisabled widow(er)s	3,913	6.8	4,772	1,219.68
- Disabled widow(er)s	256	0.4	182	709.58
- Parents of deceased workers	1	[a]	2	1,074.70
Disability Insurance	10,961	19.1	10,714	977.50
- Disabled workers	8,864	15.5	10,013	1,129.63
- Spouses of disabled workers	160	0.3	48	302.33
- Children of disabled workers	1,936	3.4	652	336.92

Source: Table is reproduced from SSA, Monthly Statistical Snapshot, April 2013, Table 2. See the latest edition of the Monthly Statistical Snapshot at http://www.socialsecurity.gov/policy

[a] Indicates a value less than 0.05%.

End Notes

[1] Social Security Administration (SSA), Monthly Statistical Snapshot, April 2013, Table 2. See the latest edition of the Monthly Statistical Snapshot at http://www.socialsecurity.gov/policy/docs/quickfacts/stat_snapshot/index.html. Details may not sum to totals due to rounding.

[2] Currently, 94% of workers in paid employment or self-employment are covered by Social Security. (SSA, 2013 Social Security/SSI/Medicare Information, February 28, 2013, at http://www.socialsecurity.gov/legislation/ 2013factsheet.pdf.)

[3] The annual limit on covered wages and net self-employment income subject to the Social Security payroll tax (the taxable wage base) is adjusted annually based on average wage growth, if a Social Security cost-of-living adjustment (COLA) is payable.

[4] In 2011, there was a temporary 2 percentage point reduction in the Social Security payroll tax rate for workers under P.L. 111-312. The temporary reduction was extended through February 2012 under P.L. 112-78, and further extended through December 2012 under P.L. 112-96. For more information, see CRS Report R41648, Social Security: Temporary Payroll Tax Reduction, by Dawn Nuschler.

[5] In this report, the OASI and DI trust funds are referred to on a combined basis as the Social Security trust funds.

[6] SSA, Trust Fund Data, http://www.ssa.gov/OACT/STATS/table4a3.html.

[7] P.L. 271, 74th Congress.

[8] P.L. 379, 76th Congress.

[9] The DI program was established by the Social Security Amendments of 1956 (P.L. 880, 84th Congress). The program became known as the Old-Age, Survivors, and Disability Insurance (OASDI) program, the formal name for Social Security.

[10] Congress has increased the Social Security payroll tax rate many times over the program's history. The payroll tax rate under current law (12.4%) was established by the Social Security Amendments of 1983 (P.L. 98-21). P.L. 98-21 increased the payroll tax rate gradually from 11.4% in 1984 to 12.4% in 1990.

[11] The taxable wage base amounts ($3,000 and $113,700) are in current dollars. The most recent legislative change to the Social Security taxable wage base was in 1977. The Social Security Amendments of 1977 (P.L. 95-216) established ad-hoc increases in the taxable wage base for 1979, 1980, and 1981, followed by a return to automatic wage indexation for 1982 and subsequent years.

[12] For example, the Social Security Amendments of 1965 (P.L. 89-97) established benefits for divorced wives aged 62 or older.

[13] See the Social Security Amendments of 1972 (P.L. 92-603). For more information, see CRS Report 94-803, Social Security: Cost-of-Living Adjustments, by Gary Sidor.

[14] See the Social Security Amendments of 1977 (P.L. 95-216).

[15] Following the Social Security Amendments of 1983 (P.L. 98-21), projections showed the re-emergence of long-range deficits as a result of changes in actuarial methods and assumptions and because program changes had been evaluated with respect to their effect on the average 75-year deficit. That is, while program changes were projected to restore trust fund solvency on average over the 75-year projection period, a period of surplus years was followed by a period of deficit years. As time passed, the inclusion of additional deficit years in the 75-year valuation period resulted in a return to projected long-range deficits.

[16] For more information, see CRS Report RL33544, Social Security Reform: Current Issues and Legislation, by Dawn Nuschler.

[17] The Patient Protection and Affordable Care Act (ACA, P.L. 111-148) imposed an additional Medicare HI tax of 0.9 percentage point on high-income workers with wages over $200,000 for single filers and $250,000 for joint filers, effective for taxable years beginning in 2013.

[18] Self-employed individuals are required to pay Social Security payroll taxes if they have annual net earnings of $400 or more. Only 92.35% of net self-employment income (up to the annual limit) is taxable.

[19] If a self-employed person does not pay him/herself wages, SECA taxes are paid annually on the Internal Revenue Service Form 1040 (U.S. Individual Income Tax Return). If a self-employed person does pay him/herself wages, FICA taxes are paid during the year along with any FICA tax payments for his or her employees.

[20] The taxes associated with including Social Security benefits in federal taxable income go to the Social Security trust funds and the Medicare HI trust fund. See CRS Report RL32552, Social Security: Calculation and History of Taxing Benefits, by Christine Scott.

[21] Social Security Act, Title II, §201(d). For more information, see SSA, Office of the Chief Actuary, Actuarial Note Number 142, Social Security Trust Fund Investment Policies and Practices, by Jeffrey L. Kunkel, January 1999, at http://www.ssa.gov/OACT/NOTES/n1990s.html.

[22] SSA, Trust Fund FAQs, http://www.socialsecurity.gov/OACT/ProgData/fundFAQ.html.

[23] The 2013 Annual Report of the Board of Trustees of the Federal Old-Age and Survivors Insurance and Federal Disability Insurance Trust Funds, May 31, 2013, at http://www.socialsecurity.gov/OACT/TR/2013/tr2013.pdf. (Hereinafter cited as 2013 Annual Report of the Social Security Board of Trustees.) See Table III.A3 on page 32.

[24] Status of the Social Security and Medicare Programs: A Summary of the 2013 Annual Reports, Social Security and Medicare Boards of Trustees, May 31, 2013, page 2, http://www.socialsecurity.gov/OACT/TRSUM/tr13summary.pdf.

[25] For more information, see CRS Report RL32552, Social Security: Calculation and History of Taxing Benefits, by Christine Scott.

[26] Projections cited in this CRS report are based on the intermediate (or "best estimate") assumptions of the 2013 Annual Report of the Social Security Board of Trustees and refer to the OASI and DI trust funds on a combined basis. For more information on the trust fund projections, see CRS Report RL33028, Social Security: The Trust Fund, by Dawn Nuschler and Gary Sidor.

[27] 2013 Annual Report of the Social Security Board of Trustees, p. 4. In 1994, the reallocation of the payroll tax rate between OASI and DI was part of the Social Security Domestic Employment Reform Act of 1994 (H.R. 4278, 103rd Congress), which became P.L. 103-387.

[28] A wage-indexed benefit formula allows initial monthly benefits for successive groups of new beneficiaries to keep pace with increases in the standard of living. An annual COLA for benefits already in payment allows benefits for current beneficiaries to keep pace with increases in prices.

[29] For more information, see CRS Report RL32822, Social Security Reform: Legal Analysis of Social Security Benefit Entitlement Issues, by Kathleen S. Swendiman and Thomas J. Nicola, and CRS Report RL33514, Social Security: What Would Happen If the Trust Funds Ran Out?, by Christine Scott.

[30] For more information, see CRS Report RL33544, Social Security Reform: Current Issues and Legislation, by Dawn Nuschler.

[31] The full retirement age is also called the normal retirement age (NRA).

[32] For more information, see CRS Report R41962, Fact Sheet: The Social Security Retirement Age, by Gary Sidor.

[33] A worker may earn a maximum of four earnings credits (or quarters of coverage, QCs) per calendar year. In 2013, a worker earns one QC for each $1,160 of covered earnings, up to a maximum of four QCs for earnings of $4,640 or more.

[34] The bend points in the benefit formula are indexed to average wage growth under current law.

[35] The replacement factors in the benefit formula are fixed under current law.

[36] A Social Security COLA was not payable in 2010 and 2011. For more information, see CRS Report 94-803, Social Security: Cost-of-Living Adjustments, by Gary Sidor.

[37] For more information on the dual entitlement rule and the GPO, see CRS Report RL32453, Social Security: The Government Pension Offset (GPO), by Christine Scott.

[38] For more information on the WEP, see CRS Report 98-35, Social Security: The Windfall Elimination Provision (WEP), by Christine Scott.

[39] For more information on the RET, see CRS Report R41242, Social Security Retirement Earnings Test: How Earnings Affect Benefits, by Dawn Nuschler.

[40] For more information, see CRS Report RL32279, Primer on Disability Benefits: Social Security Disability Insurance (SSDI) and Supplemental Security Income (SSI), by Umar Moulta-Ali.

[41] SSA, Monthly Statistical Snapshot, April 2013, Table 2. See the latest edition of the Monthly Statistical Snapshot at http://www.socialsecurity.gov/policy/docs/ quickfacts/stat_snaps hot/ index.html.

[42] To receive mother's or father's benefits, the person must be unmarried and must not be entitled to widow(er)'s benefits.

[43] For related information, see CRS Report RS22294, Social Security Survivors Benefits, by Scott Szymendera.

[44] Social Security Act, Title II, §203.

[45] Benefits for a divorced beneficiary are not taken into account for purposes of the family maximum. SSA, Program Operations Manual System (POMS), Section RS 00615.682, "Family Benefits Where a Divorced Spouse or a Surviving Divorced Spouse is Entitled," available at https://secure.ssa.gov/apps10/poms.nsf/lnx/0300615682.

In: Retirement Savings and Security
Editor: Linda A. Eisterhold
ISBN: 978-1-62948-132-6

Chapter 2

Traditional and Roth Individual Retirement Accounts (IRAs): A Primer*

John J. Topoleski

Summary

In response to concerns over the adequacy of retirement savings, Congress has created incentives to encourage individuals to save more for retirement through a variety of retirement plans. Some retirement plans are employer-sponsored, such as 401(k) plans, and others are established by individual employees, such as Individual Retirement Accounts (IRAs).

This report describes the primary features of two common retirement savings accounts that are available to individuals. Although the accounts have many features in common, they differ in some very important aspects. Both traditional and Roth IRAs offer tax incentives to encourage individuals to save for retirement.

Contributions to traditional IRAs may be tax-deductible for taxpayers who (1) are not covered by a retirement plan at their place of employment or (2) have income below specified limits. Contributions to Roth IRAs are not tax-deductible and eligibility is limited to those with incomes under specified limits.

* This is an edited, reformatted and augmented version of a Congressional Research Service publication, CRS Report for Congress RL34397, prepared for Members and Committees of Congress, from www.crs.gov, dated January 30, 2013.

The tax treatment of distributions from traditional and Roth IRAs differs. Distributions from traditional IRAs are generally included in taxable income whereas distributions from Roth IRAs are not included in taxable income. Some distributions may be subject to an additional 10% tax penalty, unless the distribution is for a reason specified in the Internal Revenue Code (for example, distributions from IRAs after the individual is age 59 1/2 or older are not subject to the early withdrawal penalty).

Individuals may rollover eligible distributions from other retirement accounts (such as an account balance from a 401(k) plans upon leaving an employer) into IRAs. Rollovers preserve retirement savings by allowing investment earnings on the funds in the retirement accounts to accrue on a tax-deferred, in the case of traditional IRAs, or a tax-free basis, in the case of Roth IRAs.

The Retirement Savings Contribution Credit (also known as the Saver's Credit) is a nonrefundable tax credit of up to $1,000. It was authorized in 2001 to encourage retirement savings among individuals with income under specified limits.

The report explains the eligibility requirements, contribution limits, tax deductibility of contributions, and rules for withdrawing funds from the accounts. It also describes the Saver's Credit and provisions enacted after the Gulf of Mexico hurricanes in 2005 and the Midwestern storms in 2008 to exempt distributions to those affected by the disasters from the 10% early withdrawal penalty.

INTRODUCTION

Individual Retirement Accounts (IRAs) are tax-advantaged accounts that individuals (or married couples) can establish in order to accumulate funds for retirement. Depending on the type of IRA, contributions may be made on a pre-tax or post-tax basis, and investment earnings are either tax-deferred or tax-free.[1]

IRAs were first authorized by the Employee Retirement Income Security Act of 1974 (ERISA; P.L. 93-406). Originally limited to workers without pension coverage, all workers and spouses were made eligible for IRAs by the Economic Recovery Act of 1981 (P.L. 97-34). The Tax Reform Act of 1986 (P.L. 99-514) limited the eligibility for tax-deductible contributions to individuals whose employers do not sponsor plans and to those whose employers sponsor plans but who have earnings below certain thresholds. The Taxpayer Relief Act of 1997 (P.L. 105-34) allowed for certain penalty-free withdrawals and authorized the Roth IRA, which provides tax-free growth from after-tax contributions.

The Economic Growth and Tax Relief Reconciliation Act of 2001 (P.L. 107-16) significantly affected the contribution limits in these plans in three ways: (1) it increased the limits, (2) it indexed the limits to inflation, and (3) it allowed for individuals aged 50 and older to make additional "catch-up" contributions. Among other provisions, the Pension Protection Act of 2006 (P.L. 109-280) temporally allowed for tax-free distributions for charitable contributions; made permanent the indexing of contribution limits to inflation; and allowed taxpayers to direct the IRS to deposit tax refunds directly into an IRA.[2]

This report describes the two kinds of IRAs that individual employees can establish: traditional IRAs and Roth IRAs.[3] It describes the rules regarding eligibility, contributions, and withdrawals. It also describes a tax credit for retirement savings contributions. An *Appendix* explains rules related to penalty-free distributions for those affected by the 2005 Gulf of Mexico hurricanes and the 2008 Midwestern floods. The appendix also describes relief provided by the IRS to those affected by Hurricane Sandy.

IRA Assets and Sources of Funds

Table 1 contains data on the end-of-year assets in traditional and Roth IRAs from 2002 to 2011. According to the Investment Company Institute, traditional IRAs held much more in assets than Roth IRAs. At the end of 2011, there was $4.3 trillion held in traditional IRAs and $266 billion held in Roth IRAs. Table 2 indicates that within traditional IRAs, more funds flowed from rollovers from employer-sponsored pensions compared to funds from regular contributions.4 For example, in 2008 (the latest year for which data are available) funds from rollovers were $272.1 billion, whereas funds from contributions were only $13.4 billion. Table 3 indicates that nearly as many households had traditional IRAs as households that had Roth and rollover IRAs combined. However, Table 4 indicates that in 2010 the median balance in rollover IRAs was 39.4% larger than the median account balance in traditional IRAs. In 2010, the total amount in rollover IRAs was only slightly larger than the total amount in traditional IRAs ($2.118 trillion versus $2.095 trillion). The number of households with a traditional or rollover IRA decreased from 2007 to 2010, whereas the number of households with a Roth IRA increased slightly from 11.0 million to 11.2 million.

Table 1. Traditional and Roth IRAs: End of Year Assets (in billions of dollars)

	2002	2003	2004	2005	2006	2007	2008	2009	2010	2011
Traditional IRAs	$2,322	$2,719	$2,957	$3,034	$3,722	$4,187	$3,257	$3,855	$4,250	$4,280
Roth IRAs	78	106	140	156	196	232	177	215	265	266

Source: CRS table using data from the Investment Company Institute, The U.S. Retirement Market, Third Quarter 2012, Table 7, available at http://www.ici.org/info/ret_12_q3_data.xls.

Table 2. Traditional IRAs: Source of Funds (in billions of dollars)

	2002	2003	2004	2005	2006	2007	2008
Rollovers from Employer-Sponsored Pensions	$204.4	$205.0	$214.9	$228.5	$282.0	$316.6	$272.1
Contributions from Account Holders	12.4	12.3	12.6	13.4	14.3	14.4	13.4

Source: CRS table using data from the Investment Company Institute, The U.S. Retirement Market, Third Quarter 2012, Table 8, available at http://www.ici.org/info/ret_12_q3_data.xls.

Table 3. Number of Households with IRAs in 2007 and 2010

	2007 Number of Households (millions)	2010 Number of Households (millions)
Traditional IRA	20.1	18.4
Roth IRA	11.0	11.2
Rollover IRA	12.0	11.8
Only rollover IRA	7.6	6.7
Rollover and also either traditional or Roth IRA	4.4	5.1
Has any kind of IRA	35.2	32.

Source: CRS Analysis of 2007 and 2010 Survey of Consumer Finances.

**Table 4. IRA Account Balances in 2007 and 2010
Inflation Adjusted 2010 Dollar Amounts**

	Traditional IRA			Roth IRA	Rollover IRA	
	2007	2010	2007	2010	2007	2010
Median balance (dollars)	$30,498	$38,000	$11,884	$15,100	$55,738	$53,000
Average balance (dollars)	$93,584	$113,990	$31,853	$48,198	$167,547	$179,001
Total of account balances (billions of dollars)	$1,884.3	$2.095.1	$351.9	$541.9	$2,006.9	$2,117.5

Source: CRS Analysis of 2007 and 2010 Survey of Consumer Finances.

Note: CRS adjusted the 2007 dollar amounts for inflation using the monthly averages for the Consumer Price Index, All Urban Consumers (CPI-U) in 2007 and 2010.

TRADITIONAL IRAS

Traditional IRAs are funded by workers' contributions, which may be tax-deductible. The contributions accrue investment earnings in an account, and these earnings are used as a basis for retirement income. Among the benefits of traditional IRAs, two are (1) pre-tax contributions provide larger bases for accumulating investment earnings and, thus, provide larger account balances at retirement than if the money had been placed in taxable accounts; and (2) taxes are paid when funds are distributed. Since income tax rates in retirement are often lower than during working life, traditional IRA holders are likely to pay less in taxes when contributions are withdrawn than when the income was earned.

Eligibility

Individuals who are less than 701/2 years old in a year and receive taxable compensation can set up and contribute to IRAs. Examples of compensation include wages, salaries, tips, commissions, self-employment income, alimony, and nontaxable combat pay. Individuals who receive income only from non-compensation sources cannot contribute to IRAs.

Contributions

Individuals may contribute either their gross compensation or the contribution limit, whichever is lower. In 2012, the contribution limit was $5,000 and in 2013 the limit is $5,500. Since 2009, the contribution limit has been indexed to inflation, although the change in the Consumer Price Index was insufficient for a cost-of-living adjustment to the 2011 or 2012 contribution limit. Individuals aged 50 and older may make additional $1,000 catch-up contributions. For households that file a joint return, spouses may contribute an amount equal to the couple's total compensation (reduced by the spouse's IRA contributions) or the contribution limit ($5,500 each, if younger than the age of 50, and $6,500 each, if 50 years or older), whichever is lower. Contributions that exceed the contribution limit and are not withdrawn by the due date for the tax return for that year are considered excess contributions and are subject to a 6% "excess contribution" tax. Contributions made between January 1 and April 15 may be designated for either the current year or the previous year.

Because IRAs were intended for workers without an employer-sponsored pension to save for retirement, contributions to an IRA may only come from income from work, such as wages and tips. The following non-compensation sources of income cannot be used for IRA contributions:

- earnings from property, interest, or dividends;
- pension or annuity income;
- deferred compensation;
- income from partnerships for which an individual does not provide services that are a material income-producing factor; and
- foreign earned income.

Investment Options

IRAs can be set up through many financial institutions, such as banks, credit unions, mutual funds, life insurance companies, or stock brokerages. Individuals have an array of investment choices offered by the financial institutions and can transfer their accounts to other financial institutions if they are unhappy with their choices. Several transactions could result in additional taxes or the loss of IRA status. These transactions include borrowing from

IRAs, using IRAs as collateral for loans, selling property to IRAs, and investing in collectibles like artwork, antiques, metals, gems, stamps, alcoholic beverages, and most coins.[5]

Deductibility of Contributions

IRA contributions may be non-tax-deductible, partially tax-deductible, or fully tax-deductible, depending on whether the individual or spouse is covered by a pension plan at work and the level of adjusted gross income. Individuals are covered by a retirement plan if (1) the individuals or their employers have made contributions to a defined contribution pension plan, or (2) the individuals are eligible for a defined benefit pension plan (even if they refuse participation).

For individuals and households not covered by a pension plan at work, *Table 5* contains the income levels at which they may deduct all, some, or none of their IRA contributions, depending on the spouse's pension coverage and the household's adjusted gross income. Individuals without employer-sponsored pensions and, if married, whose spouse also does not have pension coverage may deduct up to the contribution limit from their income taxes regardless of their adjusted gross income. For individuals and households who are covered by a pension plan at work, *Table 6* contains the income levels at which they may deduct all, some, or none of their IRA contributions, depending on the individual's or household's adjusted gross income.

Individuals may still contribute to IRAs up to the contribution limit even if the contribution is non-deductible. Non-deductible contributions come from post-tax income, not pre-tax income. One advantage to placing post-tax income in traditional IRAs is that investment earnings on nondeductible contributions are not taxed until distributed. Only contributions greater than the contribution limits as described above are considered excess contributions. Worksheets for computing partial deductions are included in IRS Publication 590, Individual Retirement Arrangements (IRAs).[6]

Withdrawals

Withdrawals from IRAs are subject to income tax in the year that they are received.[7] Early distributions are withdrawals made before the age of 591,4. Early distributions may be subject to an additional 10% penalty.

Table 5. Deductibility of IRA Contributions for Individuals Not Covered by a Plan at Work for 2012 and 2013

Filing Status	2012 Adjusted Gross Income	2013 Adjusted Gross Income	Deduction Allowed
Single, head of household, qualifying widow(er), or married filing jointly or separately with a spouse who is not covered by a plan at work	Any amount	Any amount	Full deduction
Married filing jointly or separately with a spouse who is covered by a plan at work	$173,000 or less More than $173,000 but less than $183,000 $183,000 or more	$178,000 or less More than $178,000 but less than $188,000 $188,000 or more	full deduction Partial deduction No deduction
Married filing separately with a spouse who is covered by a plan at work	Less than $10,000	Less than $10,000	Partial deduction
	$10,000 or more	$10,000 or more	No deduction

Source: CRS analysis of IRS Publication 590 and IRS News Release IR-2012-77.

Table 6. Deductibility of IRA Contributions for Individuals Covered by a Plan at Work for 2012 and 2013

Filing Status	2012 Adjusted Gross Income	2013 Adjusted Gross Income	Deduction Allowed
Single or head of household	$58,000 or less	$59,000 or less	Full deduction
	More than $58,000 but less than $68,000	More than $59,000 but less than $69,000	Partial deduction
	$68,000 or more	$69,000 or more	No deduction
Married filing jointly or qualifying widow(er)	$92,000 or less	$95,000 or less	Full deduction
	More than $92,000 but less than $112,000	More than $95,000 but less than $112,000	Partial deduction
	$112,000 or more	$115,000 or more	No deduction
Married filing separately	Less than $10,000	Less than $10,000	Partial deduction
	$10,000 or more	$10,000 or more	No deduction

Source: CRS analysis of IRS Publication 590 and IRS News Release IR-2012-77.

To ensure that IRAs are used for retirement income and not for bequests, IRA holders must begin making withdrawals by April 1 of the year after reaching the age of 701,4 (the required beginning date). The minimum amount that must be withdrawn (the required minimum distribution) is found by dividing the account balance on December 31 of the year preceding the distribution by the IRA owner's life expectancy as found in IRS Publication 590.[8] Although females live longer on average than males, separate life expectancy tables for males and females are not used for this purpose by the IRS.[9] Required minimum distributions must be received by December 31 of each year. Failure to take the required minimum distribution results in 50% excise tax on the amount not distributed as required. Congress has suspended the RMD requirement for 2009.[10]

Beginning in 2007, distributions from IRAs after the age of 701,4 could be made directly to qualified charities and excluded from gross income. This provision for Qualified Charitable Distributions expires December 31, 2013.[11]

Early Distributions

Early distributions are withdrawals made before the age of 591,4. Early distributions—just like distributions after the age of 591,4—are subject to federal income tax. In order to discourage the use of IRA funds for pre-retirement uses, most early distributions are subject to a 10% tax penalty.[12] The early withdrawal penalty does not apply to distributions before the age of 591,4 if they

- occur if the individual is a beneficiary of a deceased IRA owner;
- occur if the individual is disabled;
- are in substantially equal payments over the account holder's life expectancy;
- are received after separation from employment after the age of 55;
- are for unreimbursed medical expenses in excess of 7.5% of adjusted gross income;
- are for medical insurance premiums in the case of unemployment;
- are used for higher education expenses;
- are used to build, buy, or rebuild a first home up to a $10,000 withdrawal limit;

- occur if the individual is a reservist called to active duty after September 11, 2001;
- were distributions to residents in areas affected by Hurricanes Katrina, Rita, and Wilma from around the storms' landfalls to January 1, 2007; or
- were distributions to residents in areas affected by the Midwestern floods in 2008 from after the applicable disaster date and before January 1, 2010.

General "hardship" exceptions for penalty-free distributions from IRAs do not exist as individuals may make withdrawals from IRAs without a reason.

Rollovers

Rollovers are transfers of assets from one retirement plan to another upon separation from the original employer. Rollovers are not subject to the 591,4 rule, the 10% penalty, or the contribution limit. Rollovers can come from traditional IRAs, employers' qualified retirement plans (e.g., 401(k) plans), deferred compensation plans of state or local governments (Section 457 plans), tax-sheltered annuities (Section 403(b) plans), or the Thrift Savings Plan for federal employees.

Rollovers can be either direct trustee-to-trustee transfers or issued directly to individuals who then deposit the rollovers into traditional IRAs. Individuals have 60 days to make the rollover contributions. Rollovers not completed within 60 days are considered taxable distributions and may be subject to the 10% early withdrawal penalty. In addition, in cases where individuals directly receive a rollover, 20% of the rollover is withheld for tax purposes. Direct trustee-totrustee transfers are not subject to withholding taxes. In cases where individuals directly receive a rollover, they must have an amount equal to the 20% withheld available from other sources to place in the new IRA. If the entire distribution is rolled over within 60 days, the amount withheld is applied to the individuals' income taxes paid for the year.

Inherited IRAs

When the owner of an IRA dies, ownership passes to the account's designated beneficiary or, if no beneficiary has been named, to the decedent's estate. Federal law has different distribution requirements depending on whether the new owner is a

- designated beneficiary who is the former owner's spouse;
- designated beneficiary who is not the former owner's spouse; or
- non-designated beneficiary.

The distribution rules are summarized in *Table 7*. The distribution rules also depend on whether the IRA owner died prior to the required beginning date. The required beginning date is the date on which distributions from the account must begin. It is April 1 of the year following the year in which the owner of an IRA reaches the age of 701,4. Distributions from inherited IRAs are taxable income but are not subject to the 591,4 rule. Failure to take the required minimum distribution results in a 50% excise tax on the amount not distributed as required.

Designated spouse beneficiaries who treat inherited IRAs as their own can roll over inherited IRAs into traditional IRAs or, to the extent that the inherited IRAs are taxable, into qualified employer plans (such as 401(k), 403(b), or 457 plans). Non-spouse beneficiaries cannot roll over any amount into or out of inherited IRAs. In some cases, IRAs have requirements for distributions by beneficiaries that are more stringent than those summarized in *Table 7*. For example, an IRA's plan documents could require that a designated spouse or designated nonspouse beneficiary distribute all assets in the IRA by the end of the fifth year of the year following the IRA owner's death. In such a case, the beneficiary would not have the option to take distributions over a longer period of time. Unless the IRA plan documents specify otherwise, it is possible to take distributions faster than required in *Table 7*. For example, a beneficiary may elect to distribute all assets in a single year. In such a case, the entire amount distributed is taxable income for that year.

Roth IRAs

Roth IRAs were authorized by the Taxpayer Relief Act of 1997 (P.L. 105-34). The key differences between traditional and Roth IRAs are that contributions to Roth IRAs are made with after-tax funds and qualified distributions are not included in taxable income; hence, investment earnings accrue free of taxes.[13]

Table 7. Inherited IRA Distribution Rules

	Owner Dies Before Required Beginning Date	Owner Dies after Required Beginning Date
Spouse is named as the designated beneficiary	Treat as own, does not have to take any distribution until the age of 70½, but is subject to the 59½ rule, or Keep in decedent's name and take distributions based on own life expectancy. Distributions do not have to begin until decedent would have turned 70½.	Treat as own, does not have to take any distribution until the age of 70½, but is subject to the 59½ rule, or Keep in decedent's name and take distributions based on own life expectancy.
A nonspouse is named as the designated beneficiary	Take distributions based on life expectancy for beneficiary's age as of birthday in the year following the year of the owner's death, reduced by one for each year since owner's death. If the nonspouse beneficiary does not take a distribution in year of owner's death, then all IRA assets must be distributed by the end of the fifth year of the year following the IRA owner's death.	Take distributions based on the longer of (1) beneficiary's life expectancy, or (2) owner's life expectancy using age as of birthday in the year of death, reduced by one for year after the year of death.
Beneficiary is not named	Must distribute all IRA assets by the end of the fifth year of the year following the IRA owner's death.	Take a yearly distribution based on the owner's age as of birthday in the year of death, reduced by one for each year after the year of death.

Source: CRS analysis of IRS Publication 590.

Note: The required beginning date is the date on which distributions from the account must begin. It is April 1 of the year following the year in which the owner of an IRA reaches the age of 701/4.

Eligibility and Contribution Limits

In contrast to traditional IRAs, Roth IRAs have income limits for eligibility. *Table 8* lists the adjusted gross incomes at which individuals may make the maximum contribution and the ranges in which this contribution limit is reduced.

For example, a 40-year-old single taxpayer with income of $90,000 can contribute $5,500 in 2013. A similar taxpayer making $120,000 would be subject to a reduced contribution limit, whereas a taxpayer with come of $130,000 would be ineligible to contribute to a Roth IRA.

Individuals aged 50 and older can make additional $1,000 catch-up contributions. The adjusted gross income limit for eligibility has been adjusted for inflation since 2007; beginning in 2009, the traditional and Roth IRA contribution limit has also been adjusted for inflation. A worksheet for computing reduced Roth IRA contribution limits is provided in IRS Publication 590.

Investment Options

Roth IRAs must be designated as such when they are set up. As with traditional IRAs, they can be set up through many financial institutions. Transactions prohibited within traditional IRAs are also prohibited within Roth IRAs.

Conversions and Rollovers

Individuals may convert amounts from traditional IRAs, SEP-IRAs, or SIMPLE-IRAs to Roth IRAs.[14] Since 2008, individuals have been able to rollover distributions directly from qualified retirement plans to Roth IRAs. Amounts that would have been included in income if the conversion had not been made must be included in income. Conversions can be a trustee-totrustee transfer, a same trustee transfer by redesignating the IRA as a Roth IRA, or a rollover directly to the account holder. Inherited IRAs cannot be converted.

The rules for rollovers that apply to traditional IRAs, including completing a rollover within 60 days, also apply. Additionally, withdrawals from a converted IRA prior to five years from the beginning of the year of conversion are non-qualified distributions and are subject to a 10% penalty.

Tax-free withdrawals from one Roth IRA transferred to another Roth IRA are allowed if completed within 60 days. Rollovers from Roth IRAs to other types of IRAs or to employer-sponsored retirement plans are not allowed.

Withdrawals

The three kinds of distributions from Roth IRAs are (1) return of regular contributions, (2) qualified distributions, and (3) non-qualified distributions. Returns of regular contributions and qualified distributions are not included as part of taxable income.

Return of Regular Contributions

Distributions from Roth IRAs that are a return of regular contributions are not included in gross income nor are they subject to the 10% penalty on early distributions.

Qualified Distributions

Qualified distributions must satisfy both of the following:

- they are made after the five-year period beginning with the first taxable year for which a Roth IRA contribution was made,[15] and
- they are made on or after the age of 591,4; or because of disability; or to a beneficiary or estate after death; or to purchase, build, or rebuild a first home up to a $10,000 lifetime limit.

Non-Qualified Distributions

Distributions that are neither returns of regular contributions nor qualified distributions are considered non-qualified distributions. Although individuals might have several Roth IRA accounts from which withdrawals can be made, for tax purposes non-qualified distributions are assumed to be made in the following order:

1. the return of regular contributions,
2. conversion contributions on a first-in-first-out basis, and
3. earnings on contributions.

Non-qualified distributions may have to be included as part of income for tax purposes. A worksheet is available in Publication 590 to determine the taxable portion of non-qualified distributions. A 10% penalty applies to non-qualified distributions unless one of the exceptions in 26 U.S.C. Section 72(t) applies. The exceptions are identical to those previously listed for early withdrawals from traditional IRAs.

Distributions after Roth IRA Owner's Death

If the owner of a Roth IRA dies, the distribution rules depend on whether the beneficiary is the spouse or a nonspouse. If the beneficiary is the spouse, then the spouse can choose to treat the inherited Roth IRA as their own. If the spouse chooses not to treat the inherited Roth IRA as their own, or if the beneficiary is a nonspouse, then there are two options.

Table 8. Roth IRA Eligibility and Contribution Limits for 2012 and 2013

Filing Status	2012 Modified Adjusted Gross Income (AGI)	2012 Contribution Limits	2013 Modified Adjusted Gross Income (AGI)	2013 Contribution Limits
Single, head of household, married filing separately (and did not live with spouse at any time during the year)	Less than $110,000	$5,000 ($6,000 if 50 years or older) or AGI, whichever is smaller.	Less than $112,000	$5,500 ($6,500 if 50 years or older) or AGI, whichever is smaller.
	At least $110,000 but less than $125,000	Reduced contribution limit	At least $112,000 but less than $127,000	Reduced contribution limit
	$125,000 or more	Ineligible to contribute	$127,000 or more	Ineligible to contribute
Married filing separately and lived with spouse at any time during the year Married filing jointly, qualifying widow(er)	Less than $10,000	Reduced contribution limit	Less than $10,000	Reduced contribution limit
	$10,000 or more	Ineligible to contribute	$10,000 or more	Ineligible to contribute
	Less than $169,000	$5,000 each ($6,000 each if 50 and older) or AGI, whichever is smaller.	Less than $178,000	$5,500 each ($6,500 each if 50 and older) or AGI, whichever is smaller.
	At least $173,000 but less than $183,000 $183,000 or more	Reduced contribution limit Ineligible to contribute	At least $178,000 but less than $188,000 $188,000 or more	Reduced contribution limit Ineligible to contribute

Source: CRS analysis of IRS Publication 590 and IRS News Release IR-2012-77.

The beneficiary can distribute the entire interest in the Roth IRA (1) by the end of the fifth calendar year after the year of the owner's death, or (2) over the beneficiary's life expectancy. As with an inherited traditional IRA, a spouse can delay distributions until the decedent would have reached the age of 701,4.

Distributions from inherited Roth IRAs are generally free of income tax. The beneficiary may be subject to taxes if the owner of a Roth IRA dies before the end of (1) the five-year period beginning with the first taxable year for which a contribution was made to a Roth IRA or (2) the five-year period starting with the year of a conversion from a traditional IRA to a Roth IRA. The distributions are treated as described in the section of this report on non-qualified Roth IRA distributions.

Table 9. Retirement Saving Contribution Credit Income Limits for 2012 and 2013

Filing Status	2012 Income Limits	2013 Income Limits	Percentage Credit
Single, Married Filing Separately, Qualifying Widow(er)	$1 to $17,250	$1 to $17,750	50%
	$17,251 to $18,750	$17,751 to $19,250	20%
	$18,751 to $28,750	$19,251 to $29,500	10%
	more than $28,750	more than $29,500	0%
Head of Household	$1 to $25,875	$1 to $26,625	50%
	$25,876 to $28,125	$26,626 to $28,875	20%
	$28,126 to $43,125	$28,876 to $44,250	10%
	more than $43,125	more than $44,250	0%
Married Filing Jointly	$1 to $34,500	$1 to $35,500	50%
	$34,501 to $37,500	$35,501 to $38,500	20%
	$37,501 to $57,500	$38,501 to $59,000	10%
	more than $57,500	more than $59,000	0%

Source: CRS analysis of IRS Publication 590 and IRS News Release IR-2012-77.

RETIREMENT SAVINGS CONTRIBUTION CREDIT

The Economic Growth and Tax Relief Reconciliation Act of 2001 (P.L. 107-16) authorized a nonrefundable tax credit of up to $1,000 for eligible individuals, or $2,000 if filing a joint return, who contribute to IRAs or employer-sponsored retirement plans.[16] The tax credit is in addition to the tax deduction for contributions to traditional IRAs or other employer-sponsored pension plans. To receive the credit, taxpayers must be at least 18 years old, not full-time students, not an exemption on someone else's tax return, and have adjusted gross income less than certain limits. The limits are in Table 9. For example, individuals who make a $2,000 IRA contribution in 2013, have income of $15,000, and list their filing status as single would be able to reduce their 2013 tax liability by up to $1,000. Taxpayers must file form 1040, 1040A, or 1040NR. It is not available on form 1040EZ, which may limit the use of the credit.

APPENDIX. QUALIFIED DISTRIBUTIONS RELATED TO NATURAL DISASTERS

As part of the response to the 2005 hurricanes that affected the communities on and near the Gulf of Mexico, Congress approved provisions that exempted individuals affected by the storms from the 10% early withdrawal penalty for withdrawals from IRA. In 2008, Congress approved similar provisions in response to the storms and flooding in certain Midwestern states.

Qualified Distributions Related to Hurricanes Katrina, Rita, and Wilma

In response to Hurricanes Katrina, Rita, and Wilma, Congress approved the Gulf Opportunity Zone Act of 2005 (P.L. 109-135). The act amended the Internal Revenue Code to allow residents in areas affected by these storms who suffered economic losses to take penalty-free distributions up to $100,000 from their retirement plans, including traditional and Roth IRAs. The distributions must have been received after August 24, 2005 (Katrina), September 22, 2005 (Rita), or October 22, 2005 (Wilma), and before January 1, 2007. The distributions are taxable income and can be reported as income either in the year received or over three years (e.g., a $30,000 distribution made in May 2006, can be reported as $10,000 of income in 2006, 2007, and 2008). Alternatively, part or all of the distribution may be repaid to the retirement plan within three years of receiving the distribution without being considered taxable income.

Qualified Distributions Related to the Midwestern Disaster Relief Area

In response to severe storms, tornados, and flooding that occurred in certain Midwestern states, the Heartland Disaster Tax Relief Act of 2008 allows residents of specified Midwest areas to take penalty-free distributions up to $100,000 from their retirement plans, including traditional and Roth IRAs.

This act was passed as Division C of P.L. 110-343, the Emergency Economic Stabilization Act of 2008. The bill amends 26 U.S.C. 1400Q, which was enacted as part of the Gulf Opportunity Zone Act of 2005 (P.L. 109-135). The distributions must be received after the date in which the President declared an area to be a major disaster area and before January 1, 2010.[17] Apart from for the dates and the areas affected, the provisions are identical to the provisions for individuals who were affected by Hurricanes Katrina, Rita, and Wilma.

Hurricane Sandy Relief

As of January 29, 2013, no legislation has been introduced that would (1) exempt individuals in areas affected by Hurricane Sandy from the 10% penalty for early withdrawals from IRAs or defined contribution retirement plans or (2) ease requirements for loans from defined contribution pensions for individuals affected by Hurricane Sandy.

The IRS has eased requirements for hardship distributions in areas affected by Hurricane Sandy. Among the relief offered by the IRS in Announcement 2012-44, "Plan administrators may rely upon representations from the employee or former employee as to the need for and amount of a hardship distribution" rather than require documentation from the employee of the need.[18]

The relief offered by the IRS does not include an exemption from the 10% penalty for distributions before the age of 591/2. Exemptions from the 10% penalty require congressional authorization. Also in Announcement 2012-44, the IRS suspended the requirement that requires an individual to suspend contributions to a 401(K) and 403(b) plans for the six months following a hardship distribution.

End Notes

[1] For more information on the tax treatment of retirement savings, including IRAs, see U.S. Congress, Joint Committee on Taxation, Present Law And Background Relating To The Tax Treatment Of Retirement Savings, prepared by Joint Committee on Taxation, 112th Cong., 2nd sess., April 13, 2012, JCX-32-12.

[2] See also 26 U.S.C. §408 for traditional IRAs and 26 U.S.C. §408A for Roth IRAs.

[3] For additional information, see CRS Report RL30255, Individual Retirement Accounts (IRAs): Issues and Proposed Expansion, by Thomas L. Hungerford and Jane G. Gravelle and CRS Report RS22019, IRAs and Other Savings Incentives: A Brief Overview, by Jane G. Gravelle. There are also two kinds of IRAs established by employers for employees in small businesses: Simplified Employee Pensions (SEP-IRA) and Savings Incentive Match Plans for Employees (SIMPLE-IRA). These may be the subject of a future CRS report.

[4] Generally, rollovers are tax-free distributions of assets from one retirement plan that are contributed to a second retirement plan. Regular contributions are contributions to IRAs that are made from individuals' pre- or post-tax income (subject to the rules of the particular type of IRA).

[5] Gold, silver, and platinum coins issued by the U.S. Treasury, and gold, silver, palladium, and platinum bullion are permissible.

[6] Available at http://www.irs.gov/pub/irs-pdf/p590.pdf.

[7] For a detailed explanation of withdrawals from IRAs, see CRS Report R40192, Early Withdrawals and Required Minimum Distributions in Retirement Accounts: Issues for Congress, by John J. Topoleski.

[8] Life expectancy is calculated differently depending on whether the account holder is single and is an IRA beneficiary, has a spouse who is more than 10 years younger, has a spouse who is not more than 10 years younger, whose spouse is not the sole beneficiary, or is unmarried.

[9] The Supreme Court ruled in Arizona Governing Comm. v. Norris, 463 U.S. 1073 (1983), that employer-provided pension plans must use unisex tables in calculating monthly annuity benefits. Citing this ruling, the IRS constructs its own unisex life expectancy tables. See 26 U.S.C. §417(e)(3)(A)(ii).

[10] See CRS Report R40192, Early Withdrawals and Required Minimum Distributions in Retirement Accounts: Issues for Congress, by John J. Topoleski.

[11] See CRS Report RS22766, Qualified Charitable Distributions from Individual Retirement Accounts: A Fact Sheet, by John J. Topoleski.

[12] See 26 U.S.C. §72(t).

[13] Roth IRAs are named for former Senator William Roth (DE).

[14] Prior to January 1, 2010, only individuals with income under specified thresholds were eligible to make conversions from traditional to Roth IRAs. The Tax Increase Prevention and Reconciliation Act of 2005 (TIPRA; P.L. 109-222) eliminated the income thresholds.

[15] The five-year period is not necessarily five calendar years. Contributions made from January 1 to April 15 could be considered made in the previous tax year.

[16] See also CRS Report RS21795, The Retirement Savings Tax Credit: A Fact Sheet, by John J. Topoleski.

[17] The disaster areas are limited to Arkansas, Illinois, Indiana, Iowa, Kansas, Michigan, Minnesota, Missouri, Nebraska, and Wisconsin.

[18] See 26 CFR 1.401(k)-1.

In: Retirement Savings and Security
Editor: Linda A. Eisterhold

ISBN: 978-1-62948-132-6

Chapter 3

INDIVIDUAL RETIREMENT ACCOUNTS (IRAS): ISSUES AND PROPOSED EXPANSION*

Thomas L. Hungerford and Jane G. Gravelle

SUMMARY

Current law provides many incentives to promote saving. The goal of these provisions is to increase saving for special purposes such as education or retirement, and to increase national saving. Increased national saving can lead to faster wealth and capital accumulation, which can boost future national income.

An increasingly important retirement saving vehicle is the individual retirement account (IRA). IRA savings is encouraged by two mechanisms—a carrot approach and a stick approach. First, tax provisions allow individuals to defer taxes on IRA contributions and investment earnings or to accumulate investment earnings tax free. Second, withdrawals before the age of 591/2 are generally subject to a 10% penalty tax in addition to regular taxes.

There are two types of IRAs: the traditional IRA and the Roth IRA. The traditional IRA allows for the tax-deferred accumulation of investment earnings, and some individuals are eligible to make tax-deductible contributions to their traditional IRAs while other individuals are not. Some or all distributions from traditional IRAs are taxed at

* This is an edited, reformatted and augmented version of a Congressional Research Service publication, CRS Report for Congress RL30255, from www.crs.gov, prepared for Members and Committees of Congress, dated March 27, 2013.

retirement. In contrast, contributions to Roth IRAs are not tax deductible, but distributions from Roth IRAs are not taxed on withdrawal in retirement. Expanded contribution limits were adopted in 2001, but were scheduled to expire after 2010; the Pension Protection Act of 2006 made those increases permanent.

In November 2005, President Bush's Advisory Panel on Federal Tax Reform proposed changes to IRAs. The panel's plan would have created Save for Retirement Accounts (SRAs) to replace traditional and Roth IRAs. Additionally, President Bush proposed consolidating IRAs into a Roth-style retirement savings account. The Obama Administration appears to be taking a different tack by proposing additional incentives to increase saving by low- and moderate-income workers in existing retirement saving accounts that have proven effective in evaluations.

Neither conventional economic theory nor the empirical evidence on savings effects tends to support the argument that increased IRA contributions are primarily new savings—often increased retirement saving comes at the expense of reduced nonretirement saving. Roth-style accounts are less likely to induce new private savings than are traditional ones. Furthermore, these proposals would predominantly benefit higher-income individuals and families, who are the ones most likely to save without the added incentive.

Proposals that increase retirement saving among low- and moderate-income workers could be effective in increasing new saving because these workers typically have little or no nonretirement saving to reduce.

INTRODUCTION

Retirement experts generally argue that there are three pillars to retirement income security: Social Security, employer-provided pensions, and private savings. Coverage by Social Security is nearly universal, but its benefits are limited, and many workers reach retirement with small pensions and little savings. Over the past few decades, Congress and the President have offered tax incentives to encourage businesses to offer pensions and workers to save. The Joint Committee on Taxation estimates that tax incentives to encourage retirement saving could cost the U.S. Treasury $714 billion between 2013 and 2017.

An increasingly important retirement saving vehicle is the individual retirement account (IRA). IRAs were created by ERISA, the Employee Retirement Income Security Act of 1974 (P.L. 93- 406), which was signed into law by President Ford on Labor Day. ERISA was passed to protect the interests of pension plan participants and pension beneficiaries. IRAs were originally designed to give individuals not covered by an employer pension plan a chance to save in a tax advantaged retirement account. Since ERISA was passed in 1974, the law has been amended several times to change the tax treatment of IRAs and create new types of IRAs. Currently, nearly everyone is eligible to contribute to at least one type of IRA.

IRA savings is encouraged by two mechanisms—a carrot and a stick approach. First, tax provisions allow individuals to defer taxes on IRA contributions and investment earnings or to accumulate investment earnings tax free, effectively raising the rate of return on IRA contributions. Second, nonqualified withdrawals before the age of 591/2 are subject to a 10% penalty tax in addition to regular taxes.

Several times during his Administration, President Bush had proposed that all IRAs be combined into a single Roth-style IRA. The Obama Administration appears to be taking a different tack by proposing additional incentives to saving in existing retirement saving accounts that have proven effective in evaluations.

This report provides background information on IRAs, including a description of current law and the tax benefits of IRAs. In addition, the effects of IRAs on saving and other national objectives are discussed. A final section describes and analyzes recent IRA reform proposals. The *Appendix* contains a history of the development of IRAs.

CURRENT RULES REGARDING INDIVIDUAL RETIREMENT ACCOUNTS

Although IRAs have been around for over 30 years, the rules regarding IRAs have changed several times (see the *Appendix* for a brief history of IRAs). The current rules were set in the Economic Growth and Tax Relief Reconciliation Act of 2001 (P.L. 107-16). For 2013, both the traditional and Roth IRAs have an annual contribution limit of $5,500, which is adjusted to inflation (in $500 blocks). Individuals 50 years or older may make additional annual "catch-up" contributions of $1,000. The provisions of the Economic Growth and Tax Relief Reconciliation Act (EGTRRA) would have expired after 2010, but the Pension Protection Act of 2006 made the pension and IRA provisions of EGTRRA permanent.

Traditional (Front-loaded) IRAs

Contributions to traditional IRAs by certain individuals are tax deductible. The amount of the deduction depends on the level of the individual's modified adjusted gross income (AGI) and whether the individual or the individual's spouse is covered by an employer pension plan.[1] *Table 1* shows the income limits for the deductibility of contributions. Generally, individuals not covered by an employer pension plan and lower-income individuals are entitled to at least a partial deduction. Single individuals with modified AGI of less than $59,000 are entitled to a full deduction even if they are covered by an employer pension plan.

Table 1. Income Limits for Tax Deductions of Contributions to Traditional IRAs, 2013

Income Tax Filing Status	Modified AGI	Deduction
Individual Covered by Employer Pension Plan		
Single; or head of household	$59,000 or less	Full
	$59,000 to $69,000	Partial
	$69,000 or more	None
Married, filing jointly; or qualifying widow(er)	$95,000 or less	Full
	$95,000 to $115,000	Partial
	$115,000 or more	None
Married, filing separately	less than $10,000	Partial
	$10,000 or more	None
Individual Not Covered by Employer Pension Plan		
Single; head of household; or qualifying widow(er)	Any Amount	Full
Married, filing jointly; or married, filing separately with spouse not covered by employer pension plan	Any Amount	Full
Married, filing jointly with a spouse who is covered by employer pension plan	$178,000 or less	Full
	$178,000 to $188,000	Partial
	$188,000 or more	None
Married, filing separately with a spouse who is covered by employer pension plan	less than $10,000	Partial
	$10,000 or more	None

Source: Congressional Research Service.

Married individuals filing jointly and not covered by an employer pension plan but whose spouses are covered by a pension plan are entitled to deduct part of their traditional IRA contribution if their modified AGI is between

$178,000 and $188,000. The Tax Increase Prevention and Reconciliation Act of 2005 (P.L. 109-222), which became law in May of 2006, allows high-income individuals to convert any of their IRAs to Roth IRAs beginning in 2010, so that their partially tax-favored plans become fully tax exempt. Taxes on the conversions occurring in 2010 were due in 2011 and 2012.

Whether or not contributions are deductible, investment earnings on traditional IRA assets are tax deferred until distribution at retirement. Taxable distributions from traditional IRAs are taxed as ordinary income. All deductible contributions to traditional IRAs are fully taxable when withdrawn. However, nondeductible or after-tax contributions are not taxed when withdrawn; only the investment earnings on these contributions are taxable. Taxable distributions from traditional IRAs made before the individual has reached 591/2 years of age are subject to an additional 10% penalty tax.

Roth (Back-loaded) IRAs

Contributions to Roth IRAs are not tax deductible, but qualified distributions from Roth IRAs are tax free. Not everyone, however, is eligible to contribute to a Roth IRA—there are income limits on participation (see *Table 2*).

Table 2. Income Limits for Contributing to Roth IRA. 2013

Income Tax Filing Status	Modified AGI	Contribution
Married, filing jointly; or qualified widow(er)	less than $178,000	full contribution
	$178,000 to $188,000	reduced contribution
	$188,000 or more	no contribution
Married, filing separately and lived with spouse at any time during the year	$0	full contribution
	$0 to $10,000	reduced contribution
	$10,000 or more	no contribution
Single; head of household; or married, filing separately and did not live with spouse during the year	less than $112,000	full contribution
	$112,000 to $127,000	reduced contribution
	$127,000 or more	no contribution

Source: Congressional Research Service.

At a certain income level (for example, $110,000 for a single individual), the contribution limit is reduced. The contribution limit is eventually reduced to zero, and the individual is not eligible to contribute to a Roth IRA. Although qualified distributions from Roth IRAs are tax free, early distributions may be subject to a 10% penalty tax in addition to regular taxes.[2]

Required Minimum Distributions

Owners of traditional IRAs are required to begin taking minimum distributions from their IRA beginning at 701/2 years old (Roth IRA owners face no such requirement). The rules applying to the required minimum distribution are the same as those for qualified employer-sponsored retirement plans (e.g., 401(k)s).

The individual must receive the distribution by April 1 following the calendar year in which the owner reaches the age of 701/2. The amount that is required to be distributed depends on the IRA balance at the end of the preceding year and life expectancy. For example, an unmarried 71-year-old with an IRA balance of $26,500 would be required to take a minimum distribution of $1,000.

With the precipitous decline in the stock market in 2008, Congress was concerned that many elderly retirees would be disadvantaged because they would be required to withdraw retirement monies by selling stocks when the market is down.

Furthermore, basing the distribution amount on the account balance as of the end of the previous year could mean that the distribution is a larger proportion of the actual balance at the time of the distribution. Consequently, Congress passed the Worker, Retiree, and Employer Recovery Act of 2008 (P.L. 110-458), which provided for a one-year waiver of the required minimum distribution rules for calendar year 2009. The minimum distribution rules, however, only require that IRA owners move a certain proportion of their IRA balance from a tax-advantaged investment account to a taxable investment account and pay the appropriate taxes on the distribution (which had been deferred). Moreover, because the market will presumably recover, paying taxes at a time when asset values are low could be beneficial compared with normal circumstances, because it will defer taxes to the future when asset values rise.

TAX CONSEQUENCES OF IRAS

The main tax advantages of a traditional IRA are the deductibility of contributions for some individuals and the tax deferment of investment returns on IRA assets. The advantages are due to (1) tax-deferred compounding of interest, and (2) the possibility of postponing tax liability from a time when income is high and the individual is in a high tax bracket, to a time when income may be lower and the individual is in a lower tax bracket. However, there is no guarantee that income will be lower after retirement than before, or that the tax brackets will be the same after retirement as before.

Contributions to a Roth IRA are taxable, but the returns earned on Roth IRA assets are not taxable. Consequently, in this important respect, Roth IRAs are like a tax-exempt bond. Veryhigh-income individuals and families, however, are not eligible to establish and contribute to a Roth IRA.

Losses on both traditional and Roth IRA investments can be included on an individual's tax return.[3] The loss, however, can only be included if the individual itemizes, and after all the amounts in the IRA have been distributed with the total distributions being less than total nondeductible contributions.

When Traditional and Roth IRAs are Equivalent

The ultimate tax treatment of a front-loaded deductible traditional IRA and a back-loaded Roth IRA can be equivalent under certain circumstances. Assuming that tax rates are the same at the time of contribution and withdrawal, a deductible traditional (front-loaded) IRA offers the equivalent of no tax on the return to savings, just like a Roth (back-loaded) IRA. The initial tax benefit from the deduction is offset, in present value terms, by the payment of taxes on withdrawal. Here is an illustration: Suppose an individual had earned $100 before taxes to invest in an IRA and faces a tax rate of 25%. With a deductible traditional IRA, the individual could invest the $100, earn a 10% return, and have $110 after one year. At a 25% tax rate, the individual would receive an $82.50 after-tax distribution from his or her IRA.[4] If the individual instead chose a Roth IRA, he or she would first pay taxes on the $100 (equal to $25) and contribute $75 to the Roth IRA. After one year and a 10% return on investment, the individual would receive an $82.50 distribution from his or her Roth IRA ($75 in principal and a $7.50 return on investment, neither of which would be taxed). In this example, the after-tax distributions from each type of IRA are the same.[5]

Differences between Traditional and Roth IRAs

There are three ways in which these tax treatments can differ: if tax rates vary over time, if the dollar ceilings are the same, and if premature withdrawals are made. There are also differences in the timing of tax benefits that have some implications for individual behavior as well as revenue costs.

Variations in Tax Rates over Time

The equivalence of front-loaded and back-loaded IRAs holds only if the same tax rate applies to the individual at the time of contribution and the time of withdrawal in the case of front-loaded IRAs. Taking the same example as before, assume that the individual's tax rate at the time of contribution is 25%, but is 15% at the time of withdrawal. The individual with the Roth IRA would still receive a distribution in the amount of $82.50 after one year. The individual contributing to the deductible traditional IRA would still have $110 in pre-tax principal and interest after one year, but would be taxed at the 15% rate with an after-tax IRA distribution of $93.50.[6] In this case, the deductible traditional (front-loaded) IRA has better tax advantages than the Roth IRA. The reverse could be true if the individual faces a higher tax rate at the time of withdrawal than at the time of contribution.

Contribution Limits

The contribution limits for traditional and Roth IRAs are the same. For individuals contributing at the limit, however, the back-loaded Roth IRA is more generous than both deductible and nondeductible traditional IRAs. Suppose the contribution limit is $4,000 (the limit for 2005), the interest rate is 8%, and the tax rate is 25%. If the individual has $4,000 (after tax) for a one-time investment in an IRA, the after-tax dollar yield after 20 years is shown in Table 3 for each type of IRA and for a conventional taxable investment account.

After 20 years, the distribution to the individual from a Roth IRA would be $18,644. No taxes would be due on this amount. An individual investing in a nondeductible traditional IRA would receive a $14,983 distribution after 20 years. This individual would have to pay taxes on $14,644 in accumulated investment earnings. An individual investing $4,000 in a front-loaded deductible traditional IRA would be able to deduct the $4,000 and would consequently have an extra $1,000 to save (assuming a 25% tax rate).[7] After 20 years, the IRA balance would be $18,644, which is taxed at the 25% tax rate. The balance in the taxable investment account would be $3,207. The total after-tax income would be $17,190.[8] In comparison, with a $4,000 investment, the balance in a taxable investment account after 20 years would be $12,829.

Table 3. Net Distribution from Taxable Savings Account and Various Types of IRAs

	Net Distribution of Qualified Withdrawal After 20 Years	Net Distribution of Nonqualified Withdrawal	
		After 1 Year	After 20 Years
Roth IRA	$18,644	$4,208	$13,518
Deductible Traditional IRA	$17,190	$3,868	$15,326
Nondeductible Traditional IRA	$14,983	$4,208	$13,518
Taxable Investment Account	$12,829	$4,240	$12,829

Source: Congressional Research Service.

Nonqualified Withdrawals

Traditional and Roth IRAs differ in the tax burdens imposed if nonqualified withdrawals are made (generally before retirement age).[9] This issue is important because it affects both the willingness of individuals to commit funds to an account that might be needed before retirement and the willingness to withdraw funds already committed to an account.

The front-loaded deductible traditional IRA provides steep tax burdens for early-year withdrawals, which decline dramatically over time because the penalty applies to both principal and interest. (Without the penalty, the effective tax rate is always zero.) For example, with a 25% tax rate and an 8% rate of return, an individual taking a nonqualified distribution from a deductible IRA would face an effective interest rate of -6.4% rather than the 8% nominal return because of the 10% penalty tax. In other words, an individual would have effectively lost 6.4% of the original investment. The effective tax burden in this case would be 180%.[10] After three years the effective tax burden would be 63%, and 38% after five years. After about seven years, the tax burden would be the same as an investment made in a taxable account: 25%. Thereafter, tax benefits would occur, with the effective tax burden falling to 20% after 10 years, 10% after 20 years, and 6% after 30 years. These tax benefits would occur because taxes would be deferred, and the value of the deferral would exceed the penalty.

The case of the back-loaded Roth IRA is much more complicated. First consider the case where all such IRAs are withdrawn. In this case, the effective tax burdens would be smaller in the early years. Although premature withdrawals are subject to both regular tax and penalty, the taxes apply only to the earnings, which are initially very small. In the first year, the effective tax rate would be the sum of the ordinary tax rate (25%) and the penalty (10%), or 35%. Because of deferral, the effective tax rate would slowly decline (33% after three years, 32% after five years, 28% after 10 years). In this case, it would take 14 years to earn the same return that would have been earned in a taxable account at a 25% tax rate.[11] Partial premature withdrawals from Roth IRAs, on the other hand, would be treated more generously, as they would be considered to be a return of principal until all original contributions were recovered.

The dollar consequences of the 10% penalty tax on nonqualified distributions are shown in the final two columns of *Table 3.* After one year, a taxable investment account would yield a higher dollar amount than a nonqualified distribution from any type of IRA. The deductible traditional IRA would incur a loss after one year—not only would the net distribution be less than that for other types of IRAs, it would be less than the original $4,000 investment. Because the investment earnings from a Roth IRA would be subject to both regular and penalty taxes, the distribution would be the same as for a nondeductible traditional IRA.

After 20 years, the value of the tax deferral of the deductible traditional IRA would exceed the tax penalty, so the net distribution would be greater than that from a taxable investment account ($15,326 versus $12,829). The nonqualified distribution from a Roth IRA and nondeductible traditional IRA would be $13,518 after 20 years—greater than the return from a taxable investment account but less than a nonqualified distribution from a deductible traditional IRA.

These differences suggest that individuals should be much more willing to put funds that might be needed in the next year or two for an emergency in a back-loaded Roth account than in a front-loaded deductible traditional account, since the penalties relative to a regular savings account are much smaller. These differences also suggest that funds might be more easily withdrawn from Roth IRAs in the early years even with penalties. This feature of the back-loaded Roth IRA makes these tax-favored accounts much closer substitutes for short-term savings not intended for retirement.

It could eventually become more costly to make premature withdrawals from back-loaded accounts than from front-loaded accounts. Consider, for example, a withdrawal in the year before eligibility at the age of 591/2 of all funds that had been in the account for a long time. For a front-loaded IRA, the cost would be the 10% penalty on the withdrawal plus the payment of regular tax one year in advance—both would apply to the full amount. For a back-loaded account, in which no tax or penalty would be due if held until retirement, the cost would be the penalty plus the regular tax on the fraction of the withdrawal that represented earnings, which would be a large fraction of the account if held for many years.

ECONOMIC IMPORTANCE OF IRAS

Individual retirement accounts held $873 billion in assets in 1992, which was equivalent to almost 14% of gross domestic product (GDP). By the end of 2011, IRAs held $4.9 trillion in assets, or the equivalent of 32% of GDP (see *Figure 1*). IRAs held almost $1 of every $3 in retirement assets in 2011.[12] IRA assets grew between 1992 and 1999, fueled by the rising stock market and the introduction of Roth IRAs in 1997. After the stock market bubble burst, total IRA assets remained fairly constant at about $2.6 trillion. After the stock market recovered somewhat in 2002, IRA assets began to increase. The value of IRA assets fell in 2008 during the recession, but have since recovered as the stock market recovered.

IRAs have effects on the federal budget. On the one hand, certain IRA contributions are tax deductible, which will reduce income tax revenues. Between 1993 and 2006, annual IRA income tax deductions varied between $7.4 billion and $12.5 billion (see *Figure 2*). After Roth IRAs were introduced in 1997 (which are not deductible), IRA deductions fell from $8.7 billion in 1997 to $7.4 billion by 2001. After 2001, IRA deductions increased, reaching $12.8 billion in 2007 and then fell slightly during the 2007-2009 recession.

On the other hand, certain IRA distributions are taxable, which will increase income tax revenues. Taxable IRA distributions amounted to $27.1 billion in 1993 and grew to almost $100 billion by 2000 (see *Figure 3*). After 2000, taxable IRA distributions fell slightly until 2003 and then increased, amounting to $162.2 billion by 2008. Distributions fell in 2009 to $135.2 billion (a 17% reduction) possibly due to the fall in asset values in 2008. However, taxable distributions from IRAs increased by 44% between 2009 and 2010 as all taxpayers were allowed to convert traditional IRAs to Roth IRAs.

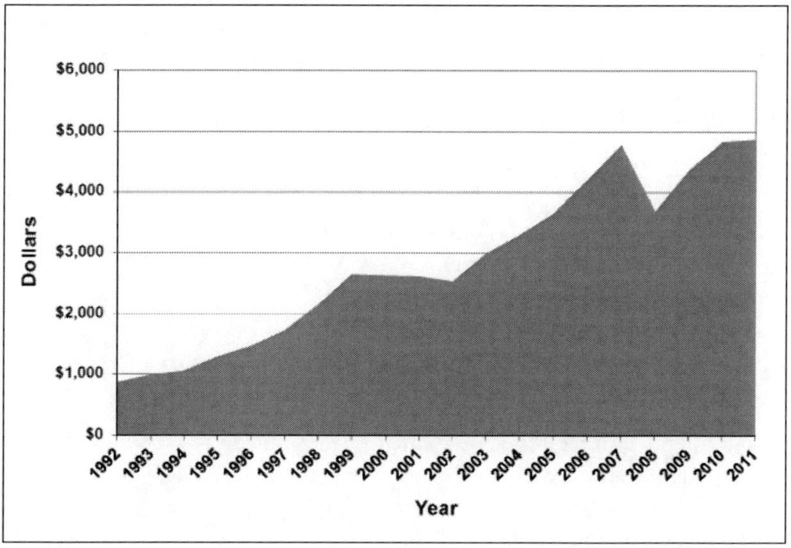

Source: Federal Reserve Board, Flow of Funds Accounts of the United States, table L.225.i.

Figure 1. Total IRA Assets, 1992-2011 (billions of dollars).

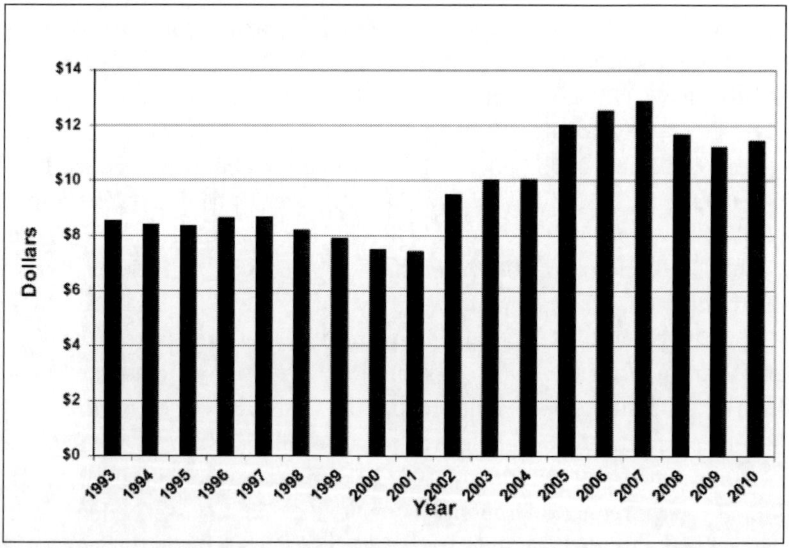

Source: Internal Revenue Service, Statistics of Income Division, Individual Income Tax Returns, Publication 1304, various years.

Figure 2. Total IRA Deductions, 1993-2010 (billions of dollars).

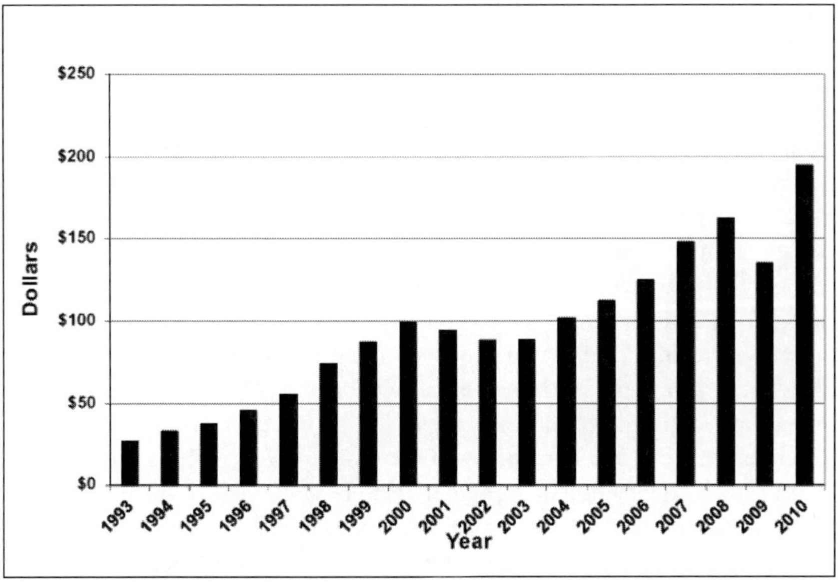

Source: Internal Revenue Service, Statistics of Income Division, Individual Income Tax Returns, Publication 1304, various years.

Figure 3. Total Taxable IRA Distributions, 1993-2010 (billions of dollars).

The cost to the government of the tax-favored treatment of IRAs can be measured by the concept of tax expenditures. Tax expenditures are defined as "revenue losses attributable to provisions of the federal tax laws that allow a special exclusion, exemption, or deduction from gross income or a deferral of tax liability."[13] The Joint Committee on Taxation estimates that the tax expenditures of individual retirement plans will be $16.3 billion in FY2008 and will amount to $98.3 billion between 2008 and 2012.[14]

Savings Effects

Higher savings rates can lead to faster wealth and capital accumulation, which can boost future national income.[15] An important question is whether or not the IRA tax incentives increase saving. The broadest measure of saving is national saving which consists of saving by households (personal saving), businesses, and the government through the budget surplus (public saving). IRA tax incentives (and many other retirement income tax incentives) can affect both personal and public saving. The tax expenditures for IRAs (discussed in the previous section) will lower public saving by reducing the budget surplus or increasing the budget deficit.

Conventional economic theory and empirical analysis do not offer unambiguous evidence that these tax incentives have increased personal or national saving.[16] From a theoretical perspective, the effect of a tax reduction on savings is ambiguous because of offsetting income and substitution effects. The increased rate of return may cause individuals to substitute future consumption for current consumption and save more (a substitution effect), but, at the same time, the higher rate of return will allow individuals to save less and still obtain their target amount of savings (an income effect). The overall consequence for savings depends on the relative magnitude of these two effects. Empirical evidence on the relationship of the rate of return to the saving rate is mixed but indicates mostly small effects of uncertain direction. Recent evidence of the uncertainty of increasing savings with a higher rate of return is the juxtaposition of high returns in the stock market in the mid- to late 1990s with a dramatic reduction in the personal savings rate. This fall in the savings rate in the face of high returns provides some evidence that expanded tax incentives for IRAs will not be successful in increasing savings rates. The increasing individual contributions to IRAs may simply have resulted from shifting existing assets into IRAs or diverting savings, which would otherwise have occurred, into IRAs.

IRAs are unlikely to increase savings because most tax benefits were provided to individuals who contributed the maximum amount, which eliminates any substitution effect. For these individuals, the effect on savings is unambiguously negative, with one exception. In the case of the front-loaded deductible traditional IRA, savings could increase to offset part of the up-front tax deduction, but only if individuals recognize that their IRA accounts will involve a tax liability upon withdrawal. The share of IRAs that were new savings would depend on the tax rate—with a 28% tax rate, one would expect that 28% would be saved for this reason; with a 15% tax rate, 15% would be saved for this reason. This effect does not occur with a back-loaded Roth IRA or a nondeductible traditional IRA. Thus, conventional economic analysis suggests that private savings would be more likely to increase with a front-loaded rather than a back-loaded IRA.

Despite this conventional analysis, some economists have argued that IRA contributions were largely new savings. Theoretical arguments have been made that IRAs increase savings because of psychological, "mental accounting," or advertising reasons. Individuals may need the attraction of a large initial tax break; they may need to set aside funds in accounts that are restricted to discipline themselves to maintain retirement funds; or they may need the impetus of an advertising campaign to remind them to save. There has also been some empirical evidence presented to suggest that IRAs increase savings. This evidence consists of (1) some simple observations that individuals who invested in IRAs did not reduce their non-IRA assets, and (2) a statistical estimate by Venti and Wise that showed that IRA contributions were primarily new savings.[17]

The fact that individuals with IRAs do not decrease their other assets does not prove that IRA contributions were new savings; it may simply mean that individuals who were planning to save in any case chose the tax-favored IRA mechanism. The Venti and Wise estimate has been criticized on theoretical grounds, and an empirical study by Gale and Scholz using similar data found no evidence of a savings effect.[18] A study by Joines and Manegold comparing savings behavior of those newly eligible for IRAs and those already eligible for IRAs found no evidence of an overall effect on savings, although increases were found for some individuals and decreases for others; a study by Attanasio and DeLeire using this approach also found little evidence of an overall savings effect.[19] And, while one must be careful in making observations from a single episode, there was no overall increase in the savings rate during the period that IRAs were universally available, despite large contributions into IRAs. Similarly, the household savings rate continued (and actually accelerated) its decline after the expansion of IRAs in 1997.

It is important to recognize that this debate on the effects of IRAs on savings concerned the effects of front-loaded deductible IRAs. Many of the arguments that suggest IRAs would increase savings do not apply to back-loaded Roth IRAs. For example, back-loaded IRAs do not involve the future tax liability that, in conventional analysis, should cause people to save for it.

Indeed, based on conventional economic theory, there are two reasons that the introduction of back-loaded Roth IRAs may decrease savings. First, those who are newly eligible for the benefits should, in theory, reduce their savings, because these individuals are higher-income individuals who are more likely to save at the limit. The closer substitutability of Roth IRAs with savings for other purposes would also increase the possibility that IRA contributions up to the limit could be made from existing savings. Secondly, those who are currently eligible for IRAs, who are switching funds from front-loaded traditional IRAs, or who are now choosing back-loaded Roth IRAs as a substitute for front-loaded ones should reduce their savings because they are reducing their future tax liabilities.

Also, many of the "psychological" arguments made for IRAs increasing savings do not apply to the back-loaded IRA. There is no large initial tax break associated with these provisions, and the funds are less likely to be locked up in the first few years because the penalty applying to early withdrawals is much smaller. In addition, funds are not as illiquid or tied up because of the possibility of withdrawing them penalty-free for special purposes, including medical expenses.

Overall, the existing body of economic theory and empirical research does not make a convincing case that the expansion of individual retirement accounts, particularly the back-loaded accounts which were included in the 1997 legislation, will increase savings.

DISTRIBUTIONAL EFFECTS

Who benefitted from the expansion of IRAs? In general, any subsidy to savings tends to benefit higher-income individuals who are more likely to save. The benefits of IRAs for high-income individuals are limited, however, compared to many other savings incentives because of the dollar and income limits. Nevertheless, the benefits of IRAs when universally allowed tended to go to higher-income individuals. In 1986, 82% of IRA deductions were taken by the upper third of individuals filing tax returns (based on adjusted gross income); since these higher-income individuals had higher marginal tax rates, their share of the tax savings would also be larger.

In addition, when universal IRAs were available from 1981-1986, they were nevertheless not that popular. In 1986, only 15% of tax returns reported contributions to IRAs. Participation rates were lower in the bottom and middle of the income distribution: only 2% of taxpayers in the bottom third of tax returns and only 9% of individuals in the middle third contributed to IRAs. Participation rose with income: 33% of the upper third contributed, 54% of taxpayers in the top 10% contributed, and 70% of taxpayers in the top 1% contributed.

Ownership of IRAs has increased substantially since 1986, however. In 2004, the Investment Company Institute estimates that 40% of U.S. households owned an IRA.[20] Not surprisingly, households that own IRAs have higher income and more wealth than households not owning IRAs. Although there are income limits on the deductibility of IRA contributions, a disproportionate share of the tax benefits accrue to upper-income taxpayers. In 2003, tax returns reporting $75,000 or more in adjusted gross income accounted for 23.5% of all taxable returns. While only 4.5% of these higher-income returns reported a tax-deductible IRA contribution, they accounted for 40% of all reported deductible IRA contributions.

Overall, as one might expect, the expansion of IRAs tends to benefit higher-income individuals, although the benefits are constrained for very-high-income individuals because of the contribution and income limits. An expansion in contribution limits (as occurred in 2003) would be more focused, however, on higher-income individuals who are more likely to be contributing at the limit and more likely to take full advantage of higher limits.

ADMINISTRATIVE ISSUES

The more types of IRAs that are available, the larger the administrative costs associated with them. With the introduction of back-loaded Roth accounts in 1997, three types of IRAs now exist: the front-loaded that have been available since 1974 (and universally available in 1981-1986), the non-deductible tax-deferred accounts, and the back-loaded Roth accounts. Treatment on withdrawal will also be more complex, since some are fully taxable, some partially taxable, and some not taxable at all.

Another administrative complexity that arises is the possibility of penalty-free withdrawals prior to retirement for special purposes. These special purposes include using the distribution for unreimbursed medical expenses, buying or building a first home, and higher-education expenses. Each special purpose has separate conditions placed on the distribution. For example, the firsttime-homebuyer early distribution is limited to $10,000, and the medical expenses early distribution can occur only if unreimbursed medical expenses exceed 7.5% of adjusted gross income.[21]

POLICY IMPLICATIONS OF TRADITIONAL AND ROTH IRAS

Many individuals now have a choice between a front-loaded deductible traditional IRA and a back-loaded Roth IRA. An earlier section discussed the relative tax benefits of the alternatives to the individual. This section discusses the relative advantages and disadvantages to these different approaches in achieving national policy objectives. These objectives include reducing the federal budget deficit and federal debt, increasing national savings, and increasing retirement savings.

From a budgetary standpoint, the short-run estimated cost of the front-loaded deductible traditional IRA will better reflect the eventual long-run budgetary costs of IRAs than does the back-loaded Roth IRA. Roth IRAs have probably made it harder to meet long-run budgetary goals because the budget cost is incurred in the future as the nontaxed account earnings grow and budget targets do not take into account the out-year costs (that is, the costs beyond the five- or 10- year budget window). This issue can be important if the long-term objective is balancing the budget or generating surpluses. Achieving this goal can be compromised if the costs of IRAs are rising. In addition, if distributional tables are based on cash flow measures, as in the case of the Joint Tax Committee distributional estimates, a more realistic picture of the contribution of IRA provisions to the total distributional effect of the tax package will emerge with the front-loaded IRA.

The deductible traditional IRA is more likely to result in more private savings than the Roth IRA, from the perspective of either conventional economic theory or the "psychological" theories advanced by some. In fact, Roth IRAs may not have contributed to private savings. Of course, a traditional IRA also has a revenue cost which offsets any positive private savings effect. The ultimate impact of traditional IRAs on national saving depends on the relative magnitudes of the revenue costs and the private saving effect.

While the IRA tax incentives may not have appreciably increased national savings, they have probably increased retirement savings by individuals.[22] The severe penalties for early withdrawals increase the likelihood these funds will be available at retirement. The increase in retirement savings is becoming more important as the old-style defined benefit pension plans are either eliminated or replaced by less generous and riskier defined contribution plans such as 401(k) plans.

There are, however, some policy advantages of Roth IRAs. The Roth IRA avoids one planning problem associated with deductible traditional IRAs: individuals may fail to recognize the tax burden associated with accumulated IRA assets. If this is the case, the deductible IRA would leave them with less after-tax assets in retirement than they had planned for, a problem that would not arise with the Roth IRA, in which no taxes are paid at retirement. Another possible advantage of Roth IRAs is that the effective tax rate is always known (zero), unlike the front-loaded IRA where the effective tax rate depends on the tax rate today vs. the tax rate in retirement.

RECENT PROPOSALS

In 2005, the President's Advisory Panel on Federal Tax Reform proposed consolidating the traditional and Roth IRAs. This plan would create Save for Retirement Accounts (SRAs) to replace traditional and Roth IRAs. Contributions up to $10,000 annually could be made regardless of adjusted gross income. The contribution limit would be indexed to inflation. Contributions would not be tax deductible but investment earnings would accumulate tax free. Early distribution exceeding the value of contributions would be subject to regular and penalty taxes.

The Advisory Panel also proposed the creation of Save for Family Accounts (SFAs) to replace existing education and medical savings accounts. This proposal would allow every taxpayer to contribute up to $10,000 each year to an SFA on an after-tax basis. The earnings would accumulate tax free in the same way as in the current Roth IRA. Tax-free withdrawals would be allowed at any time for qualified educational and medical costs, or to purchase a primary residence. In addition, taxpayers would be able to withdraw up to $1,000 tax free each year for any purpose. Nonqualified distributions in excess of the $1,000 limit would be subject to income taxes and a 10% penalty tax, similar to the penalty paid on nonqualified distributions from the current Roth IRA.

For the same reasons that apply to Roth IRAs, none of these proposals would appreciably increase national saving. Furthermore, it is unlikely that these proposals would appreciably increase retirement saving. The SFA is probably more attractive savings vehicles for workers than the SRA because they have the same tax advantages as the retirement accounts, but can be accessed penalty-free before retirement. Because less than a third of U.S. families report that retirement is the most important reason for saving, it seems likely most workers would save in the nonretirement accounts before saving in the retirement accounts.[23]

With no income limits on owning any of these accounts, it also seems likely that a considerable amount of existing savings would be transferred to these accounts. Consequently, tax expenditures would increase, especially beyond the typical budget 5- or 10-year horizon. This could dramatically increase future budget pressures.

Although 60% of U.S. families saved in 2000, there are income disparities: 30% of the poorest 20% of families saved while over 80% of the richest 10% of families saved.[24] These proposals would predominantly benefit higher-income individuals and families who are the ones likely to save.

The Obama Administration is taking a different tack on incentives to encourage retirement saving. The Administration has proposed incentives to save in traditional and Roth IRAs rather than creating new savings accounts. One proposal would require employers that do not offer a retirement plan to offer employees automatic enrollment in a Roth IRA (that is, all employees would be enrolled in an IRA but would have the option to opt out of the plan or enroll in a traditional IRA). Evaluations of automatic enrollment in voluntary retirement plans (with the option to opt out) show that participation is significantly increased.

Another Administration proposal would increase the tax credit to small business for adopting a new qualified retirement plan or SIMPLE IRA. The proposal is to increase the credit from $500 to $1,000 per year for three years.

Lastly, the Administration has proposed expanding the saver's credit.[25] The proposal would essentially convert the credit to a 50% match on the first $500 contributed to a qualified retirement plan and would make the credit refundable. Evidence from the current saver's credit suggests that many eligible taxpayers are unable to receive the full benefit of the credit because of insufficient tax liability. Furthermore, the saver's credit appears to be substantially less effective in boosting retirement saving than a simple matching contribution because of the complexity of the credit. Research has shown that small matching contributions increase employee's contributions to retirement plans. Making the saver's credit refundable and simplifying the rules may contribute to increasing retirement saving.

CONCLUSION

The initial purpose of IRAs in 1974 was to extend the tax advantages allowed to employees with pension plans to individuals with no pension coverage. The major focus of IRAs today is generally to encourage savings, especially for retirement. If the main objective of individual retirement accounts is to encourage private and national savings, the analysis in this study suggests that this objective has not been achieved. Moreover, the back-loaded Roth approach is less likely to induce savings than the traditional form of IRAs. However, IRAs have undoubtedly increased longer-term saving for retirement. But, the ability to withdraw amounts for purposes other than retirement somewhat dilutes this focus on preparing for retirement. The recent and planned expansions in the IRA limit may make the provisions more likely to provide a marginal incentive, but will also direct the benefits towards higher-income individuals.

IRAs have often been differentiated from other tax benefits for capital income as the plan focused on moderate income or middle class individuals. The IRA has been successful to the extent that more of the benefits are targeted to moderate-income individuals than is the case for many other tax benefits for capital (e.g., capital gains tax reductions). Nevertheless, data on participation and usage of IRAs suggest that the benefits still accrue primarily to higher-income individuals.

Appendix. A History of IRA Proposals

Individual retirement accounts of the traditional type (front-loaded) were first allowed in 1974 (up to $1500 or 15% of earnings) to extend some of the tax benefits of employer pension plans to those whose employers did not have such plans. IRAs were made universally available in 1981 (and the limits increased to $2000) as a general savings incentive.

In 1986, IRAs were restricted for higher-income individuals already covered by employer pension plans, as part of the general base broadening needed to reach the distributional and revenue neutrality goals of the Tax Reform Act of 1986. Those covered by employer plans with incomes less than $50,000 for married individuals and $35,000 for single individuals were not eligible. There was a $10,000 phaseout range (i.e., $40,000 to $50,000) where partial benefits were allowed. Deductible contributions were limited to $2,000 or total earnings, whichever was less; contributions could also be made for a non-working spouse (but total contributions for a married couple could not exceed total earnings). Individuals above the income limits could make nondeductible contributions and take advantage of tax deferral on investment earnings.

In the 101st Congress (1989-1990) several proposals to restore IRA benefits were made: the Super IRA, the IRA-Plus, and the Family Savings Account (FSA).

The Super-IRA proposal, suggested by Senator Bentsen and approved by the Senate Finance Committee in 1989 (S. 1750), would have allowed one half of IRA contributions to be deducted and would have eliminated penalties for "special purpose" withdrawals (for first time home purchase, education, and catastrophic medical expenses). The IRA proposal was advanced as an alternative to the capital gains tax benefits proposed on the House side.

The IRA-Plus proposal (S. 1771), sponsored by Senators Packwood, Roth, and others, proposed an IRA with the tax benefits granted in a different fashion from the traditional IRA. Rather than allowing a deduction for contributions and taxing all withdrawals similar to the treatment of a pension, this approach simply eliminated the tax on earnings, like a tax-exempt bond. (This type of IRA is commonly referred to as a back-loaded IRA.) The IRA-Plus would also be limited to a $2,000 contribution per year. Amounts in current IRAs could have been rolled over and would not have been subject to tax on earnings (only on original contributions); there were also special purpose withdrawals with a five-year holding period.

The Administration's proposal in 1990 for FSAs also used a back-loaded approach with contributions allowed up to $2500. No tax would have been imposed on withdrawals if held for seven years, and no penalty (only a tax on earnings) if held for three years. There was also no penalty if funds were withdrawn to purchase a home. Those with incomes below $60,000, $100,000, and $120,000 (single, head of household, joint) would have been eligible.

In 1991, S. 612 (Senators Bentsen, Roth, and others) would have restored deductible IRAs, and also allowed an option for a nondeductible or back-loaded "special IRA." No tax would have been applied if funds had been held for five years and no penalties would have applied if used for "special purpose withdrawals."

In 1992, the President proposed a new IRA termed a FIRA (Flexible Individual Retirement Account), which would have allowed individuals to establish back-loaded individual retirement accounts in amounts up to $2,500 ($5,000 for joint returns) with the same income limits as proposed in the 101st Congress. No penalty would have been applied for funds held for seven years.

Also in 1992, the House passed a limited provision (in H.R. 4210) to allow penalty-free withdrawals from existing IRAs for "special purposes." The Senate Finance Committee proposed, for the same bill, an option to choose between back-loaded IRAs and front-loaded ones, with a five-year period for the back-loaded plans to be tax free and allowing "special purpose" withdrawals. This provision was included in conference, but the bill was vetoed by the President for unrelated reasons. A similar proposal was included in H.R. 11 (the urban aid bill) but only allowed IRAs to be expanded to those earning $120,000 for married couples and $80,000 for individuals (this was a Senate floor amendment that modified a Finance Committee provision). That bill was also vetoed by the President for other reasons.

The Contract with America and the 1995 budget reconciliation proposal included proposed IRA expansions similar to the 1997 proposals (discussed below), but this package was not adopted. The Health Insurance Portability and Accountability Act of 1996 allowed penalty-free withdrawals from IRAs for medical costs.

In 1997, the President proposed to increase the adjusted gross income limits for the current IRAs to $100,000 for married couples (with a phaseout beginning at $80,000), and to $70,000 for individuals (with a phaseout beginning at $50,000). Part of this expansion would have occurred in 1997-1999 (a joint phaseout between $70,000 and $90,000 and a single phaseout between $45,000 and $65,000). Such a proposal would have extended individual retirement account eligibility to the vast majority of taxpayers. Taxpayers would have had the option of choosing instead special, nondeductible IRAs, with no taxes applying if the funds are held in the account for at least five years. The 10% penalty would not have been due for withdrawals during that period for post-secondary education, first-home purchase, or unemployment spells of 12 weeks or more. Existing deductible IRAs could have been rolled over into nondeductible accounts with the payment of tax on withdrawals.

The House-proposed revisions were generally the same as those proposed in the House Republican Contract With America and included in the 1995 budget reconciliation proposal, and as those reported out of the Ways and Means Committee. This change would have allowed individuals to contribute up to $2,000 to a nondeductible or "back-loaded" IRA regardless of income, termed the American Dream Savings (ADS) account. The back-loaded IRA did not provide a tax deduction up front, and did not impose taxes on qualified withdrawals. The $2,000 would have been indexed for inflation after 1998. This provision would have been in addition to deductible IRAs (but would have replaced the current nondeductible accounts); earnings on withdrawals would not have been be taxed if held for at least five years and used for qualified purposes: withdrawals after the age of 591/2, left in the estate, attributable to being disabled, or withdrawn for down payment on a first home.

A 10% early withdrawal penalty would have continued to apply to nonqualified withdrawals, but withdrawals to pay for higher-education expenses would not have been subject to the penalty tax. No minimum distribution requirements would have applied. Taxes and penalties would not have applied until the original contribution was recovered, and all IRAs would be aggregated for this purpose.

Amounts in current IRAs could have been withdrawn and placed into the nondeductible IRAs without penalty prior to 1999. Amounts rolled over must have been included in income in equal increments over four years.

The Senate 1997 version would have raised the income limits on deductible IRAs from $50,000 to $60,000 for single returns and $80,000 to $100,000 for joint returns by 2004. These limits would have been phased in: $30,000 to $40,000 for single and $50,000 to $60,000 for joint in 1998-1989; $35,000 to $45,000 for single and $60,000 to $70,000 for joint 2000-2001; $40,000 to $50,000 for single and $70,000 to $80,000 for joint in 2002-2003. Individuals whose spouses were participants in an employer plan would have been eligible regardless of the income limit.

This proposal would also have introduced back-loaded accounts as a substitute for nondeductible accounts; individuals would have had to reduce the contributions to these accounts by the amounts deductible from front-loaded accounts. These accounts were called IRA Plus accounts. The rules regarding withdrawals and penalties were similar to those in the House bill, except that withdrawals without penalty were also allowed for long-term unemployment. There were no income limits for back-loaded IRAs.

The final bill followed the Senate version, with some alterations to the phaseouts. The provision allowing exemption from withdrawal penalties for long-term unemployment was dropped.

The Senate version of Taxpayer Refund and Relief Act of 1999 would have increased contribution limits to $5,000, increased income limits for deductible IRAs, and eliminated income limits for Roth IRAs. The House bill's provisions were much more limited: Roth IRA limits would have been increased. The final bill more closely followed the Senate version, although the income limits for Roth IRAs were to have been increased with no change for deductible IRAs. The President vetoed the tax cut because of its large revenue cost. Several bills including IRA provisions saw some legislative action in 2000, but not one was enacted.

The Economic Growth and Tax Relief Reconciliation Act of 2001 (EGTRRA) gradually increases the contribution limits to IRAs. IRA limits increased to $3,000 in 2002-2004, to $4,000 in 2005- 2007, and $5,000 in 2008. The limits will then be indexed for inflation in $500 increments. Limits for catch-up contributions by individuals over 50 years of age were $500 in 2002-2005 and $1,000 in 2006. A nonrefundable tax credit for contributions to a qualified retirement plan including IRAs beginning at 50%, but phasing down, is allowed for lower-income individuals. Many of the provisions in EGTRRA would have expired in 2010, but the Pension Protection Act of 2006 made those expansions permanent.

End Notes

[1] Modified adjusted gross income does not include certain deductions and income exclusions that are included in adjusted gross income from the 1040 or 1040A tax form.

[2] A qualified distribution is a payment from a Roth IRA made at least five years after the contribution was placed in the IRA account and the individual is at least 591/2 years old.

[3] The loss is claimed as a miscellaneous itemized deduction, subject to the 2% of adjusted gross income limit, on schedule A of the 1040 tax form.

[4] By deducting the $100 the individual does not have to pay $25 in taxes in the year the contribution is made to the IRA. However, this $25 will be paid as taxes a year later when the individual withdraws the funds from the IRA. This is essentially equivalent to borrowing $25 from the government at a 0% annual interest rate and investing the loan in the financial markets.

[5] The tax treatment is different from those who are not eligible for either a deductible traditional IRA or Roth IRA. This individual would contribute the after-tax $75 to an IRA, earn a return of $7.50 which will be taxed at the 25% tax rate. The after-tax IRA distribution will be $80.62.

[6] This is essentially equivalent to the individual borrowing $25 from the government (the taxes not paid because of deductibility), investing the money, and paying the government back $15. The individual is borrowing at a -40% interest rate.

[7] The individual could spend this $1,000. But it is assumed in this example that he saves this amount in a taxable investment account that earns the nominal yield of 8%. This $1,000 "loan" is eventually paid back to the government because the original deductible $4,000 (the investment principal) is taxed at the 25% tax rate when it is withdrawn.

[8] The ranking of a Roth IRA and deductible traditional IRA depends on the tax rate the individual faces when the money is withdrawn from the account. However, qualified distributions from both Roth IRAs and deductible traditional IRAs will always be greater than from a nondeductible traditional IRA if the rate of return is positive.

[9] A qualified withdrawal from an IRA is either a withdrawal taken after the age of 591/2 or a penalty-free withdrawal prior to retirement for special purposes. These special purposes include using the distribution for unreimbursed medical expenses, buying or building a first home, and higher-education expenses.

[10] The effective tax burden is the ratio of what the individual lost (compared to what they would have gained without the penalty tax) to what they would have gained in the absence of the 10% penalty tax.

[11] These patterns are affected by the tax rate.

[12] At the end of 2011, public and private pensions and IRAs held $15.4 trillion in assets.

[13] Congressional Budget and Impoundment Control Act of 1974 (P.L. 93-344).

[14] Joint Committee on Taxation, "Estimates of Federal Tax Expenditures for Fiscal Years 2008-2012," October 31, 2008, table 2, p. 63.

[15] Other factors also affect future income and living standards. Productivity growth, for example, directly raises future national income even without an increase in national saving.

[16] For a more complete discussion of the savings literature, see Jane G. Gravelle, The Economic Effects of Taxing Capital Income (Cambridge, MA: MIT Press, 1994), p. 27 for a discussion of the general empirical literature on savings and pp. 193-197 for a discussion of the empirical studies of IRAs. Subsequent to this survey, a paper by Orazio P. Attanasio and Thomas C. DeLeire, "The Effect of Individual Retirement Accounts on Household Consumption and National Savings," Economic Journal, vol. 112 (July 2002), pp. 504-538,

found little evidence that IRAs increased savings. For additional surveys see the three articles published in the Journal of Economic Perspectives, vol. 10, no. 3 (fall 1996): R. Glenn Hubbard and Jonathan Skinner, "Assessing the Effectiveness of Savings Incentives," (pp. 73-90); James M. Poterba, Steven F. Venti, and David A. Wise, "How Retirement Savings Programs Increase Saving," (pp. 91- 113); Eric M. Engen, William G. Gale, and John Karl Scholz, "The Illusory Effects of Savings Incentives on Saving," (pp. 113-138). A working paper by Alun Thomas and Christopher Towe, "U.S. Private Saving and the Tax Treatment of IRA/401(k)s: A Re-examination Using Household Saving Data," International Monetary Fund Working Paper 96/87, August1996, found that IRAs did not increase private household saving. A more recent study by Eric M. Engen and William G. Gale found that 401(k) plans, which are similar to IRAs in some ways, had a negligible to modest effect on savings. See "The Effects of 401(k) Plans on Household Wealth: Differences Across Earnings Groups," National Bureau for Economic Research Working Paper 8032, December 2000. See also Orazio P. Attanasio, James Banks, and Matthew Wakefield, "Effectiveness of Tax Incentives to Boost (Retirement) Savings: Theoretical Motivation and Empirical Evidence," OECD Economic Studies no. 39, 2004/2, pp. 145-172, which presents evidence that retirement saving tax incentives induce very little new saving.

[17] This material has been presented by Steven Venti and David Wise in several papers; see for example, "Have IRAs Increased U.S. Savings?" Quarterly Journal of Economics, vol. 105, no. 3 (August 1990), pp. 661-698.

[18] See William G. Gale and John Karl Scholz, "IRAs and Household Savings," American Economic Review, vol. 84 (December 1994), pp. 1233-1260. A detailed explanation of the modeling problem with the Venti and Wise study is presented in Jane G. Gravelle, "Do Individual Retirement Accounts Increase Savings?" Journal of Economic Perspectives, vol. 5 (spring 1991), pp. 133-148.

[19] See Douglas H. Joines and James G. Manegold, "IRAs and Savings: Evidence from a Panel of Taxpayers," Federal Reserve Bank of Kansas City Research Working Paper 91-05, October 1991; Orazio P. Attanasio and Thomas C. DeLeire, "The Effect of Individual Retirement Accounts on Household Consumption and National Savings," Economic Journal, vol. 112 (July 2002), pp. 504-538.

[20] Sarah Holden, Kathy Ireland, Vicky Leonard-Chambers, and Michael Bogden, "The Individual Retirement Account at Age 30: A Retrospective," ICI Perspective, vol. 11, no. 1 (February 2005).

[21] The tax rules are explained in the 100-page guide for preparing 2012 tax returns. See Internal Revenue Service, Individual Retirement Arrangements (IRAs), Publication 590, 2012.

[22] See Employee Benefit Research Institute, Universal IRAs and Deductible Employee Contributions, EBRI Issue Brief #1, January 1982, at http://www.ebri.org/publications/ib.

[23] Ana M. Aizcorbe, Arthur B. Kennickell, and Kevin B. Moore, "Recent Changes in U.S. Family Finances: Evidence from the 1998 and 2001 Survey of Consumer Finances," Federal Reserve Bulletin, vol. 89 (January 2003), pp. 1-32.

[24] Ana M. Aizcorbe, Arthur B. Kennickell, and Kevin B. Moore, "Recent Changes in U.S. Family Finances: Evidence from the 1998 and 2001 Survey of Consumer Finances," Federal Reserve Bulletin, vol. 89 (January 2003), pp. 1-32.

[25] The saver's credit is a nonrefundable credit provided to low- and moderate-income workers who contribute to a qualified retirement plan. The credit is for up to 50% of workers' contribution to a retirement plan (the maximum amount of the credit is $2,000 for joint taxpayers and $1,000 for a single taxpayer).

In: Retirement Savings and Security
Editor: Linda A. Eisterhold

ISBN: 978-1-62948-132-6

Chapter 4

401(K) PLANS AND RETIREMENT SAVINGS: ISSUES FOR CONGRESS*

John J. Topoleski

SUMMARY

Over the past 25 years, defined contribution (DC) plans—including 401(k) plans—have become the most prevalent form of employer-sponsored retirement plan in the United States. The majority of assets held in these plans are invested in stocks and stock mutual funds, and the decline in the major stock market indices in 2008 greatly reduced the value of many families' retirement savings. The effect of stock market volatility on families' retirement savings is just one issue of concern to Congress with respect to defined contribution retirement plans.

This report describes seven major policy issues with respect to defined contribution plans:

1) *Access to employer-sponsored retirement plans.* In 2007, only 61% of employees in the private sector were offered a retirement plan of any kind at work. Fifty-five percent were offered a DC plan. Only 45% of workers at establishments with fewer than 100 employees were offered a retirement plan of any kind in 2007. Forty-two percent were offered a defined contribution plan.

* This is an edited, reformatted and augmented version of a Congressional Research Service publication, CRS Report for Congress R40707, from www.crs.gov, dated January 7, 2011.

2) *Participation in employer-sponsored plans.* Between 20% and 25% of workers whose employer offers a DC plan do not participate. Workers under age 35 are less likely than older workers to participate.
3) *Contribution rates.* On average, participants in DC plans contributed 6% of pay to the plan in 2007. The median contribution by household heads who participated in a DC plan in 2007 was $3,360. This was just 22% of the maximum allowable contribution of $15,500 in that year.
4) *Investment choices.* At year-end 2007, 78% of all DC plan assets were invested in stocks and stock mutual funds. This ratio varied little by age, indicating that many workers nearing retirement were heavily invested in stocks and risked substantial losses in a market downturn like that in 2008. Investment education and target date funds could help workers make better investment decisions.
5) *Fee disclosure.* Retirement plans contract with service providers to provide investment management, record-keeping, and other services. There can be many service providers, each charging a fee that is ultimately paid by participants in 401(k) plans. The arrangements through which service providers are compensated can be very complicated and fees are often not clearly disclosed.
6) *Leakage from retirement savings.* Pre-retirement withdrawals from retirement accounts are sometimes called “leakages.” Current law represents a compromise between limiting leakages from retirement accounts and allowing people to have access to their retirement funds in times of great need. In general, borrowing from a 401(k) plan poses less risk to retirement security than a withdrawal. Pre-retirement withdrawals can have adverse long-term effects on retirement income.
7) *Converting retirement savings into income.* Retirees face many financial risks, including living longer than they expected, investment losses, inflation, and possible large expenses for medical care and long-term care. Annuities can protect retirees from some of these risks, but few retirees purchase them. Developing polices that motivate retirees to convert assets into a reliable source of income will be a continuing challenge for Congress and other policymakers.

New Challenges to a Secure Retirement Income

Over the past 25 years, defined contribution (DC) plans have become the most prevalent form of employer-sponsored retirement plan in the United States. According to the Bureau of Labor Statistics (BLS), 51% of workers in the private sector participated in an employer-sponsored retirement plan of some kind in 2007. Only 20% of all private-sector workers were covered by traditional pensions—also called defined benefit or "DB" plans—whereas 43% participated in 401(k) plans and other DC plans.[1] Twelve percent of workers participated in both types of plan.[2]

One of the key distinctions between a defined benefit plan and a defined contribution plan is that in a DB plan, it is the employer who bears the investment risk. The employer must ensure that the pension plan has sufficient assets to pay the benefits promised to workers and their surviving dependents. In a DC plan, the worker bears the investment risk. The worker's account balance at retirement will depend on how much has been contributed to the plan over the years and on the performance of the assets in which the plan is invested. In a typical 401(k) plan, a worker must decide whether to participate, how much to contribute, how to invest the contributions, what to do with the account if he or she changes jobs, and how to take money out of the account after retiring.

The majority of assets held in DC plans are invested in stocks and stock mutual funds, and as a result, the decline in the major stock market indices in 2008 greatly reduced the value of many families' retirement savings.[3] According to the Federal Reserve Board, assets held in DC plans fell from $3.73 trillion at year-end 2007 to $2.66 trillion at year-end 2008, a decline of 28.7%.[4] The decline would have been even greater if not for ongoing contributions to the plans by workers and employers.

The effect of stock market volatility on families' retirement savings is just one issue of concern to Congress with respect to DC plans. Other issues that have received attention in hearings and through proposed legislation include increasing access to employer-sponsored plans, raising participation and contribution rates, helping participants make better investment choices, requiring clearer disclosure of fees charged to plan participants, preserving retirement savings when workers face economic hardship or change jobs, and promoting life annuities as a source of retirement income.

This report describes these seven major policy issues with respect to DC plans:

- access to employer-sponsored retirement plans,
- participation in employer-sponsored plans,
- contribution rates,
- investment choices,
- fee disclosure,

- leakage from retirement savings, and
- converting retirement savings into income.

Access to Employer-Sponsored Retirement Plans

According to the National Compensation Survey (NCS), 61% of private-sector workers were employed at establishments that offered one or more retirement plans in 2007. Twenty-one percent worked for employers that offered a DB plan, 55% worked for employers that offered a DC plan, and 15% worked for employers that offered both types of plan.[5] Thus, almost 4 out of 10 workers in the private sector did not have the opportunity to participate in a retirement plan where they worked. Moreover, there is a substantial disparity in sponsorship of retirement plans between large employers and small employers. Workers at establishments with fewer than 100 employees are much less likely to have access to an employer-sponsored retirement plan than are workers at larger establishments. (See Table 1.) Policies that would increase the number of small employers that offer retirement plans could expand access to these plans to include millions more workers.

Plan Sponsorship by Small Employers

Surveys of households and employers illustrate the gap in retirement plan sponsorship between large and small employers. Data collected by the Bureau of the Census indicate that there were 75 million private-sector workers between the ages of 25 and 64 who were employed year-round, full-time in 2007. Thirty million of these workers, or 40%, worked for employers that did not sponsor a retirement plan of any kind. Of these 30 million workers, 19.1 million, or 64%, worked for firms with fewer than 100 employees.[6] Likewise, data from the Department of Labor's 2007 National Compensation Survey show that 78% of workers at establishments with 100 or more employees worked for employers that sponsored retirement plans in 2007, compared with just 45% of workers at establishments with fewer than 100 employees.

Although workers at small establishments are less likely to be offered a retirement plan, when one is offered, they are as likely as employees at larger businesses to participate in the plan. In 2007, for example, 70% of workers at establishments with 100 or more employees were offered a DC plan, and the take-up rate among those offered a DC plan was 76%. At establishments with fewer than 100 employees, 42% of workers were offered a DC plan, and the take-up rate among those offered a DC plan was 79%.[7]

Table 1. Participation in Employer-Sponsored Retirement Plans, 2003 and 2007 (Private-sector workers; in percentages)

Establishment Size	2003	2007	2003	2007	2003	2007
	Offered any plan		Participated in any plan		Take-up rate	
100 or more workers	75	78	65	66	87	85
Under 100 workers	42	45	35	37	83	82
All Workers	57	61	49	51	86	84
	Offered a DB Plan		Participated in DB plan		Take-up rate	
100 or more workers	34	34	33	32	97	94
Under 100 workers	9	9	8	9	89	100
All Workers	20	21	20	20	100	95
	Offered a DC Plan		Participated in DC plan		Take-up rate	
100 or more workers	65	70	51	53	78	76
Under 100 workers	38	42	31	33	82	79
All Workers	51	55	40	43	78	78

Source: U.S. Department of Labor, Bureau of Labor Statistics, National Compensation Survey.

Notes: Data represent 102 million workers in 2003 and 108 million workers in 2007. The take-up rate is the percentage of workers offered a plan who participated in the plan. In 2007, for example, 55% of workers were offered a DC plan and 43% of workers participated in a DC plan. Therefore, the take-up rate was .43/.55 = .78.

Workers at firms with fewer than 100 employees comprised 44% of all private-sector workers in the United States in 2007. If employees at small firms had been offered DC plans at the same rate as employees of larger firms, an additional 11.4 million workers would have had the opportunity to participate in employer-sponsored retirement plans in 2007. If take-up rates among these employees had been the same as at firms that already offered DC plans, an additional 9.0 million workers would have participated in DC plans in 2007.[8]

Defined Contribution Plans for Small Employers

Qualified retirement plans, including 401(k) plans, must comply with the Employee Retirement Income Security Act (ERISA) and the Internal Revenue Code (IRC). Among the requirements for retirement plans to receive favorable tax treatment is that they are prohibited from discriminating in favor of highly-compensated employees (HCEs) in terms of contributions or benefits.[9] This assures that rank and file employees as well as owners and managers benefit from the tax breaks that Congress has granted to tax-qualified retirement plans. The nondiscrimination tests compare the participation rates and plan contributions for HCEs to those of other employees.[10] In a small firm, relatively modest changes in employee participation or contributions can make the difference between the plan passing or failing the nondiscrimination test. If the plan fails, some of the contributions made by HCEs must be returned to them and included in their taxable income for the year. A plan that fails the nondiscrimination test also can lose its tax-qualified status, but this penalty is applied only in rare circumstances.

To encourage more employers, especially small employers, to sponsor retirement plans, Congress has authorized several kinds of defined contribution plans that are exempt from some administrative requirements that otherwise would apply. In some cases, plans that adopt certain characteristics that favor rank-and-file workers are exempt from nondiscrimination testing.

"Safe-Harbor" 401(k) Plans

In 1996, Congress authorized a "safe-harbor" 401(k) plan that exempts the plan sponsor from the annual nondiscrimination tests in exchange for the employer agreeing to make contributions to the plan. In a safe-harbor 401(k), the employer must either contribute an amount equal to 3% of pay on behalf of each *eligible* employee or match the first 3% of salary deferrals of each *participating* employee on a dollar-for-dollar basis and match the next 2% of employee deferrals at 50 cents per dollar.[11] Any firm with one or more employees can establish a safe-harbor 401(k).

Savings Incentive Match Plans for Employees of Small Employers (SIMPLE)

The Small Business Job Protection Act of 1996 (P.L. 104-188) authorized the Savings Incentive Match Plan for Employees of Small Employers (SIMPLE). In exchange for mandatory employer contributions, the plan is exempt from the nondiscrimination tests. An employer that sponsors a

SIMPLE must either contribute an amount equal to 2% of pay on behalf of every *eligible* employee or match 100% of the first 3% of each *participating* employee's contributions to the plan. The maximum allowable employee contribution to a SIMPLE is $11,500 per year in 2010 and 2011. Participants aged 50 and older can make additional contributions of up to $2,500 to a SIMPLE plan. SIMPLE plans can be established only by employers with fewer than 100 employees that do not already have retirement plans.

Simplified Employee Pension (SEP)

In the Revenue Act of 1978 (P.L. 95-600), Congress authorized a defined contribution plan called the Simplified Employee Pension (SEP) for firms that do not already sponsor a retirement plan. Only the employer can make contributions to a SEP, and the employer can decide from year to year whether to contribute to the plan. Employer contributions must be made on behalf of all eligible employees, and the contributions must be the same percentage of pay for all eligible employees. Contributions cannot exceed an amount equal to 25% of pay up to a maximum of $49,000 in each year 2010 and 2011 (indexed to inflation). Participants are fully and immediately vested in the employer's contributions to the plan. Any firm with one or more employees can establish a SEP.

Plan Sponsorship Remains Low among Small Employers

Despite the availability of the SEP, SIMPLE, and safe-harbor 401(k), there has been relatively little growth in retirement plan sponsorship among small firms over the past 20 years. According to the Bureau of Labor Statistics, 36% of employees at small private-sector establishments participated in an employer-sponsored retirement plan of some kind in 1990.[12] By 2007, the participation rate in all types of retirement plans among employees at small private-sector establishments had increased by just one percentage point to 37%.[13]

One reason that small firms are less likely than large firms to offer retirement plans is that small employers are much more likely than large employers to go out of business in any given year. For example, over the six years from 2000 through 2005, an average of 10.2% of firms with fewer than 20 employees went out of business each year. Among firms with 20 to 99 employees, an average of 4.6% of firms went out of business annually, whereas among firms with 500 or more employees, an average of 2.3% of firms went out of business each year.[14] Because small firms face relatively greater uncertainty about their survival from year to year, their owners are less likely to offer a retirement plan to their employees.

Policy Issue: Automatic IRAs

Because small employers are less likely to sponsor retirement plans for their employees, policy analysts have continued to search for ways to help employees of these firms save for retirement. One proposal that has received considerable attention is to promote the adoption of payroll deduction IRAs by employers who do not sponsor retirement plans. Some such proposals would require employers above a certain size who do not sponsor a retirement plan to allow employees to contribute to an IRA through payroll deduction.[15]

Payroll deduction IRAs are not subject to the Employee Retirement Income Security Act. Small business owners who are concerned about the administrative burden of complying with ERISA might be willing to set up a payroll deduction IRA for their employees. Although some small business owners who already have retirement plans for their employees might drop these plans in favor of payroll deduction IRAs, many will not because it would reduce their opportunity to save for retirement on a tax-deferred basis. In 2011, the annual contribution limit for an IRA is $5,000 whereas the maximum employee contribution to a 401(k) is $16,500. A small business owner who sponsors and participates in a 401(k) plan can save more for retirement on a tax-deferred basis than he or she could save in an IRA. If IRA contribution limits were the same as 401(k) contribution limits, small business owners would be more likely to drop 401(k) plans for IRAs.

One possible area of concern with respect to payroll deduction IRAs is that because they are not subject to ERISA, workers who save through these plans do not have the same rights and protections as participants in 401(k) plans. The participation and vesting requirements of ERISA are not relevant to payroll deduction IRAs, but ERISA has rigorous fiduciary standards that provide important protections to plan participants. Not all of these protections extend to IRAs.

PARTICIPATION IN EMPLOYER-SPONSORED RETIREMENT PLANS

Even when an employer offers a retirement plan, not all employees choose to participate. In 2007, about 75% of employees whose employer sponsored a 401(k) plan participated in the plan, and about 78% of eligible employees participated in DC plans of all types.[16] Participation in a 401(k) plan usually requires the employee to elect to contribute to the plan. Although some 401(k) plans now automatically enroll eligible employees, almost two-thirds of DC plans continue to require employees to elect to participate.[17]

Sponsorship Rates and Take-up Rates

Participation rates are affected both by access to retirement plans and take-up rates among employees who are offered a plan. The take-up rate is the percentage of employees offered a plan who choose to participate. For example, only 32% of workers under the age of 35 participated in DC plans in 2007.[18] (See Table 2.) Although this was due in part to the relatively low percentage of these workers whose employers sponsored plans, another important factor was the low take-up rate among younger workers who were offered a plan. Only 70% of workers under age 35 whose employer sponsored a DC plan participated in the plan in 2007. In contrast, the take-up rate among workers aged 35 to 44 was 82%, and the take-up rate among workers aged 45 to 54 was 83%.[19]

In contrast to the lower participation rate of younger workers compared with older workers, participation rates among employees of small firms are lower than those of employees of larger firms mainly because a smaller proportion of workers at small firms are employed by firms that sponsor retirement plans. Among employees who are offered a retirement plan, take-up rates are similar for employees of small firms and large firms. The data presented in Table 2 show that in 2007, only 9% of workers employed at firms with fewer than 20 employees participated in a DC plan, compared with 35% of workers at firms with 20 to 99 employees, 46% of those at firms with 100 to 499 employees, and 57% of those at firms with 500 or more employees. However, only 12% of workers at firms with fewer than 20 employees were *offered* a DC plan, compared with 46% of those at firms with 20 to 99 employees, 59% of those at firms with 100 to 499 employees, and 70% of workers at firms with 500 or more employees. Take-up rates were similar among employees at small firms and large firms. The take-up rate in 2007 among employees at firms with fewer than 20 employees was 77%, whereas the take-up rates among workers at firms with 20 to 99 employees and firms with 100 to 499 employees were 75% and 78%, respectively. The take-up rate at firms with 500 or more employees was slightly higher (81%).[20]

Table 2. Participation in Defined Contribution Plans: 2004 and 2007 (Working household heads and spouses under age 65)

	Offered a DC Plan		Participated in DC Plan		Take-up Rate	
	2004	**2007**	**2004**	**2007**	**2004**	**2007**
Age						
55 to 64	49.9	48.2	43.1	40.2	86.5	83.5
45 to 54	50.1	54.6	40.0	45.3	79.9	83.0
35 to 44	48.4	49.0	38.2	40.2	79.1	82.1
Under 35	42.4	45.6	28.6	31.8	67.5	69.7
Size of Firm						
500+ employees	67.7	70.4	52.8	57.0	78.0	80.9
100-499 employees	56.1	58.7	41.4	45.8	73.7	78.0
20-99 employees	43.6	46.3	34.3	34.9	78.8	75.4
Under 20 employees	14.9	11.9	11.9	9.2	80.1	76.9
Education						
College graduate	58.6	59.5	49.1	50.6	83.8	85.0
Some college	46.3	50.5	35.1	39.3	75.7	77.9
High school less	37.8	39.4	26.5	28.6	70.2	72.7
Household Income						
Top quartile	60.9	61.5	53.0	53.9	87.1	87.5
Second quartile	52.6	54.5	41.4	45.6	78.7	83.8
Third quartile	43.5	46.3	31.1	33.6	71.4	72.5
Bottom quartile	25.8	29.7	13.9	17.0	54.1	57.4
Total	**47.3**	**49.4**	**36.7**	**39.2**	**77.5**	**79.3**

Source: CRS analysis of the Federal Reserve Board's 2004 and 2007 *Survey of Consumer Finances*.

Notes: Data represent 112 million workers in 2004 and 115 million workers in 2007. Education is the highest level of education completed by the head of household. The take-up rate is the percentage of workers offered a plan who participated in the plan. In 2007, for example, 49.4% of workers were offered a DC plan and 39.2% of workers participated in a DC plan. Therefore, the take-up rate was .392/.494 = .793.

Access to employer-sponsored retirement plans and participation in plans also differ between better-educated and less-educated workers and between workers in higher-income and lower-income households. Only 39% of workers in households in which the household head had a high school education or less worked for an employer that sponsored a DC plan in 2007, compared with 60% of workers in households in which the household head was a college graduate. The take-up rate among the less-educated group was 73%, compared with 85% for those in the better-educated group. Similarly, only 30% of workers in households in the bottom quartile of household income worked for an employer that sponsored a DC plan in 2007, compared with 62% of workers in households in the top income quartile. The take-up rate among workers in the bottom income quartile was just 57%, compared with 88% among workers in the top income quartile.

These results imply that policies intended to raise participation in retirement plans should be designed with the situation of the target population in mind. Efforts to increase plan participation among younger workers should be focused on the low take-up rate among young employees who are offered a plan, perhaps by encouraging firms to adopt automatic enrollment or to provide more education for workers about the importance of saving for retirement. Policies designed to raise participation among employees of small firms will need to target the low sponsorship rate among small employers, which may require finding new ways to make offering a retirement plan less burdensome and costly to small employers. Less-educated workers may need more guidance, perhaps in the form of investment education and investment advice, than better-educated workers. Workers in lower-income households, who may be hesitant to opt into a 401(k) plan that will reduce take-home pay, may be more receptive to plans that devote a portion of future pay increases to the retirement plan.

Policy Issue: The Retirement Savings Tax Credit

Congress has established tax incentives to encourage employers to sponsor retirement plans and employees to participate in these plans. Employer contributions to qualified plans are a tax-deductible business expense, and neither contributions—whether made by the employer or the employee—nor the investment earnings on those contributions are taxed as income to the employee until they are withdrawn from the plan.[21]

Because higher-earning workers pay higher marginal tax rates than lower-earning workers, the tax deduction for contributing to a retirement plan is worth more to a worker in a higher tax bracket than it is to a worker in a lower tax bracket. For a worker with a marginal income tax rate of 35%, contributing $1 to a 401(k) plan costs just 65 cents after taking the tax deduction into account. For a worker with a marginal income tax rate of 20%, contributing $1 to a 401(k) plan costs 80 cents on an after-tax basis. Moreover, both economic theory and empirical evidence suggest that the propensity to save rises with income. Because higher-earners would save much of their income even without tax incentives to do so, a substantial share of the tax revenue lost through the deduction for contributions to retirement plans does not result in a net increase in national saving. Consequently, some economists have suggested that the tax incentives for retirement saving are "upside down." Most of these tax breaks are enjoyed by higher-wage workers who would be likely to save part of their income even without a tax deduction, rather than by low-wage workers who might respond to an effective tax incentive with new saving.

One strategy for increasing contributions to retirement plans would be to provide tax incentives that are targeted to low- and middle-income workers. To provide an additional incentive for lower-income workers to contribute to retirement savings plans, Congress in 2001 authorized a new retirement savings tax credit, sometimes called the "saver's credit." In 2011, single taxpayers with adjusted gross income (AGI) up to $17,000 are eligible for a credit of 50% on qualified retirement contributions up to $2,000. For single filers with AGI of $17,001 to $18,250, the credit is 20%, and for single filers with AGI of $18,251 to $28,250, the credit is 10%. Married couples filing jointly with AGI up to $34,000 are eligible for a credit of 50% on qualified retirement contributions up to $2,000. For married couples with AGI of $34,001 to $36,500, the credit is 20%, and for married couples with AGI of $36,501 to $56,500, the credit is 10%.

The saver's credit is now claimed on about 5 million tax returns each year.[22] The maximum credit is $1,000. The average credit in 2007 was $167. Although the saver's credit provides an incentive for lower-income workers to save for retirement, its effect has been limited because the credit is non-refundable and phases out steeply over a range of income that is relatively low. A nonrefundable credit reduces taxes owed by the amount of the credit. However, if the individual or family owes no income tax after having taken the exemptions and deductions for which they are eligible, a nonrefundable credit has no value.[23] This is the case for many households with modest earnings who might benefit from the saver's credit if the credit were refundable.[24]

H.R. 1961 of the 111th Congress would have increased the rate of the tax credit for retirement savings contributions, mad the credit refundable, and required the credit to be paid into retirement accounts. The income limit for the maximum credit of 50% of contributions would have been increased to an adjusted gross income of $32,500 for individuals and $65,000 for couples. The credit would have phased out between $32,500 and $42,500 for individuals and between $65,000 and $85,000 for married couples filing jointly. The bill would have set the maximum amount of an employee contribution that is eligible for the credit at $500 for an individual and $1,000 for a couple. The contribution limits would have increased by $100 and $200, respectively, each year until 2020. After that time, the limits would have been indexed to the rate of inflation.

CONTRIBUTIONS TO RETIREMENT SAVINGS PLANS

If an employee elects to participate in a 401(k) plan, the next important decision he or she must make is how much to contribute to the plan. Studies have shown that employees are more likely to contribute to a plan if it provides matching contributions, and the amount that an employee contributes to a plan can be influenced by the formula for the matching contribution.[25] About two-thirds of all 401(k) plans offered an employer matching contribution in 2007.[26] The most common matching formula was 50% of the first 6% of pay contributed by the employee, for a total employer contribution equal to 3% of employee pay.

The maximum permissible annual contribution to a retirement plan is limited by federal law, but very few workers contribute amounts near the annual legal maximum.[27] Many employees contribute only enough to receive the full amount of the employer matching contribution. Those who elect not to contribute to a plan that offers a match, or who contribute less than the amount necessary to receive the full match, are in effect choosing to reduce their own compensation below the maximum available to them.[28]

In defined contribution plans, the benefit available to the worker at retirement is the amount in his or her account. The account balance depends on the amount that the employer and employee have contributed to the plan, the investment gains or losses on those contributions, and the fees charged to participants. Research has shown that, historically, the most important factors affecting workers' retirement account balances at retirement are the number of years over which they have contributed and the amounts that they contributed each year to their retirement plans.[29] Consequently, persuading workers to save more and to begin saving earlier are two of the most effective ways of increasing workers' income in retirement.

Household Contributions to DC Plans in 2007

Table 3 shows households' monthly contributions to DC plans in 2007 both in dollars and as a percentage of household earnings. The top panel of the table shows contributions categorized by the age of the household head, the middle panel shows contributions categorized by household income, and the bottom panel shows contributions by all households that contributed to a DC plan.

In 2007, the median monthly contribution to defined contribution plans by households in which at least one worker aged 25 to 64 participated in a DC plan was $290. This is equivalent to $3,480 on an annual basis.[30] As a percentage of household earnings, the median contribution by households in which one or more workers participated in a DC plan was 5.1% of earnings. Twenty-five percent of households that contributed to a DC plan in 2007 contributed $660 or more per month, and 25% contributed $130 per month or less. As a percentage of earnings, 25% of households participating in DC plans contributed 8.3% of earnings or more to the plan in 2007, and 25% of participating households contributed 2.9% of earnings or less to the plan.

Household Contributions by Age of Household Head

Households headed by persons under age 35 contribute less to DC plans, both in dollars and as a percentage of household earnings, than households headed by individuals aged 35 and older. In 2007, the median monthly contribution to DC plans by households headed by persons under age 35 in which at least one worker participated in a plan was $190. Among households headed by persons aged 35 to 44, the median monthly contribution was $310, and among households headed by persons aged 45 to 44, the median monthly contribution was $368. The median monthly DC plan contribution among households headed by persons aged 55 to 64 was $330 in 2007.

As a percentage of total household earnings, the median monthly contribution to DC plans by households headed by persons under age 35 in which at least one worker participated in a plan was 4.2% of earnings. The median contribution among households headed by persons aged 35 to 44 was 5.2% of earnings. Among both households headed by persons aged 45 to 54 and households headed by persons aged 55 to 64, the median contribution to DC plans in 2007 was 5.7% of household earnings.

Household Contributions by Household Income

As one might expect, household contributions to DC plans vary substantially by household income. This is likely to be the case both because higher-income households have more disposable income to save and also because, as was discussed earlier, the tax deduction for retirement savings is more valuable to higher-income households than to lower-income households. In addition, higher-income households are more likely than lower-income households to have more than one worker contributing to a DC plan.

In 2007, the median monthly contribution to DC plans among households in the top income quartile in which one or more workers participated in a plan was $750. Among households in the bottom income quartile in which one or more workers participated in a DC plan, the median monthly contribution to DC plans was $100. As a percentage of income, the median contribution among households in the top income quartile was 6.6% of household earnings, whereas among households in the bottom income quartile, the median contribution was 4.3% of household earnings.[31]

Table 3. Monthly Household Contributions to Defined Contribution Plans in 2007

	Monthly Contributions in Dollars	**Percentage of Household Earnings**
Age of Householder		
55 to 64		
75th percentile of contributions	$790	9.9%
50th percentile of contributions	330	5.7
25th percentile of contributions	133	3.1
45 to 54		
75th percentile of contributions	810	8.5
50th percentile of contributions	368	5.7
25th percentile of contributions	158	3.1
35 to 44		
75th percentile of contributions	750	8.6
50th percentile of contributions	310	5.2
25th percentile of contributions	150	2.9

Table 3. (Continued)

	Monthly Contributions in Dollars	Percentage of Household Earnings
Under 35		
75th percentile of contributions	360	6.0
50th percentile of contributions	190	4.2
25th percentile of contributions	87	2.5
Household Income		
Top income quartile		
75th percentile of contributions	1,292	10.0
50th percentile of contributions	750	6.6
25th percentile of contributions	380	3.6
Second income quartile		
75th percentile of contributions	500	8.2
50th percentile of contributions	303	5.1
25th percentile of contributions	170	3.0
Third income quartile		
75th percentile of contributions	250	6.1
50th percentile of contributions	160	4.4
25th percentile of contributions	90	2.5
Bottom income quartile		
75th percentile of contributions	160	6.2
50th percentile of contributions	100	4.3
25th percentile of contributions	50	2.5
All Contributing Households		
75th percentile of contributions	660	8.3
50th percentile of contributions	290	5.1
25th percentile of contributions	130	2.9

Source: CRS analysis of the Federal Reserve Board's 2007 Survey of Consumer Finances.

Notes: Households are grouped by total income, including earnings and all other income. Contributions are reported as a percentage of total household earnings. Among households in which there was a worker under age 65 in 2007, those with income of $100,780 or more were in the top income quartile and those with income under $33,940 were in the bottom income quartile. Median income for these households was $59,650.

POLICY ISSUE: AUTOMATIC CONTRIBUTION ESCALATION

Employer matching contributions have been shown to raise participation rates in 401(k) plans. Many employees, however, contribute just enough to receive the full employer match. Employer matching contributions usually phase out at relatively low employee contribution rates. Matching contributions on employee salary deferrals of more than 6% of pay are relatively uncommon. Consequently, employer matching contributions are not as effective at raising employee contribution rates over time as they are at inducing employees to start contributing to the plan. Just as automatic enrollment has proven to be an effective means of raising participation rates in 401(k) plans, automatic contribution escalation can raise contribution rates.

The Pension Protection Act of 2006 sought to encourage employers to adopt automatic enrollment as a feature of their retirement plans by granting an exemption to certain regulations to plans that include a "qualified automatic contribution arrangement."[32] One of the features that a qualified automatic contribution arrangement must include is automatic escalation of employee contributions. Employee deferrals must be equal to specific percentages of pay unless the employee elects a different percentage. The minimum required deferral amount is 3% of pay in the employee's first year of participation, 4% in the second year, 5% in the third year, and 6% in the fourth and later years. The automatic deferral cannot exceed 10% of pay, but participants can elect a higher deferral rate, provided their total deferrals for the year do not exceed the annual limit under I.R.C. § 402(g). In 2011, this limit is $16,500.

A qualified automatic contribution arrangement also must include employer contributions. The employer contribution can be either a non-elective contribution equal to at least 3% of pay for all employees or a matching contribution equal to 100% of the first 1% of salary deferred and 50% of deferrals from 1% of pay to 6% of pay. Other matching formulas are permitted if they result in matching contributions that are at least equal to the amount provided under the prescribed matching formula, do not increase as the employee's rate of deferral increases, and do not apply to deferrals in excess of 6% of pay.

In 2007, the median employee salary deferral into employer-sponsored defined contribution plans was 6% of pay; however, 25% of workers who contributed to a DC plan deferred 3.9% of pay or less. Qualified automatic contribution arrangements that include automatic contribution escalation could raise employee contribution rates for a substantial percentage of participants. Employees could elect not to participate or to lower their contributions. The experience of most plans with automatic enrollment has been that the majority of participants who are automatically enrolled continue to participate. There is less evidence on the long-term effects of automatic contribution escalation on employee contributions because not as many plans have yet adopted automatic escalation.

INVESTMENT CHOICES AND INVESTMENT RISK

A worker who has elected to participate in a 401(k) plan and has decided how much to contribute to the plan usually also must decide how to invest these contributions. More than 90% of 401(k) plans allow employees to direct the investment of their contributions, and three-fourths of plans allow employees to direct the investment of the employer's contributions.[33] In order for a plan sponsor to be relieved of liability for investment losses in a participant-directed retirement plan, participants must be given a choice of at least three investment alternatives, each of which must have different risk and return characteristics.[34] Most plans offer participants more than the minimum number of investment choices required by law. In 2007, the average 401(k) plan offered participants 18 investment options.[35] The investment options most commonly offered were actively managed U.S. stock funds (77% of plans), actively managed international stock funds (73%), indexed U.S. stock funds (70%), and actively managed U.S. bond funds (64%).[36]

Participants in 401(k) plans bear the risk of investment losses. An individual's retirement account might suffer investment losses because the particular stocks, bonds, or other assets in which he or she has chosen to invest decline in value. Diversification can reduce the risk associated with investing in specific assets because declines in the value of some assets may be fully or partially offset by gains in the value of other assets. Stock and bond mutual funds, for example, help protect individuals from investment risk by purchasing securities from many companies in a variety of industries. In a stock mutual fund, investment losses from companies that are performing poorly may be offset by investment gains from companies that are performing well.

A broader form of investment risk is *market risk*, which is the possibility of an overall decline in a broad class of assets, such as stocks. Even a well-diversified portfolio of stocks, for example, will not protect the value of an individual's retirement account from depreciating if stock values fall across the board, as they did in 2008. This is why most investment advisors recommend diversification not only within a class of assets—by buying broadly diversified stock mutual funds instead of individual stocks, for example—but also diversification across asset classes. Bond prices have historically been less volatile than stock prices, and there have been long periods when returns on stocks and bonds have not been closely correlated. Life-cycle funds and target date funds diversify across classes of assets by buying shares in stock mutual funds, bond funds, and sometimes other investments as well.

Although most financial advisors recommend diversifying investments across classes of assets and periodically re-balancing accounts to maintain appropriate diversification, relatively few plan participants put this advice into practice. The assets of DC plans are heavily invested in stocks and stock mutual funds. At year-end 2007, 78% of all DC plan assets were invested in stocks and stock mutual funds. Investment in stocks and stock mutual funds varied little by age, indicating that many workers nearing retirement were heavily invested in stocks, and risked substantial losses in a market downturn like that in 2008. According to the 2007 Survey of Consumer Finances, nearly 30% of DC plan participants between the ages of 35 and 54 had 100% of their account balance invested in stocks in 2007. Twenty-eight percent of participants aged 55 to 64 had their entire account balance invested in stocks and stock mutual funds. (See Figure 1.)

Because many plan participants lack basic financial literacy, policy analysts have suggested that plans should take steps to help participants make better investment choices or adopt plans that automatically allocate contributions among various classes of investments. Investment education and target date funds are two approaches to achieving asset diversification in DC plans.

Policy Issue: Investment Education and Investment Advice

To make informed decisions about how much to save for retirement and how to invest these savings, plan participants need to understand certain basic principles of finance. For example, an individual who understands the risk-

and-return characteristics of stocks and bonds will be better able to balance the risk of investment losses with the expected rate of return from each kind of investment compared to someone who lacks this understanding. Not everyone understands investment risk, however, and many people make decisions about their investments that are not well-informed. Some 401(k) plan sponsors have attempted to help employees make better investment decisions by providing investment education, offering investment advice, and adding "life-cycle funds" or "target date funds" to their plans.

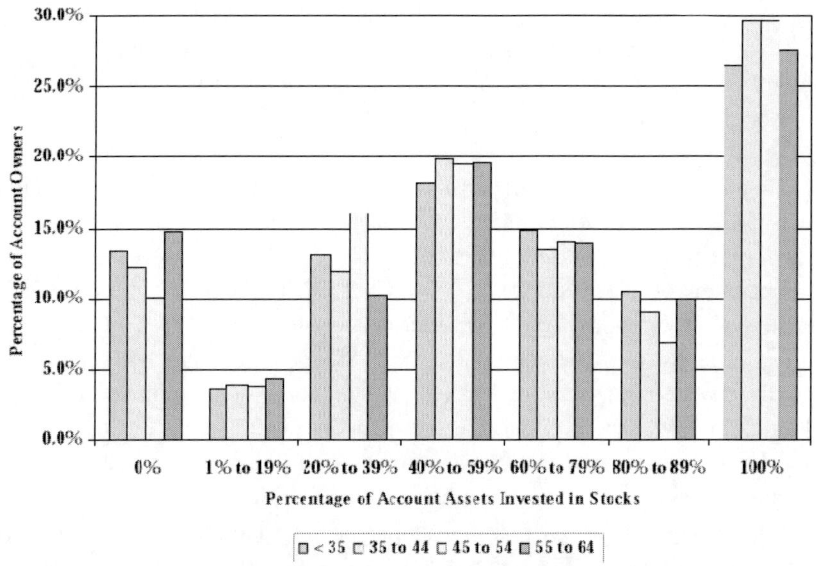

Source: CRS analysis of the Federal Reserve Board's 2007 Survey of Consumer Finances.

Notes: Household heads under age 65 with a defined contribution plan.

Figure 1. Percentage of Defined Contribution Plan Assets Invested in Stocks, 2007; (By age of account owner).

Investment Education

According to Hewitt Associates, more than 90% of all 401(k) plans offer some form of investment education. Typically, investment education is offered through enrollment kits, seminars and workshops, and internet sites. Investment education helps plan participants understand the importance of saving for retirement. It typically focuses on educating individuals about basic tenets of finance, such as the effects of compound interest and the difference between stocks and bonds. Employees who understand how investment gains compound over time are more likely to start contributing to the plan, to continue to contribute to the plan, and to raise their contributions as their earnings rise over time. Participants who understand that the higher expected rate of return on stocks compared to bonds comes at the cost of greater price volatility will be better able to balance their tolerance for risk with their desire for higher returns when choosing investments. Even with more investment education, some employees will choose not to participate in retirement savings plans because they prefer higher current income to higher income in retirement. For workers who discount future income heavily, changing their default participation status to automatic enrollment may be more effective than investment education.

Investment Advice

Investment education consists mainly of giving plan participants general information about the basic principles of finance that they need to be informed investors. Investment advice, on the other hand, is tailored to the individual and often involves recommending specific investments. Some plan sponsors have been reluctant to offer investment advice both because of the cost of paying professional advisors and concerns about possible legal liability for investment losses incurred by plan participants. Almost half (49%) of all 401(k) plans offered investment advice to plan participants in 2007, up from 35% in 2000.[37]

Even if a plan offers a range of low-cost, diversified investment options and offers investment education and investment advice, it is not unusual for some participants to make investment choices that may prove to be unwise in the long run. For example, some participants invest too much of their retirement savings in the stock of their employers. This exposes them to the risk of losing their retirement savings as well as their jobs if the firm goes out of business. Others invest too conservatively while they are young—putting most of their contributions into low-yielding money market funds, for example—even though their longer investment horizon would suggest that they could take on more risk. Sound investment advice can help plan participants avoid these common mistakes.

Under ERISA, providing investment advice is a fiduciary act. A plan sponsor could be held liable for investment losses incurred by a participant who follows investment advice offered by a plan or its agent. The Pension Protection Act of 2006 (PPA) amended ERISA to allow plan sponsors who follow certain procedures to provide investment advice without being held liable for investment losses of participants who act on the advice.[38] In general, to be permissible under the provisions of the PPA, the advice must be provided for a fee rather than a commission, or it must be based on a computer model that meets requirements set forth in statute and regulations. The advisors must disclose their fee arrangements to plan participants and inform them of their affiliations with investments they recommend and with the developer of the computer model. The model on which the advice is based must "operate in a manner that is not biased in favor of investments offered by the fiduciary adviser or a person with a material affiliation or contractual relationship with the fiduciary adviser."[39]

Investment Advice Regulations and Legislation

On January 21, 2009, the Department of Labor (DOL) published a final regulation on the investment advice provisions of the PPA. On March 19, the department delayed the effective date of the regulation for 60 days, pending further review and receipt of additional public comments. On May, 21, 2009, the department announced that the regulation would not be implemented until November 18, 2009. On November 20, 2008, DOL announced that it was withdrawing the final rule. [40]

The investment advice provisions of the PPA allow investment advice to be provided to plan participants by individuals with a financial interest in the investments that they recommend, provided that they disclose this information to plan participants. On April 23, 2009, Representative Robert Andrews introduced H.R. 1988, the Conflicted Investment Advice Prohibition Act of 2009. This bill would allow investment advice to be provided to plan participants only by independent investment advisers who are registered under the Investment Advisers Act of 1940 and who meet certain other qualifying requirements. The bill would prohibit advisers from managing any investments in which any of the assets of the plan are invested, and it would prohibit plans in which individuals direct the investment of their accounts from contracting with investment advisers who are not independent advisers. Independent advisers would be required to provide participants with documentation of the historic rates of return of investment options available to the plan, and to notify participants that the investment adviser is acting as a fiduciary of the plan.

Policy Issue: Life-cycle Funds and Target Date Funds

Even if a plan participant understands the basic principles of finance, he or she may have neither the time nor the inclination to monitor and manage a retirement account. Because many plan participants lack either the aptitude, interest, or time to manage their retirement accounts, plan sponsors have begun to add "life-cycle funds" or "target date funds" to their 401(k) plans. These plans are designed to allocate the participant's investments between stocks and bonds in a way that takes into account his or her risk tolerance and expected date of retirement. Although these funds have proved popular with participants and have won the approval of many investment professionals, the sharp downturn in stock prices in 2008 showed that they are not without problems. Many target-date funds for people expecting to retire in 2010 or 2011 were heavily invested in stocks and lost 25% to 30% of their value in 2008.

Life-cycle funds and target date funds are similar. Many financial analysts consider target date funds to be a subset of the category of funds called life-cycle funds. A life-cycle fund is a mutual fund in which the allocation of assets among stocks, bonds, and cash-equivalents (money market funds, for example) is automatically adjusted during the course of the participant's working life. As the participant nears retirement age, the investment allocation is shifted away from higher-risk investments, such as stocks, and moves toward lower-risk investments, such as bonds and cash equivalents. A target-date fund is a life-cycle fund designed to achieve a particular (generally conservative) mix of assets at a specific date in the future, which is usually the year when the participant expects to retire.

Although life-cycle funds and target date funds are typically designed with the intent of achieving more rapid growth in the early years of the participant's career and greater stability of asset values in the later years, they can contain any mix of stocks, bonds, and cash. There are no industry standards or federal regulations that specify what allocation of assets is required for a life-cycle fund or a target date fund that is intended for plan participants of a given age or with a particular investment time horizon. Currently, less than 5% of DC plan assets are invested in life-cycle funds. Analysts expect this percentage to rise over the next 10 years because the Pension Protection Act allows companies to use life-cycle funds as the default investment option for employees who are automatically enrolled in a 401(k) plan and who do not select an investment fund for their 401(k) contributions.[41]

Allocation of assets among stocks, bonds, and cash-equivalents varies greatly among target date funds with the same target retirement date. A recent study by Morningstar, Inc. found that among target-date 2010 funds that were at least three years old, stock allocations ranged from 14% of assets to 63% of assets. In December 2008, the average 2010 fund had more than 45% of its assets invested in stocks. Fund performance also varied greatly during the bear market of 2008. The S&P Target Date 2010 Index Fund, a benchmark of fund performance, fell 17% in 2008. The fund holds 60% of its assets in bonds and other fixed-income securities and 40% in equities. In comparison, the Deutsche Bank DWS Target 2010 Fund fell just 4% in 2008, whereas Oppenheimer's Transition 2010 fund fell 41%. In January, 2009, the Thrift Savings Plan's "L2010 Fund" for federal employees who plan to retire in 2010 held 70% of its assets in bonds and 30% in stocks. Shares of the L2010 Fund fell 10.5% in 2008.

In a letter sent to Secretary of Labor Hilda Solis in February 2009, Senator Herb Kohl, chairman of the Senate Special Committee on Aging, urged the Secretary to "immediately commence a review of target date funds and begin work on regulations to protect plan participants."[42] In her reply to Senator Kohl on March 26, Secretary Solis stated that the Department of Labor would, in coordination with the Securities and Exchange Commission, begin a review of target date funds to determine if these funds should be subject to further federal regulation.[43]

FEES AND FEE DISCLOSURE

Another issue that has concerned Congress is the effect of fees on retirement account balances. Retirement plans contract with service providers to provide investment management, record-keeping, and other services. There can be many service providers, each charging a fee that is ultimately paid by plan participants. The arrangements through which service providers are compensated can be very complicated. Because the structure of 401(k) fees is opaque to most plan participants, it is very difficult for them to judge whether they are receiving services at a price they would be willing to pay in a more transparent market transaction.

The Administrative Structure of 401(k) Plans

Figure 2 illustrates the administrative structure of a typical 401(k) plan. Plan participants have individual accounts to which the employees, the employer, or both contribute. As the plan sponsor, the employer arranges for one or more third parties to provide various services for the plan. Services include recording transactions, arranging for loans, cashing out departing employees' accounts, and contracting with the funds into which participants can direct their contributions. Employers can purchase services separately from several service providers or they might purchase two or more services from a single service provider. Services may be priced individually or purchased in a bundled arrangement. In a bundled arrangement, several services are offered to the plan for a single fee. The service provider sometimes contracts out the provision of these services to one or more third parties.

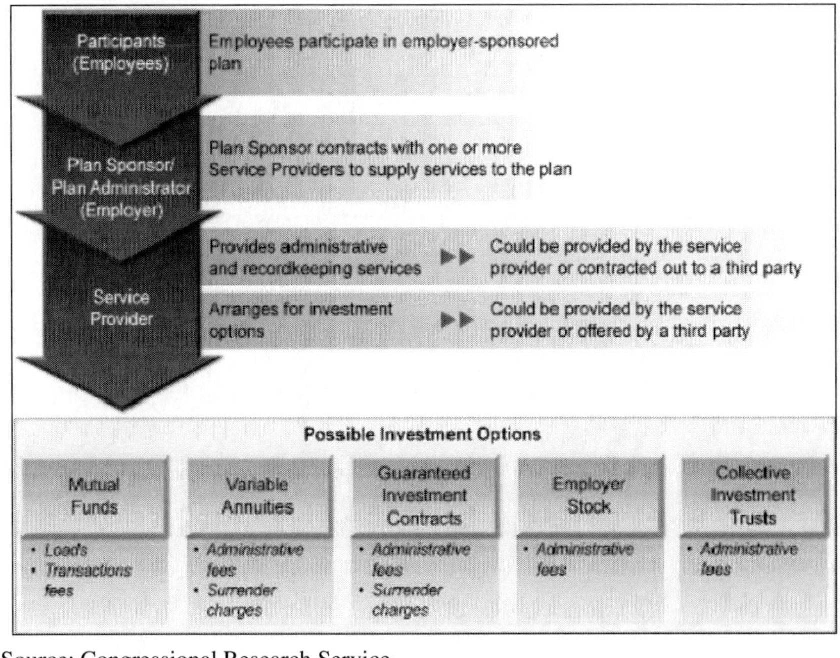

Source: Congressional Research Service.

Figure 2. The Structure of a Typical Defined Contribution Plan.

Fees vary from plan to plan. They are affected by the amounts and kinds of services offered to plan participants and also by the size of the plan. As a percentage of plan assets, fees are negatively correlated with the number of plan participants and the average account balance. In general, the greater the number of plan participants and the larger the average account balance, the lower the fees will be as a percentage of plan assets. A recent survey conducted by Deloitte Consulting for the Investment Company Institute looked at fees in plans ranging in size from those with fewer than 100 participants and less than $1 million in total assets to plans with more than 10,000 participants and assets of more than $500 million.[44] The study looked at fees for administration, recordkeeping, and investment management, which were combined into a single "all-in" fee, expressed as a percentage of plan assets. The median fee for all plans in the survey was 0.72% of plan assets, or approximately $350 for an account with the median balance of plans in the survey, which was $48,500. The study found that 10% of plans had total fees of 0.35% of assets or less and that 10% of plans had total fees of 1.72% of assets or more.

Policy Issue: Requiring Clearer Disclosure of Fees

The firms that provide record-keeping, investment management, and other services to 401(k) plans charge fees for these services, and many of these fees are passed on to plan participants. Fees for some services are charged for each transaction, while others are charged as a flat fee per account per year, and still others—such as investment management—are typically charged as a percentage of total plan assets. Small differences in fees can yield large differences in account balances at retirement, especially in the case of yearly or recurring fees.[45] For example, after 20 years, an initial $20,000 account balance earning 7% yearly would be worth about $70,000 if fees were equal to 0.5% of plan assets each year. The account would have a balance of about $58,000, or 17% less, if fees amounted to 1.5% per year. Over the course of 30 years, a participant in a plan charging fees equal to 1.5% of assets would pay almost $33,000 more in fees than he or she would have paid if the annual fees were 0.5% of assets.[46]

Section 404(a) of ERISA states that plan sponsors are responsible for "defraying reasonable expenses of administering the plan." This has been interpreted by the Department of Labor as imposing a duty on plan sponsors to assure that expenses—including fees—are reasonable. Plan sponsors are not required to minimize fees, but they are required to make sure that plan fees are "reasonable." This standard allows for wide variation in fees across plans. Although sponsors of DC plans are required by law to assure that fees are reasonable, they do not have the same financial incentive to keep fees low as do the sponsors of DB plans. In a DC plan, many fees are passed through to the plan participants, while in a DB plan most fees are paid by the plan sponsor.[47] If plan participants were better-informed about the fees that they pay and the services they receive in return for those fees, they could question plan sponsors about fees that they believe to be unreasonable. Therefore, policies that increase the transparency of fee arrangements could result in participants paying lower fees.

Plans are required by law to disclose some of the fees that plan participants pay. However, the information is not always easily accessible or easily understood by the average participant. On July 16, 2010, DOL issued final regulations requiring greater disclosure of fees.[48]

Members of Congress have been developing legislation that would require greater disclosure of fees to participants. Several bills were introduced in the 111th Congress to increase fee disclosure.

On February 10, 2009, Senator Tom Harkin introduced S. 401, the Defined Contribution Fee Disclosure Act. On April 21, 2009, Representative George Miller introduced H.R. 1984, the 401(k) Fair Disclosure for Retirement Security Act. On June 24, the House Education and Labor Committee ordered the 401(k) Fair Disclosure and Pension Security Act reported to the House. The bill reported by the committee was numbered H.R. 2989. This bill combined H.R. 1984 with H.R. 1988, the Conflicted Investment Advice Prohibition Act, which was introduced by Representative Robert Andrews. On June 9, 2009, Representative Richard Neal introduced H.R. 2779, the Defined Contribution Plan Fee Transparency Act, which was referred to the Committee on Ways and Means.

LEAKAGE FROM RETIREMENT SAVINGS PLANS

The tax incentives that Congress has authorized for retirement savings accounts are designed to assure that the money workers have set aside for retirement remains in the account until they are near retirement age. In recognition of needs that may arise over the course of an individual's life, Congress has allowed certain exceptions to the general restriction on access to these accounts before retirement. Each exception, however justifiable on its own merits, increases the danger that workers will reduce their retirement savings before they have reached retirement.

Pre-retirement withdrawals from retirement accounts are sometimes described as "leakages" from the pool of retirement savings. Congress has used a combination of regulation and taxation to limit and discourage pre-retirement access to money in retirement accounts, but it has not completely prohibited pre-retirement access to these accounts because this access is important to many plan participants. Research has shown that workers are less likely to put money into a retirement account if they believe that the money will be inaccessible in the event of emergency. Consequently, current law represents a compromise between limiting leakages from retirement accounts and allowing people to have access to their retirement funds in times of great need.

Leakages from retirement plans can take a variety of forms, including "hardship" withdrawals from the plan prior to retirement, borrowing against plan assets, and cashing out plan assets upon separation from employment.

Hardship Distributions

The tax code permits 401(k) plans to make distributions available "upon hardship of the employee."[49] Although the Internal Revenue Code (IRC) allows plans to make these distributions available, it does not require them to do so. Federal regulations specify that a hardship distribution can be made only on account of "an immediate and heavy financial need of the employee" and cannot exceed the amount of the employee's previous elective contributions.[50] Qualifying expenses include medical care for the participant or family members, the purchase of a principal residence, college tuition and education expenses, expenses to prevent eviction or foreclosure on a principal residence, and funeral expenses.

A hardship distribution must be limited to the amount needed to meet the employee's immediate financial need plus any taxes that will result from the distribution. Plan participants are prohibited from making contributions to a plan for a period of six months after a hardship distribution, and consequently they forego any employer match on contributions during that time. Hardship distributions are always subject to ordinary income taxes, and unless the distribution is used for a purpose specifically designated in law, the distribution will be subject to a 10% early withdrawal tax penalty unless the plan participant is over age 591/2.[51]

Borrowing from Retirement Plans

The IRC allows participants in employer-sponsored retirement plans to borrow from their accounts, but plans are not required to allow such loans. A loan cannot exceed the greater of $10,000 or 50% of the participant's vested benefit in the plan, up to a maximum of $50,000. Most loans from retirements plans must be paid back within five years, although loans used to purchase a home can be repaid over 15 years. If repayment ceases, the IRS will treat the full amount of the loan as a distribution from the plan, and it will be subject to income tax and possibly to an early distribution penalty. Most plans require employees who separate from the employer before the loan is repaid to repay the balance immediately or the loan will be treated as a taxable distribution from the plan.[52]

For the plan participant, borrowing from a 401(k) plan is usually preferable to taking a hardship withdrawal. With a loan, the account balance is not permanently reduced because the loan will be repaid into the account, generally within five years. Unlike a hardship distribution, after which employee contributions must be suspended for six months, the participant can continue to contribute to the plan while the loan is outstanding. Also unlike hardship distributions, loans are not subject to income taxes or the early withdrawal penalty if repayments continue on schedule.

According to the Federal Reserve Board's Survey of Consumer Finances, 9.5% of households in which the householder or spouse participated in a DC plan had one or more plan loans outstanding in 2007. The mean balance of all loans from DC plans was $6,683 and the median loan balance was $5,000. Ten percent of households with loans from DC plans had outstanding loan balances of $15,000 or more and 10% of households had loan balances of $1,000 or less.

Leakages When Switching Jobs

Leakages from retirement savings can occur when workers change jobs.[53] A participant in a retirement plan usually has several options to choose from when leaving a job. He or she can

- keep the account in the former employer's plan;
- roll over the account into the new employer's retirement plan;

- roll over the account into an Individual Retirement Account (IRA); or
- receive the account balance directly as a distribution from the plan.[54]

Policy Issue: Preserving Retirement Savings

Congress has amended the IRC several times to encourage workers who change jobs to leave their accrued retirement benefit in the former employer's plan or to roll over the account into an IRA or another qualified retirement plan. For example:

- Section 72(t) of the IRC imposes a 10% tax in addition to ordinary income taxes on distributions from retirement plans received before age 591/2 that are not rolled over into an IRA or another tax-qualified plan within 60 days.[55]
- The Unemployment Compensation Amendments of 1992 (P.L. 102-318) require employers to give departing employees the option to transfer a distribution directly to an IRA or to another employer's plan. If the participant instead chooses to receive the distribution, the employer is required to withhold 20%, which is applied to any taxes due on the distribution.[56]
- IRC §411(a)(11) allows a plan sponsor to distribute to a departing employee his or her accrued benefit under a retirement plan without the participant's consent only if the present value of the benefit is less than $5,000.[57] The Economic Growth and Tax Relief Reconciliation Act of 2001 (P.L. 107-16) requires that if the present value of the distribution is at least $1,000, the plan sponsor must deposit the distribution into an IRA unless otherwise instructed by the participant.

In developing policies to prevent leakages from retirement savings, Congress has attempted to promote the preservation of savings until workers retire while recognizing that they may have to take money from their accounts in times of financial hardship. An example of how these goals have been balanced is the treatment of distributions when a worker leaves a job in which he or she participated in a retirement plan. In this situation, Congress has sought to *encourage* recipients to roll over pre-retirement distributions from retirement plans, but it has not *required* such distributions to be rolled over into an IRA or another retirement plan. Current law allows accrued benefits worth less than $5,000 to be cashed out automatically, but it requires the plan participant to agree in writing to a distribution of more than $5,000. The law allows workers to take cash distributions from plans when they leave a job, but it requires 20% to be withheld against taxes owed, and it places an additional 10% tax on amounts that are not rolled over into another retirement account within 60 days of the distribution.

Current law on pre-retirement distributions represents a compromise between competing goals. Stricter limits on access to retirement savings prior to retirement could lower participation or contributions. Research has shown that participation in plans that do not permit plan loans or hardship distributions is lower than in plans that allow these kinds of access to funds held by the plan. Allowing easier pre-retirement access to retirement accounts could lead to more leakages from the plans, depleted account balances, and poorer retirements for many. Moreover, to the extent that retirement accounts could be freely tapped before retirement, they would not be retirement accounts at all, but merely tax-deferred general-purpose savings accounts.

In summary, the laws that Congress has passed with respect to taxation of early distributions from retirement plans represent a compromise among several competing objectives, including

- encouraging employees to participate in retirement plans;
- promoting the preservation of retirement assets;
- allowing participants to have access to their retirement savings when they would otherwise face substantial economic hardship; and
- assuring that the tax preferences granted to retirement savings plans are not used for purposes other than to fund workers' financial security during retirement.

CONVERTING RETIREMENT SAVINGS INTO INCOME

A retiree who is deciding how to convert retirement savings into income will have to take into account many risks. Increases in average life expectancy mean that many retirees will have to ensure that their savings will last through a retirement that could span 30 or 40 years. Volatility in equity markets, the effects of inflation on purchasing power, and the possibility of substantial expenses for medical treatment and long-term care will further complicate this decision. Many retirees may find it more challenging to manage their financial assets in retirement than it was during their working years.[58]

There are a number of ways to convert retirement savings into income. One option is to purchase an annuity. A life annuity—also called an immediate annuity—is an insurance contract that provides regular income payments for life in return for an initial lump-sum premium. Life annuities can help protect retirees against some of the financial risks of retirement, especially longevity risk and investment risk. A life annuity pays income to the purchaser for as long as he or she lives, and in the case of a joint-and survivor annuity, for as long as the surviving spouse lives. Some annuities offer limited protection against inflation through annual increases in income; however, the annual increases must be paid for by accepting a lower initial monthly annuity income. Other annuities allow the purchaser to share in investment gains from growth in equity markets as a way to offset the effects of inflation. These annuities also require the purchaser to share in the investment losses if markets fall.

Relatively few 401(k) plans provide the opportunity for retiring workers to convert all or part of their 401(k) accounts into life annuities at retirement. Only 21% of plans offered an annuity option in 2007, down from 26% in 2000.[59] One reason few plans offer annuities is that they have proven to be unpopular in plans that offer them. Fewer than 10% of participants in plans that offer an annuity choose this option.[60] At retirement, most DC plan participants either take periodic withdrawals or roll the account balance into an IRA from which they take withdrawals.

Few people purchase life annuities for a number of reasons. Social Security provides benefits in the form of an inflation-adjusted annuity, and some retirees may consider this to be sufficient protection against the risk of spending all of their retirement assets before they die. In addition, about one-third of retirees receive income from defined benefit pensions, and they therefore have less need to purchase an annuity with their retirement savings. Some potential purchasers of annuities are concerned that the fees charged by insurers are too high and that the insurance companies do a poor job of explaining the fees that they charge. Others are concerned that purchasing an annuity will reduce the financial assets that they have available to meet unexpected expenses. Finally, some older persons prefer not to purchase an annuity in the hope that they will be able to leave their assets as an inheritance for their children. For these and other reasons, the number of retirees who purchase income annuities has remained relatively low compared with the number who elect to take periodic withdrawals from their retirement accounts.

Policy Issue: The Role of Income Annuities in Retirement

Defined benefit pension plans are required by law to offer participants a joint and survivor annuity as the default form of benefit.[61] No such requirement applies to defined contribution plans. Congress could require DC plan sponsors to contract with insurance companies to offer participants the option of taking their retirement benefits in the form of an annuity, but most policy proposals have focused on making annuities a more appealing option rather than a mandatory form of benefit. For example, H.R. 2748 of the 111th Congress (Pomeroy) would amend the Internal Revenue Code to exclude from gross income up to 50% of annuity income up to an annual maximum of $5,000 for single tax filers and $10,000 for couples filing jointly.

Because most 401(k) plans do not offer an annuity option, retirees who wish to purchase annuities have to withdraw money from their accounts and buy annuities in the individual market. Individual annuities are more expensive than group annuities, and they place the responsibility for finding the best deal from a financially sound insurer on individuals who usually have had little or no experience shopping for annuities. Many consumers may not feel competent to do this on their own. They may be more comfortable taking periodic withdrawals from their accounts. Some retirees are reluctant to purchase a life annuity because canceling the annuity contract can be costly. The charge for canceling an annuity—the "surrender charge"—can account for more than 10% of the principal in the first year of the contract.[62]

Many economists have found the low demand for life annuities to be puzzling in light of the protection they provide against longevity risk. Recent research has found that the appeal of annuities to potential purchasers depends greatly on whether prospective buyers understand and appreciate the value of the income security that annuities provide. Researchers have found that when annuities are portrayed—or "framed"—as investment vehicles, the lower rates of return on life annuities (which are backed mainly by bonds) can put them at a competitive disadvantage with respect to stocks and stock mutual funds. However, when the insurance aspects of annuities are emphasized—in particular, the insurance against outliving one's assets—potential buyers have been found to be more receptive to the idea of buying a life annuity.[63]

Automatic Trial Income

As a way to familiarize people with annuities, researchers at the Retirement Security Project have suggested a strategy they call "automatic trial income." This would allow retirees to "test drive" an annuity for 24 months.[64] They suggest that if the default form of benefit from a 401(k) plan were a monthly check, even for only a 24-month period with the option to take the remainder as a lump-sum at the end of two years – it would help change the public's perception of retirement accounts by framing them as an income stream rather than as a lump sum.

Under automatic trial income, at least part of the assets in a worker's 401(k) account would be automatically paid out as income at retirement unless the individual chooses another option. Retirees would receive monthly payments from the automatic trial income plan for 24 months, at the end of which they could choose to take the remainder as a lump sum or have it converted to an annuity. To assure that only people who are near retirement have their accounts distributed as income when they leave an employer, automatic trial income could apply only to those who are 55 or older when they leave a job. To prevent small account balances from being converted to annuities, the policy could apply only to accounts above a minimum value of perhaps $50,000.

Advanced Life Deferred Annuity

Another annuity product, the Advanced Life Deferred Annuity (ALDA) is purchased at retirement but does not begin paying income until the purchaser reaches an advanced age, such as 80 or 85. If the purchaser dies before the age at which income payments are scheduled to begin, he or she forfeits the premium. On the other hand, because income payments are deferred until an advanced age, premiums would be relatively low compared to immediate income annuities. A recent analysis concluded that "this product would provide a substantial proportion of the longevity insurance provided by an immediate annuity, at a small fraction of the cost," and that "few households would suffer significant losses were it used as a 401(k) plan default."[65] Although the ALDA could provide substantial insurance against living into very old age for a comparatively low premium, "it remains to be seen whether such a product would overcome annuity aversion."[66]

One way to help participants in 401(k) plans to begin thinking of their accounts as a source of retirement income rather than as a savings account would be to report the value of the participant's accrued benefits as a stream of monthly income beginning at age 65 in addition to reporting the account balance. To make these presentations comparable across plans, it might be necessary for the federal government to set standards on the appropriate interest rates and mortality tables for plans to use in restating account balances as streams of future income.

Some financial firms are designing managed withdrawal programs as alternatives to annuities. These are typically investment accounts with periodic distributions that are designed to assure that the account balance will not be exhausted before a specified number of years have passed. Unlike annuities, however, these accounts do not provide longevity insurance. The account owner bears the risk that investment losses or living longer than he or she anticipated will result in the account being exhausted during his or her lifetime.

CONCLUSION

About half of all workers in the United States participate in employer-sponsored retirement plans, a proportion that has remained essentially unchanged since the early 1970s. Since the 1980s, the proportion of workers in defined benefit pension plans has fallen while the proportion in defined contribution plans has risen. Sponsorship of retirement plans is substantially lower among small employers than among large employers. Efforts to increase retirement plan sponsorship among small employers have had only limited success. Some policy analysts have suggested that expanding access to payroll deduction IRAs could greatly increase the number of employees at small firms who have a retirement savings account.

Even among employers who offer a retirement plan, not all workers participate. Roughly 20% to 25% of workers employed at firms that sponsor a defined contribution plan do not participate in the plan. Participation rates may rise if more firms adopt automatic enrollment, but currently, almost two-thirds of DC plans continue to require employees to elect to participate in the plan.

On average, individual workers who participate in DC plans contribute about 6% of their pay to the plan, and households with one or more participants contribute about 5% of total household earnings. One way to boost employee savings rates would be for employers to adopt automatic escalation of contributions. Employee contributions can be increased slightly each year until reaching a target contribution rate, such as 10% of pay. As with automatic enrollment, employees must be permitted to opt out of the increase or to choose another contribution rate.

In most DC plans, workers must decide not only whether to participate in the plan and how much to contribute, but also how to invest the contributions. As employers have become more aware of how daunting these choices can be for their employees, some have begun to add life-cycle funds that automatically adjust the allocation of contributions between stocks, bonds, and other investments based on the employee's expected date of retirement. The majority of plan sponsors also offer investment education for participants. Some employers arrange for financial planners or other professionals to offer investment advice to their employees.

Excessive fees can substantially reduce retirement account balances, but plan participants often are unable to discern from their account statements how much they are paying in fees and what services they are receiving in exchange for the fees charged to their accounts. Improving the disclosure of fees charged to participants in 401(k) plans could help to drive down fees because participants and plan sponsors would be better able to compare fees across plans and to evaluate the services provided relative to the fees charged for those services.

Although pre-retirement access to money held in 401(k) plans is limited by law, money sometimes "leaks" from workers' accounts before they retire. This happens when a worker withdraws funds from a 401(k) plan when changing jobs, or through a hardship distribution from the plan. Current law imposes a 10% tax penalty on most withdrawals from 401(k) plans before age 591/2. The tax penalty creates a disincentive for withdrawing money from the account before retirement and also helps assure that 401(k) accounts remain dedicated to preparing for retirement rather than functioning as tax-deferred general-purpose savings accounts.

Workers who are approaching retirement today are less likely than those who retired 20 or more years ago to have a defined benefit pension. Those who have retirement savings in a 401(k) plan or an IRA will have to decide how to convert their retirement savings into retirement income. One of the risks that they will face is the possibility that if they withdraw money too quickly, they might exhaust their savings while they still have many years to live. Income annuities insure retirees against the possibility of outliving their retirement savings, but for a variety of reasons income annuities have not yet proved to be a popular option for providing retirement income. One of the most important public policy challenges of the next several years will be to develop strategies that will help retirees manage their retirement savings wisely so that they can remain financially independent throughout retirement.

ACKNOWLEDGMENTS

Patrick Purcell was also a co-author of this report.

End Notes

[1] Not all DC plans are 401(k) plans, but 401(k) plans hold about 67% of DC plan assets. Other DC plans include 403(b) plans for non-profit employers, 457 plans for state and local governments, and miscellaneous other DC plans. Increasingly, 403(b) plans and 457 plans operate similarly to 401(k) plans. In this report the terms "401(k)" plan and "defined contribution" plan are used interchangeably unless a distinction is noted in the text.

[2] U.S. Department of Labor, Bureau of Labor Statistics, *National Compensation Survey: Employee Benefits in Private Industry in the United States, March 2007*, Summary 07-05, August 2007. The sample represented 108 million workers.

[3] On October 11, 2007, the Standard & Poor's 500 Index of common stocks reached an intra-day high of 1,576, an all-time record for the index. On March 6, 2009, the S&P 500 fell to an intra-day low of 667, a decline of 57.7% from its all-time high. Over the next three months, stock prices climbed 41%. The S&P 500 closed at a value of 943 on June 1, 2009. This was 40% lower than the index's highest level in October 2007. By July 7, the S&P 500 had fallen to 881.

[4] Board of Governors of the Federal Reserve System, *Flow of Funds Accounts of the United States: Flows and Outstandings*, Fourth Quarter 2008, March 12, 2009, p. 113.

[5] U.S. Department of Labor, Bureau of Labor Statistics, *National Compensation Survey, March 2007*, Summary 07-05, August 2007. In contrast, the BLS data indicate that 89% of workers in state and local governments were offered a retirement plan of some kind. Eighty-three percent of state and local workers were offered a DB plan, 29% were offered a DC plan, and 23% were offered both types of plan. See *National Compensation Survey: Employee Benefits in State and Local Governments in the United States, September 2007*, Summary 08-01, March 2008.

[6] The Census Bureau data are from a CRS analysis of the March 2008 Current Population Survey (CPS). The National Compensation Survey is a survey of business establishments. The CPS is a survey of households. The CPS asks households about the number of workers employed by the firm where the respondent is employed. A firm may consist of more than one establishment. Some small establishments are operating units of larger firms.

[7] Bureau of Labor Statistics, National Compensation Survey, March 2007.

[8] CRS calculations based on analysis of the Census Bureau's March 2008 Current Population Survey.

[9] Under I.R.C. §414(q), for 2009 a highly compensated employee is anyone who owned 5% or more of the firm at any time during 2008 or 2009 or anyone whose compensation in 2009

exceeds $110,000. The employer can elect to count only workers in the top 20% of employee compensation as an HCE, but must count all 5% owners.

[10] A plan must satisfy one of two tests: either the proportion of non-highly compensated employees (NHCEs) covered by the plan must be at least 70% of the proportion of highly compensated employees (HCEs) covered by the plan, or the average contribution percentage for NHCEs must be at least 70% of the average contribution percentage for HCEs. Plans that have employer matching contributions are subject to the "actual contribution percentage" (ACP) test, which measures the contribution rate to HCEs' accounts relative to the contribution rate to NHCEs' accounts.

[11] The maximum annual employee salary deferral into a 401(k) plan is $16,500 in 2009 (I.R.C. §402(g)). Employees aged 50 and older can contribute an additional $5,500. The total annual addition to a 401(k) plan—comprising the sum of employer and employee contributions—is limited to $49,000 in 2009 (I.R.C. §415(c)).

[12] U.S. Department of Labor, Bureau of Labor Statistics, *Employee Benefits in Small Private Establishments, 1990*, Bulletin 2388, September 1991.

[13] U.S. Department of Labor, Bureau of Labor Statistics, *National Compensation Survey, March 2007*, Summary 07-05, August 2007.

[14] U.S. Small Business Administration, Office of Advocacy.

[15] In the 111th Congress, Sen. Jeff Bingaman introduced S. 3760, the Automatic IRA Act of 2010, which would provide for Auto IRAs. Rep. Richard Neal introduced companion legislation, H.R. 6099. Further background on the Auto IRA proposal can be found in Pursuing Universal Retirement Security Through Automatic IRAs, by J. Mark Irwy and David C. John, available at http://www.brookings.edu/papers/2009/07_automatic_ira_iwry.aspx.

[16] U.S. Department of Labor, Bureau of Labor Statistics, *National Compensation Survey, March 2007*, Summary 07-05, August 2007.

[17] The participation rate in 401(k) plans is from the Profit Sharing/401(k) Council of America's 51st Annual Survey of Profit Sharing and 401(k) Plans. The participation rate in DC plans of all types is from the Department of Labor's National Compensation Survey.

[18] This participation rate is based on a CRS analysis of the Federal Reserve Board's 2007 Survey of Consumer Finances. Similarly, a CRS analysis of the Census Bureau's Survey of Income and Program Participation (SIPP) showed that only 30% of workers under age 35 participated in a defined contribution plan in 2006.

[19] The take-up rate is calculated as the percentage of workers who participated divided by the percentage offered a plan. For workers under age 35, the take-up rate in 2007 was .318/.456 = .697.

[20] All figures cited in this paragraph are from the Federal Reserve Board's 2007 Survey of Consumer Finances.

[21] A notable exception to this rule is the Roth 401(k). In a Roth 401(k), the employee's salary deferrals into the plan are made with after-tax income. In retirement, the part of the withdrawals attributable to the employee's contributions and investment earnings on those contributions is tax free.

[22] For more information, see CRS Report RS21795, *The Retirement Savings Tax Credit: A Fact Sheet*, by John J. Topoleski.

[23] Some tax credits—such as the earned income tax credit (EITC) for low-income families—are refundable.

[24] Consider, for example, a young married couple with one child, for whom the husband is the sole breadwinner. In 2007, 25% of all workers aged 18 to 34 who worked year-round, full-time had earnings of $21,000 or less. Taking into account the standard deduction in effect

for 2007 ($10,700) and three personal exemptions ($3,400 X 3 = $10,200), a couple with gross income of $21,000 would have had taxable income of $100. The child tax credit of $1,000 would reduce their tax liability to zero. For this couple, the saver's credit would have no value because it is not refundable.

[25] See, for example, CRS Report RL33116, *Retirement Plan Participation and Contributions: Trends from 1998 to 2006*, by Patrick Purcell, and CRS Report RL30922, *Retirement Savings and Household Wealth in 2007*, by Patrick Purcell.

[26] Employers often suspend the match during difficult times. According to the Pension Rights Center, between June 2008 and June 2009, nearly 300 medium and large employers had announced plans to suspend, reduce, or delay their 401(k) matching contributions.[26] See http://www.pensionrights.org/pubs/facts/401(k)-match.html#.

[27] The limit in 2009 is $16,500 (I.R.C. §415(c)).

[28] With respect to after-tax income, even non-participants in plans that do not offer a matching contribution are reducing their total income by not contributing. Nevertheless, because contributions to a 401(k) plan reduce a worker's take-home pay, some workers are willing to give up higher future retirement income for higher current income.

[29] For more information, see CRS Report RL33845, *Retirement Savings: How Much Will Workers Have When They Retire?*, by Patrick Purcell and Debra B. Whitman.

[30] This takes into account contributions by both the household head and his or her spouse. Among household heads who contributed, the median monthly contribution was $280, or $3,360 on an annual basis. This was just 22% of the maximum permissible employee salary deferral under I.R.C. §402(g) in 2007, which was $15,000.

[31] In Table 3, households are grouped by income quartile. Income includes earnings and unearned income, such as interest, dividends, rent, and transfer payments. Contributions are reported as a percentage of total household earnings.

[32] Section 902 of P.L. 109-280exempts plans with a qualified automatic contribution arrangement from the nondiscrimination tests.

[33] U.S. Department of Labor, Bureau of Labor Statistics, National Compensation Survey.

[34] ERISA §404(c). Employer stock cannot be one of the three core investment choices.

[35] Profit Sharing/401(k) Council of America, 51st Annual Survey.

[36] Profit Sharing/401(k) Council of America, 51st Annual Survey.

[37] Profit Sharing/401(k) Council of America, 44th Annual Survey and 51st Annual Survey.

[38] Section 406(a)(1)(C) of ERISA prohibits a fiduciary from engaging in a transaction when he knows or should know that such transaction constitutes a direct or indirect furnishing of goods, services, or facilities between the plan and a party in interest. Section 601 of the PPA amended §408(b) of ERISA to add an exception to the transactions prohibited by ERISA for an "eligible investment advice arrangement." For more information, see CRS Report RS22514, *Investment Advice and the Pension Protection Act of 2006*, by Jon O. Shimabukuro.

[39] 29 U.S.C. § 1108(g)(3)(B)(i)-(v).

[40] *Federal Register*, Vol. 74, No. 223, November 20, 2009, p. 60156.

[41] Under the PPA, a target date fund is a "Qualified Default Investment Alternative" (QDIA).

[42] See http://aging.senate.gov/record.cfm?id=308665.

[43] *Investment News*, "Labor Department, SEC to probe target date funds," April 3, 2009.

[44] Defined Contribution/401(k) Fee Study, Deloitte Consulting LLP, Spring 2009. The report is available on the ICI website at http://www.idc.org/pdf/rpt_09_dc_401k_fee_study.pdf.

[45] See CRS Report RL34678, *Fee Disclosure in Defined Contribution Retirement Plans: Background and Legislation*, by John J. Topoleski.

[46] The examples are based on an account with an initial balance of $20,000 growing at an average annual rate of 7.0%.

[47] Even if fees charged to a DB plan are paid for from plan assets, this increases the sponsor's funding obligation.

[48] *Federal Register*, Vol. 75, No. 135, July 16, 2010, p. 41599-41638.

[49] 26 U.S.C. §401(k)(2)(B)(i)(IV). All distributions are taxable, except any portion that is attributable to after-tax contributions. I.R.C. §72(t) lists limited cases in which distributions made before age 591/2 are not subject to the 10% additional tax on early distributions.

[50] 26 C.F.R. §1.401(k)-1(d). Regular matching contributions and discretionary profit-sharing contributions may also be distributed on account of hardship if the plan so provides. See 26 C.F.R. §1.401(k)-1(d)(3)(ii).

[51] The exceptions to the 10% additional tax are listed at 26 USC, §72(t).

[52] Loans are not permitted from IRAs, but money in an IRA can, in effect, be "borrowed" for 60 days because the law states that any distribution from an IRA that is not deposited in the same or another IRA within 60 days is a taxable distribution. (26 U.S.C. § 408(d)).

[53] More information is available in CRS Report RL30496, *Pension Issues: Lump-Sum Distributions and Retirement Income Security*, by Patrick Purcell, *Pension Issues: Lump-Sum Distributions and Retirement Income Security*, by Patrick Purcell.

[54] If the individual chooses this option, federal law requires 20% of the account balance to be withheld and forwarded to the IRS toward any income tax and tax penalties owed.

[55] Under IRC §72(t), the 10% penalty is waived if the distribution is made in a series of "substantially equal periodic payments" based on the recipient's life expectancy or if the recipient has retired from the plan sponsor at age 55 or older. Other exceptions to the 10% additional tax apply under special circumstances. See CRS Report R40192, *Early Withdrawals and Required Minimum Distributions in Retirement Accounts: Issues for Congress*, by John J. Topoleski.

[56] If the distribution is not rolled over within 60 days, the 20% withheld is applied to the taxes owed on the distribution. If the distribution is rolled over within 60 days, the 20% withheld is credited toward the income tax that the individual owes for the year. If the participant has received the distribution in cash, then to roll over the full amount of the distribution, the recipient must have access to other funds that are at least equal to 20% withheld by the employer.

[57] Distributions of $5,000 or more require the participant's written consent. The $5,000 limit was established by the Taxpayer Relief Act of 1997 (P.L. 105-34). The amount had been set at $3,500 by Retirement Equity Act of 1984. It was originally established at $1,750 by ERISA in 1974.

[58] For more information, see CRS Report R40008, *Converting Retirement Savings into Income: Annuities and Periodic Withdrawals*, by Janemarie Mulvey and Patrick Purcell.

[59] Profit Sharing/401(k) Council of America, 51st Annual Survey.

[60] Hewitt Associates, survey of 401(k) plans, various years.

[61] ERISA § 205; 29 USC § 1055.

[62] Typically, surrender charges drop by about one percentage point per year, eventually allowing penalty-free withdrawals from the annuity.

[63] See "Why Don't People Insure Late Life Consumption? A Framing Explanation of the Under-Annuitization Puzzle," by J. R. Brown, J. R. Kling, S. Mullainathan, and M. V. Wrobel, TIAA-CREF Institute, April 2008.

[64] See *Increasing Annuitization in 401(k) Plans with Automatic Trial Income* by William Gale, J. Mark Iwry, David C. John, and Lina Walker at

http://www.retirementsecurityproject.org/pubs/File/RSP_TrialIncomev4(2).pdf.

[65] Guan Gong and Anthony Webb, *Evaluating the Advanced Life Deferred Annuity*, Boston College Center for Retirement Research, Working Paper no. 2007-15, September 2007.

[66] Ibid.

In: Retirement Savings and Security
Editor: Linda A. Eisterhold

ISBN: 978-1-62948-132-6

Chapter 5

FEDERAL EMPLOYEES' RETIREMENT SYSTEM: BENEFITS AND FINANCING*

Katelin P. Isaacs

SUMMARY

Most civilian federal employees who were hired before 1984 are covered by the Civil Service Retirement System (CSRS). Federal employees hired in 1984 or later are covered by the Federal Employees' Retirement System (FERS). Both CSRS and FERS require participants to contribute toward the cost of their pensions through a payroll tax. Employees who are covered by CSRS contribute 7.0% of pay to the Civil Service Retirement and Disability Fund (CSRDF). They do not pay Social Security taxes or earn Social Security benefits. Employees enrolled in FERS and first hired before 2013 contribute 0.8% of their pay to the CSRDF. Employees enrolled in FERS and first hired in 2013 or later contribute 3.1% of pay to the CSRDF. All employees enrolled in FERS contribute 6.2% of wages up to the Social Security taxable wage base ($113,700 in 2013) to the Social Security trust fund.

The minimum retirement age (MRA) under CSRS is 55 for workers who have at least 30 years of service. The FERS MRA was 55 for employees born before 1948. The MRA for employees born between 1953 and 1964 is 56, increasing to the age of 57 for those born in 1970 or

* This is an edited, reformatted and augmented version of a Congressional Research Service publication, CRS Report for Congress 98-810, from www.crs.gov, prepared for Members and Committees of Congress, dated January 9, 2013.

later. Both FERS and CSRS allow retirement with an unreduced pension at the age of 60 for employees with 20 or more years of service and at the age of 62 for employees with at least 5 years of service.

The Thrift Savings Plan (TSP) is a retirement savings plan similar to the 401(k) plans provided by many employers in the private sector. In 2013, employees covered under either CSRS or FERS can contribute up to $17,500 to the TSP. Employees aged 50 and older can contribute an additional $5,500 to the TSP. Employees under FERS receive employer matching contributions of up to 5% of pay from the federal agency by which they are employed. Federal workers covered by CSRS also can contribute to the TSP, but they receive no matching contributions from their employing agencies.

The Office of Personnel Management (OPM) estimates the cost of CSRS to be an amount equal to 26.0% of employee pay. The federal government pays 19.0% of this amount and the other 7.0% is paid by employees. OPM estimates the cost of the FERS basic annuity at an amount equal to 12.7% of pay. For FERS employees first hired before 2013, the federal government contributes 11.9% of this amount and the other 0.8% is paid by employees. For FERS employees first hired in 2013 or later, the federal government contributes 9.6% of this amount and

employees pay the remaining 3.1%. There are three other employer costs for employees under FERS. Both the employer and employee pay Social Security taxes equal to 6.2% of pay up to the maximum taxable amount; agencies automatically contribute an amount equal to 1% of employee pay to the TSP; and agencies make matching contributions to the TSP equal to up to 4% of pay.

At the start of FY2011, the CSRDF had an unfunded liability of $622.3 billion, consisting of a $634.5 billion deficit for CSRS and a $12.2 billion surplus for FERS. Although the civil service trust fund has an unfunded liability, it is not in danger of becoming insolvent. OPM projects that the balance of the CSRDF will continue to grow through at least 2080, at which point it will hold assets equal to more than 4.7 times total payroll and about 20 times total annual benefit payments.

Background on Retirement Plan Design

Employers establish retirement plans both to help them attract workers with valuable skills and to enable older workers to retire without facing the prospect of inadequate income. Employers must balance the goals of providing adequate retirement income with controlling the cost of the retirement plan. For employers in the private sector, another important consideration is the regulatory environment in which their retirement plans must operate. Private-sector retirement plans must comply with the relevant provisions of federal law, including the Employee Retirement Income Security Act (ERISA), the Age Discrimination in Employment Act (ADEA), and the Internal Revenue Code.

Two Types of Retirement Plans

Retirement programs generally can be classified as either *defined benefit* (DB) plans or *defined contribution* (DC) plans. In a defined benefit plan, a worker's retirement benefit is typically paid as a life annuity based on years of service and average salary. A defined contribution plan is much like a savings account maintained by the employer on behalf of each participating employee. The employer and/or employee contribute a specific dollar amount or percentage of pay into an account, which is usually invested in stocks and bonds. When the worker retires, he or she receives the balance in the account, which is the sum of all the contributions that have been made plus interest, dividends, and capital gains (or losses), net of fees and expenses. The retiring worker usually has the choice of receiving these funds as a series of payments over a period of years or as a lump sum.

An important difference between the two types of retirement plans is that in a defined benefit plan it is the *employer* who bears the financial risk, whereas in a defined contribution plan it is the *employee* who bears the financial risk. In a defined benefit plan, the employer promises to provide retirement benefits in the form of a life annuity or its actuarial equivalent.[1] To pay the promised benefit, the employer must make contributions to a pension fund, which is invested in stocks, bonds, and other assets. The employer's contributions plus the expected investment earnings on the contributions must be sufficient to pay the pension benefits that workers have earned under the plan. The employer is at risk for the full amount of retirement benefits that have been earned by employees. If the pension plan is underfunded, the employer must make additional contributions so that the promised benefits can be paid.

In a defined contribution plan, the employee bears the investment risk. If the contributions to the plan have been insufficient or if the securities in which the contributions have been invested lose value or appreciate too slowly, the employee might reach retirement age without the financial resources needed to maintain his or her desired standard of living in retirement. If this occurs, the worker might have little choice but to delay retirement.

CSRS and FERS

Most civilian federal employees who were hired before 1984 are covered by the Civil Service Retirement System (CSRS). Under CSRS, employees do not pay Social Security taxes or earn Social Security benefits. Federal employees first hired in 1984 or later are covered by the Federal Employees' Retirement System (FERS). All federal employees who are enrolled in FERS pay Social Security taxes and earn Social Security benefits. Federal employees enrolled in either CSRS or FERS also may contribute to the Thrift Savings Plan (TSP); however, only employees enrolled in FERS are eligible for employer matching contributions to the TSP.

Origins of the Federal Civilian Retirement System

Congress passed the Civil Service Retirement Act of 1920 (P.L. 66-215) to provide pension benefits for civilian federal employees. In 1935, Congress created the Social Security system for workers in the private sector. During the 1950s, Congress allowed state and local governments to bring their employees into Social Security, and today about three-fourths of state and local employees are covered by Social Security. Federal employees remained outside of Social Security until Congress passed the Social Security Amendments of 1983 (P.L. 98-21). This law required all civilian federal employees hired into permanent employment on or after January 1, 1984, to participate in Social Security.

Enrolling federal workers in both CSRS and Social Security would have resulted in substantial duplication of benefits and would have required employees to contribute more than 13% of pay to the two programs. Consequently, Congress directed the development of a new retirement system for federal workers with Social Security as its cornerstone. The new plan was designed to include many features of the retirement plans of large employers in the private sector. The result of this effort was the Federal Employee Retirement System Act of 1986 (P.L. 99-335), enacted on June 6, 1986. The FERS has three elements:

- Social Security,
- the FERS basic retirement annuity and the FERS supplement, and
- the Thrift Savings Plan.

The FERS covers federal employees initially hired into federal employment on or after January 1, 1984, and employees who voluntarily switched from CSRS during "open seasons" in 1987 and 1998.[2] Former federal employees who had completed at least five years of service under CSRS and were later rehired by the government after a break in service could either join FERS or participate in the "CSRS offset plan." Under the CSRS offset plan, 6.2 percentage points of the employee's payroll contribution and an equal share of the employer contribution are diverted from CSRS to the Social Security trust fund. Later, the retiree's CSRS annuity is reduced (offset) by the amount of his or her Social Security benefit. Both CSRS and the CSRS offset program will terminate with the death of the last worker or survivor still covered under that program, which the Office of Personnel Management (OPM) estimates will occur around the year 2070.

ELIGIBILITY AND BENEFIT AMOUNTS UNDER FERS AND CSRS

Under both CSRS and FERS, the date of an employee's eligibility to retire with an annuity depends on his or her age and years of service. The amount of the retirement annuity is determined by three factors: the number of years of service, the accrual rate at which benefits are earned for each year of service, and the salary base to which the accrual rate is applied.[3]

Retirement Age and Years of Service

Under CSRS, a worker with at least 30 years of service can retire at the age of 55; a worker with at least 20 years of service can retire at the age of 60; and a worker with 5 or more years of service can retire at the age of 62.

Federal employees are fully vested in the FERS basic retirement annuity after five years of service. The FERS minimum retirement age (MRA) for an employee with 30 or more years of service was 55 for workers born before 1948. The MRA under FERS began to increase in 2003 for workers born after 1947. The MRA for employees born between 1953 and 1964 is 56. It will increase to 57 for those born in 1970 or later. (See *Table 1.*) A worker who has reached the minimum retirement age and has completed at least 30 years of service can retire with an immediate, unreduced annuity. A worker with 20 or more years of service can retire with an unreduced annuity at age 60, and a worker with at least 5 years of service can retire at age 62.

Table 1. Minimum Retirement Age Under FERS

Year of Birth	Minimum Retirement Age
1947 or earlier	55 years
1948	55 years, 2 months
1949	55 years, 4 months
1950	55 years, 6 months
1951	55 years, 8 months
1952	55 years, 10 months
1953 to 1964	56 years
1965	56 years, 2 months
1966	56 years, 4 months
1967	56 years, 6 months
1968	56 years, 8 months
1969	56 years, 10 months
1970 or later	57 years

Source: U.S. Office of Personnel Management.

Under FERS, an employee can retire with a reduced benefit at the minimum retirement age if he or she has completed at least 10 years of service.

The retirement benefit is permanently reduced by 5% multiplied by the difference between 62 and the retiree's age at the time the annuity begins. For example, an employee with at least 10 years of service who retires at 56 would receive a pension benefit that is reduced by 30% below the amount that would be paid to an individual with the same salary and years of service who retired at the age of 62.

Retirement Income Adequacy

Replacement Rates

A commonly used measure of retirement income adequacy is the percentage of pre-retirement income replaced by pension income. This measure—the *replacement rate*—is expressed by the following ratio:

$$\frac{\textit{annual retirement benefits}}{\textit{annual pre - retirement earnings}}$$

Replacement rates usually are based on the sum of the employee's pension benefit and Social Security benefit. Because retirees do not have the expenses that are associated with having a job, most people are able to maintain their previous standard of living with less income than they had while working. Although there is no fixed rule about what comprises an adequate replacement rate, most pension analysts believe retirement income should replace at least 70% to 80% of pre-retirement income.[4] Workers who had low-wage jobs generally need a replacement rate near the high end of this range because a higher proportion of their income is expended on non-discretionary items, such as food, clothing, shelter, health care, and taxes.

Determinants of the Replacement Rate

The basic retirement annuity under both CSRS and FERS is determined by multiplying three factors: the *salary base*, the *accrual rate*, and the number of *years of service*. This relationship is shown in the following formula:

Pension Amount = salary base x *accrual rate* x *years of service*

Salary Base

In both CSRS and FERS, the salary base is the average of the highest three consecutive years of basic pay.[5] This is often called "high-three" pay.

Accrual Rates

The accrual rate is the pension benefit earned for each year of service, expressed as a percentage of the salary base. Under FERS, workers accrue retirement benefits at the rate of 1% per year.

A worker with 30 years of service will have accrued a pension benefit equal to 30% of high-three pay. For employees in FERS who have at least 20 years of service and who work until age 62, the accrual rate is 1.1% for each year of service.

For example, a worker under FERS who retires at 61 with 29 years of service would receive an annuity equal to 29% of his or her high-three average pay. Delaying retirement by one year would increase the annuity to 33% of high-three average pay (30 x 1.1 = 33).

CSRS pension accrual rates increase with length of service. CSRS pensions equal 1.5% of high-three average pay for each of the first 5 years of service, 1.75% for the 6th through 10th years; and 2.0% of high-three average pay for each year of service after the 10th year. This formula yields a replacement rate of 56.25% for a worker who retires with 30 years of service. FERS accrual rates are lower than the accrual rates under CSRS because employees under FERS pay Social Security payroll taxes and earn Social Security retirement benefits.

Some Members of Congress, some congressional staff, all federal law enforcement officers, all firefighters, and all air traffic controllers accrue benefits at higher rates under both CSRS and FERS than do other federal employees. Under CSRS, all Members of Congress and all congressional staff accrue benefits at the rate of 2.5% for each year of service. This results in a replacement rate of 75% after 30 years of service. All law enforcement officers and all firefighters enrolled in CSRS accrue benefits at the rate of 2.5% for each of their first 20 years of service and 2.0% for each year thereafter.

Under FERS, Members of Congress and congressional staff first hired before 2013 accrue pension benefits at the rate of 1.7% per year for their first 20 years of service and 1.0% for each year of service after the 20th year. All law enforcement officers, all firefighters, and all air traffic controllers also accrue pension benefits at the rate of 1.7% per year for their first 20 years of service and 1.0% for each year of service after the 20th year. These accrual rates yield a pension equal to 34% of the FERS salary base after 20 years of service and 44% after 30 years of service.

With enactment of P.L. 112-96, Members of Congress and congressional staff covered by FERS and first elected or hired in 2013 or later, accrue pension benefits at the same rate as regular FERS employees (i.e., 1% per year; or, for Members and congressional employees in this category with at least 20 years of service and who work until age 62, the accrual rate is 1.1% for each year of service). The replacement rate for these Members and congressional staff is, therefore, the same as for regular FERS employees.[6]

Replacement Rates for Federal Retirees

For a regular federal employee with 30 years of service, CSRS provides a replacement rate equal to 56.25% of high-three average pay. Estimating replacement rates under FERS is complicated by the fact that income from two of its components—Social Security and the TSP—will vary depending on the individual's work history, contributions to the TSP, and the investment performance of his or her TSP account.[7]

Social Security and the "FERS Supplement"

Because Social Security retirement benefits cannot begin before the age of 62, Congress included in FERS a temporary supplemental benefit for workers who retire before age 62.

This "FERS supplement" is paid to workers who retire at the age of 55 or older with at least 30 years of service or at the age of 60 with at least 20 years of service. It is also paid to law enforcement officers, firefighters, and air traffic controllers who retire at the age of 50 or later with 20 or more years of service.

The supplement is equal to the estimated Social Security benefit that the individual earned while employed by the federal government. It is paid only until the age of 62, regardless of whether the retiree chooses to apply for Social Security retired worker benefits at 62 years old.

Cost-of-living Adjustments

Cost-of-living adjustments (COLAs) protect the purchasing power of retirement benefits from being eroded by inflation in the prices of goods and services. COLAs do not raise the real value of income. They merely prevent the real value of income from falling. In 1972, Congress passed legislation providing for automatic COLAs for Social Security. COLAs have been in effect since 1962 for CSRS. Social Security COLAs and CSRS COLAs are equal to the annual change in the Consumer Price Index for Urban Wage and Clerical Workers (CPI-W).[8]

As a cost-control measure, Congress limited the annual COLA applied to the FERS retirement annuity. Under FERS, the basic retirement annuity is fully indexed if inflation is under 2% per year and partially indexed if inflation exceeds 2%.

If the CPI-W increases by up to 2%, then the FERS annuity increases by the same percentage. If the CPI-W increases by 2% to 3%, the FERS annuity increases by 2%. If the CPI-W increases by more than 3%, the FERS annuity increases by the rise in the CPI-W minus one percentage point. Under FERS, COLAs are applied only to annuities of retirees aged 62 or older, individuals who retired by reason of disability, and to survivor annuitants. Other FERS retirees receive no COLAs while they are under the age of 62.

THE THRIFT SAVINGS PLAN

The Thrift Savings Plan (TSP) is a defined contribution (DC) retirement plan similar to the 401(k) plans provided by many employers in the private sector. The TSP is a key component of FERS, especially for workers in the middle and upper ranges of the federal pay scale, who are unlikely to achieve adequate retirement income—as measured by the replacement rate—from Social Security and the FERS basic annuity.

In 2013, federal employees can contribute up to $17,500 to the TSP.[9] Employees aged 50 and older can contribute an additional $5,500. These employee contributions may be made on a pretax basis, in which case neither the contributions nor investment earnings that accrue to the plan are taxed until the money is withdrawn. Alternatively, P.L. 111-31 authorized a qualified Roth contribution option to the TSP. Under a Roth contribution option, employee salary deferrals into a retirement plan are made with after-tax income.

Qualified distributions from the Roth TSP plan option—generally, distributions taken five or more years after the participant's first Roth contribution and after he or she has reached the age of 591/2—are tax-free.

For all federal workers under FERS, the agencies where they are employed contribute an amount equal to 1% of each employee's base pay to the TSP, whether or not the employee chooses to contribute anything to the plan. In addition, employees enrolled in FERS can receive employer matching contributions equal to 4% of pay, according to the schedule shown in *Table 2.* Federal workers covered by CSRS also may contribute to the TSP, but they receive no matching contributions from their employing agencies.

Table 2. Government Matching Rate on TSP Contributions by FERS Participants

Employee	Government	Total
0.0%	1.0%	1.0%
1.0%	2.0%	3.0%
2.0%	3.0%	5.0%
3.0%	4.0%	7.0%
4.0%	4.5%	8.5%
5.0% or more	5.0%	10.0%

Source: Federal Retirement Thrift Investment Board.

TSP participants are immediately vested in their contributions to the plan, all federal matching contributions, and any interest, dividends, or capital gains attributable to those contributions. Participants are fully vested in the 1% agency automatic contribution to the TSP after three years (two years for congressional employees and executive branch political appointees).

TSP Investment Options

The value of an individual's TSP account at retirement will depend on how much he or she contributed to the TSP each year, the number of years over which contributions were made, and the investment earnings of the TSP funds. Participants in the TSP may choose among five funds in which they can invest their TSP contributions:

- The "C" fund invests in a stock market index fund that replicates the *Standard and Poor's 500* Index of 500 large to medium-sized U.S. companies.
- The "F" fund invests in bonds in the same proportion as they are represented by the Barclays Capital U.S. Aggregate Bond Index.
- The "G" fund invests in U.S. government securities and pays interest equal to the average rate of return on government securities with maturities of four years or more.
- The "S" fund invests in a stock index fund that tracks the Dow Jones U.S. Completion Total Stock Market Index.
- The "I" fund invests in a stock index fund that replicates the Morgan Stanley Capital International EAFE (Europe, Australasia, Far East) Index.[10]

In 2005, the TSP added a "Lifecycle Funds" option. Lifecycle Funds are invested in various combinations of the five existing TSP funds. According to the Federal Retirement Thrift Investment Board, participants who invest in these funds "benefit from having professionally designed asset allocation models available to optimize their investment performance by providing portfolios that are appropriate for their particular time horizon."[11] The participant's time horizon is based on the future date he or she expects to begin withdrawing money from the TSP. There are currently four TSP Lifecycle Funds: Lifecycle 2050 (with a target date for leaving federal service of 2045 or later); Lifecycle 2040 (with a target date of 2035 through 2044); Lifecycle 2030 (with a target date of 2025 through 2034); and Lifecycle 2020 (with a target date of now through 2024). When a particular "Lifecycle Fund" reaches its target date, it is automatically rolled into the "L Income Fund," to produce income for TSP participants who anticipate withdrawing from their TSP accounts in the near term or who are already receiving TSP monthly payments.

Historical rates of return for the TSP are shown in *Table 3*. For the years before 2001, the rates of return for the S and I funds are the rates of return for the indices on which those funds are based.

Table 3. Annual Rates of Return for Thrift Savings Plan Funds

Year	G Fund	C Fund	F Fund	S Fund	I Fund
1988	8.8%	11.8%	3.6%	20.5%	26.1%
1989	8.8%	31.0%	13.9%	23.9%	10.0%
1990	8.9%	-3.2%	8.0%	-13.6%	-23.6%
1991	8.1%	30.8%	15.7%	43.5%	12.2%
1992	7.2%	7.7%	7.2%	11.9%	-12.2%
1993	6.1%	10.1%	9.5%	14.6%	32.7%
1994	7.2%	1.3%	-3.0%	-2.7%	7.8%
1995	7.0%	37.4%	18.3%	33.5%	11.3%
1996	6.8%	22.8%	3.7%	17.2%	6.1%
1997	6.8%	33.2%	9.6%	25.7%	1.5%
1998	5.7%	28.4%	8.7%	8.6%	20.1%
1999	6.0%	21.0%	-0.8%	35.5%	26.7%
2000	6.4%	-9.1%	11.7%	-15.8%	-14.2%
2001	5.4%	-11.9%	8.6%	-2.2%	-15.4%
2002	5.0%	-22.1%	10.3%	-18.1%	-16.0%
2003	4.1%	28.5%	4.1%	42.9%	37.9%
2004	4.3%	10.8%	4.3%	18.0%	20.0%
2005	4.5%	5.0%	2.4%	10.5%	13.6%
2006	4.9%	15.8%	4.4%	15.3%	26.3%
2007	4.9%	5.5%	7.1%	5.5%	11.4%
2008	3.8%	-37.0%	5.5%	-38.3%	-42.4%
2009	3.0%	26.7%	6.0%	34.9%	30.0%
2010	2.8%	15.1%	6.7%	29.1%	7.9%
2011	2.5%	2.1%	7.9%	-3.4%	-11.8%
Average Return, 1988-2011	5.8%	10.9%	7.2%	12.4%	6.9%

Sources: http://www.tsp.gov, http://www.wilshire.com, and http://www.msci.com.

Note: Rates of return for the TSP funds are shown net of expenses.

TSP Withdrawal Options

There are three ways an employee can withdraw funds from the TSP. Funds can be withdrawn

- as a life annuity,[12]
- in a single lump-sum payment, or
- in a series of monthly payments, either for a fixed number of months or in a fixed dollar amount until the account is depleted.

A retiree can choose to have payments begin immediately or at a later date. There is a 10% tax penalty for those who withdraw funds before the age of 591/2. The penalty does not apply if the individual has retired and is aged 55 or older, or if the withdrawals are taken as a series of substantially equal periodic payments based on the person's remaining life expectancy.

EMPLOYER AND EMPLOYEE CONTRIBUTIONS TO CSRS AND FERS

Both CSRS and FERS require participants to contribute toward the cost of their future pensions through a payroll tax. Under CSRS, employees contribute 7.0% of base pay to the Civil Service Retirement and Disability Fund (CSRDF). Under FERS, employees first hired before 2013 contribute 0.8% of pay to the CSRDF and they also pay Social Security taxes (6.2% on salary up to the maximum taxable wage base of $117,700 in 2013). FERS employees first hired in 2013 contribute 3.1% of pay to the CSRDF as well as Social Security taxes. Participants in CSRS are not covered by Social Security.[13] Members of Congress contribute 8.0% of salary to the CSRDF if covered by CSRS; 1.3% of salary to the CSRDF if under FERS and first elected prior to 2013; and 3.1% of salary to the CSRDF if under FERS and first elected in 2013 or later. All Members of Congress pay Social Security taxes, regardless of whether they are under CSRS or FERS.[14]

In the private sector, employers are required by the Employee Retirement Income Security Act of 1974 (ERISA, P.L. 93-406) to pre-fund the benefits that workers earn under defined benefit plans. Pre-funding of future pension obligations is required because there is always the possibility that a firm could go out of business. A firm that closes down will no longer have revenues to pay its pension obligations, and if these obligations were not fully funded, retirees and employees of the firm would lose some or all of their pension benefits. Private-sector employers with defined benefit pensions are required to pay premiums to the Pension Benefit Guaranty Corporation (PBGC), which insures the pensions of workers whose employer terminates a pension plan that has unfunded liabilities. For plans that terminate in 2013, the PBGC guarantees a maximum annual benefit of approximately $57,477 for a worker retiring at the age of 65. The maximum benefit is lower for workers who retire before the age of 65. The PBGC does not insure federal, state, or local government pensions. The ultimate guarantors of government pensions are the taxpayers.

The federal government requires firms in the private sector to pre-fund employees' pension benefits to ensure that if a firm goes out of business, there will be funds available to pay its pension obligations. Although the federal government is unlikely to "go out of business," there are other reasons that Congress has required federal agencies and their employees to contribute money to the CSRDF.[15] First, by providing a continuous source of budget authority, the CSRDF allows benefits to be paid on time, regardless of any delays that Congress may experience in passing its annual appropriations bills. Secondly, the balance in the trust fund acts as a barometer of the government's future pension obligations. Given a fixed contribution rate and benefit structure, a rising trust fund balance indicates that the government is incurring obligations to make higher pension payments in the future.[16] Finally, prefunding pension obligations forces federal agencies to recognize their full personnel costs when requesting annual appropriations from Congress. Otherwise, these costs would be recognized only in the central administrative accounts of the Office of Personnel Management, and not by the agencies where the costs are incurred.

Employee Contributions

Contributions to CSRS and FERS are not deposited into individual employee accounts. Nor is the amount of a federal worker's pension based on the amount of his or her contributions. All contributions are paid into—and all benefits are paid out of—the Civil Service Retirement and Disability Fund. Employee contributions pay for a comparatively small part of the retirement annuities paid by CSRS and FERS. There are, however, both budgetary and actuarial reasons that federal employees are required to contribute to CSRS and FERS.

Employee Contributions from a Budgetary Perspective

Employee contributions are revenues of the federal government. These revenues reduce the proportion of pension costs that must be borne by the public. In FY2012, employee contributions to CSRS and FERS totaled an estimated $3.0 billion, equal to 2.9% of the cash income of the Civil Service Retirement and Disability Fund. The other major sources of revenue to the CSRDF are agency contributions, contributions of the U.S. Postal Service on behalf of its employees, interest on the federal bonds held by the fund, and transfers from the general revenues of the U.S. Treasury. These transfers are necessary because the costs of the older of the two federal retirement programs, the CSRS, are not fully covered by employee and agency contributions. FERS benefits are required by law to be fully funded by the sum of contributions from employees and their employing agencies and the interest earnings of the CSRDF.

Employee Contributions in Actuarial Terms

Actuaries calculate the cost of defined benefits pension plans in terms of "normal cost." The normal cost of a pension plan is the level percentage of payroll that must to be set aside each year to fund the pension benefits that participants have earned. Normal cost is based on estimates of attrition and mortality among the workforce, future interest rates, salary increases, and inflation.

OPM has estimated the current normal cost of CSRS to be 26.0% of payroll. The federal government's share of the normal cost of CSRS is 19.0% of payroll. The Civil Service Retirement Amendments of 1969 (P.L. 91-93) require participating employees and their employing agencies each to contribute an amount equal to 7.0% of basic pay to the CSRDF to finance retirement benefits under CSRS. The combined contribution of 14% of employee pay does not fully finance the retirement benefits provided by the CSRS. The costs of the CSRS that are not financed by the 7.0% employee and 7.0% agency contributions are attributable mainly to increases in future CSRS benefits that result from (1) employees' annual pay raises, and (2) annual COLAs to CSRS annuities. In actuarial terms, the employee and agency contributions totaling 14% of pay are equal to the *static normal cost* of CSRS benefits.[17] This is the benefit that would be paid if employees received no future pay raises and annuitants received no future COLAs. The *dynamic normal cost* of CSRS pensions includes the cost of financing future benefit increases that result from pay raises and COLAs provided to annuitants.[18]

Contributions from employees and their employing agencies meet about 54% of the normal cost of CSRS (14.0/26.0 = .538). The remaining 46% of the cost of CSRS is paid from the interest earned by bonds held by the retirement and disability trust fund, special contributions by the U.S. Postal Service for retired postal workers, and transfers from the general revenues of the U.S. Treasury. If each federal agency were to pay the full cost of CSRS benefits on an accrual basis, as is done under FERS, they would contribute an amount equal to 19.0% of payroll. This represents the dynamic normal cost of CSRS minus the required employee contribution of 7.0% of pay.

OPM has estimated the normal cost of the FERS basic annuity to be 12.7% of payroll. Federal law requires agencies to contribute an amount equal to the normal cost of FERS minus employee contributions to the program. Employees first hired before 2013 contribute 0.8% of pay toward their FERS annuities. Consequently, the normal cost of the FERS basic annuity to the federal government for these employees is equal to 11.9% of payroll (12.7-0.8=11.9). Under P.L. 112-96, FERS employees first hired in 2013 or later contribute 3.1% of pay toward their FERS annuity. The cost for this category of FERS employees is equal to 9.6% of payroll (12.7-3.1=9.6).

The federal government has three other mandatory costs for employees enrolled in FERS: Social Security, the 1% agency automatic contribution to the TSP, and agency matching contributions to the TSP. Social Security taxes are 6.2% of payroll on both the employer and the employee up to the maximum taxable amount of earnings ($113,700 in 2013). All agencies must contribute an amount equal to 1% of employee pay to the TSP. The normal cost of FERS to the federal government is therefore is at least 19.1% of pay for employees first hired before 2013 and 16.8% for employees hired in 2013 or later. Federal matching contributions to the TSP can add up to 4 percentage points to that amount. For an employee enrolled in FERS and first hired before 2013 who contributes 5.0% or more of pay to the TSP, his or her employing agency must finance retirement costs equal to 23.1% of employee pay. For an employee enrolled in FERS and first hired in 2013 or later who contributes 5.0% or more of pay to the TSP, his or her employing agency must finance retirement costs equal to 20.8% of pay.

CSRS and FERS differ in the way that each federal agency must budget its contributions toward employee pension benefits. Under FERS, each agency must include the *full normal cost* of the FERS basic benefit (11.9% of pay for FERS employees hired before 2013; 9.6% of pay for FERS employees hired in

2013 or later) in its annual budget request. In addition, each agency must include in its budget request the cost of the employer share of Social Security payroll taxes, the 1.0% automatic contribution to the TSP, and employer matching contributions to the TSP. Under CSRS, each agency must budget only a 7.0% contribution to the CSRDF, even though this is less than the full cost of the program. The costs associated with CSRS that are not paid by the employee contribution of 7.0% and the agency contribution of 7.0% are treated as a general obligation of the U.S. Treasury.

In both CSRS and FERS, government contributions to the Civil Service Retirement and Disability Fund result in the Treasury issuing securities that are credited to the fund. The contributions for both programs are commingled, and benefits for retirees and survivors in both programs are paid from the CSRDF. In contrast, government contributions to the TSP are deposited into individual accounts for each TSP participant. The accounts are managed by the Federal Retirement Thrift Investment Board. The TSP is not a trust fund of the U.S. government. TSP accounts are individually owned by the participants in the TSP in the same way that 401(k) accounts are owned by workers in the private sector.

FINANCING PENSION BENEFITS FOR FEDERAL EMPLOYEES

As of September 30, 2010, the CSRDF had net assets of $784.6 billion available for benefit payments under both CSRS and FERS. At the same time, the accrued actuarial liability under the CSRS and FERS plans was $1,406.9 billion.[19] In other words, on October 1, 2010, the civil service trust fund had an *unfunded actuarial liability* of $622.3 billion. Although FERS currently has a surplus of $12.2 billion, there is $634.5 billion in unfunded liability attributable to CSRS. Federal law has never required that employee and agency contributions must equal the present value of benefits that employees accrue under the CSRS. In contrast, the FERS Act requires that the benefits accrued each year by employees must be fully funded by contributions from employees and their employing agencies.

Although the CSRDF has an unfunded liability, it is not in danger of becoming insolvent. According to the projections of the actuaries at OPM, the assets of the CSRDF will continue to grow over the next 70 years. The fund's assets are projected to reach $1.1 trillion in 2020, $2.2 trillion in 2040, $5.3

trillion in 2060, and $11.5 trillion in 2080. Actuarial projections indicate that the CSRDF will be able to meet its financial obligations in perpetuity. According to OPM, "the total assets of the CSRDF, including both CSRS and FERS, continue to grow throughout the term of the projection, and ultimately reach a level of about 4.7 times payroll, or about 20 times the level of annual benefit outlays."[20] One reason that the CSRDF will not exhaust its resources is that all federal employees hired since 1984 are enrolled in FERS. By law, the benefits that employees earn under FERS must be fully funded by the sum of employer and employee contributions and interest earnings.

Federal Trust Funds and Pre-Funding of Benefits

The CSRDF is similar to the Social Security Trust Fund in that 100% of the monies deposited must be used to purchase special-issue U.S. Treasury bonds. This exchange between the trust fund and the Treasury does not result in revenues or outlays for the federal government. It is an intra-governmental transfer, which has no effect on the size of the government's budget surplus or deficit.[21]

Federal trust funds are not a "store of wealth" like private pension funds. The assets of the civil service retirement trust fund are U.S. Treasury bonds that function solely as a record of available budget authority. The bonds cannot be sold by the trust fund to the general public in exchange for cash. They can only be returned to the Treasury, which recognizes each bond as representing an equivalent dollar-value of budget authority to be used for the payment of benefits to federal retirees and their survivors. The Office of Management and Budget has stated that

> These [trust fund] balances are available for future benefit payments and other trust fund expenditures, but only in a bookkeeping sense. The holdings of the trust funds are not assets of the Government as a whole that can be drawn down in the future to fund benefits. Instead, they are claims on the Treasury. From a cash perspective, when trust fund holdings are redeemed to authorize the payment of benefits, the Department of the Treasury finances the expenditure in the same way as any other Federal expenditure—by using current receipts or by borrowing from the public. The existence of large trust fund balances, therefore, does not, by itself, increase the Government's ability to pay benefits. Put differently, these trust fund balances are assets of the program agencies

and corresponding liabilities of the Treasury, netting to zero for the Government as a whole.[22]

Government trust funds, however, *can* ease the burden of future benefit payments if an increase in the trust fund balance represents a net increase in national saving. Again, quoting OMB:

> From an economic standpoint, the Government is able to prefund benefits only by increasing saving and investment in the economy as a whole. This can be fully accomplished only by simultaneously running trust fund surpluses equal to the actuarial present value of the accumulating benefits while maintaining an unchanged Federal fund deficit, so that the trust fund surplus reduces the unified budget deficit or increases the unified budget surplus. This would reduce Federal borrowing by the amount of the trust funds surplus and increase the amount of national saving available to finance investment. As long as the increase in Government saving is not offset by a reduction in private saving, greater investment would increase future national income, which would yield greater tax revenue to support the benefits.[23]

Investment Practices of Federal Trust Funds

Federal trust funds do not represent a store of wealth for the government because they consist entirely of U.S. government bonds. A bond represents wealth only when it is held by someone other than the individual, company, or government that issued it. A bond is an I.O.U.—that is, a promise to pay. An I.O.U. received from someone else might be considered an asset, provided that the issuer is willing and able to pay the debt when it is due, but writing an I.O.U. to oneself does *not* create an asset. This analogy applies to the U.S. Treasury bonds held by the federal government's trust funds: they are I.O.U.s issued by one agency of the U.S. government and held by another agency of the same government. Both the issuer and holder are part of the same entity: the U.S. government. When federal trust funds redeem their bonds, the Treasury has only one source from which to obtain the required cash: the public. It can do this either by collecting taxes or by borrowing.

Many state and local government pension funds invest in stocks, bonds, mortgages, real estate, and other private assets. If Congress were to permit the CSRDF to acquire assets other than U.S. Treasury bonds—such as the stocks and bonds issued by private corporations—these assets could be sold to the public for cash as pension liabilities come due. This would represent a major change in public policy that would have important effects on the federal budget and on private businesses that would, in effect, be partly owned by an agency of the federal government.[24]

Among the possible drawbacks of allowing the CSRDF to invest in private assets are that the stocks and bonds purchased by the trust fund would displace purchases of these assets by private citizens, so that while civil service retirement benefits would be prefunded, it would be at the cost of reducing the amount of private-sector assets held by private citizens. In a scenario of "full displacement," there would be no net increase in the amount of saving and investment in the economy, just a reallocation of assets in which the government would own more private sector stocks and bonds and private investors would hold more Treasury bonds.

A second issue that would have to be considered if the trust fund were to purchase private investment securities would be the fund's management and investment practices. Who would make the investment decisions, and what would be the acceptable level of investment risk for the funds? The most fundamental risk is that poor investment choices would result in the trust fund losing value over time. Another question would be how the fund would decide what assets to purchase. Deciding what would constitute an appropriate investment for a fund that consists mainly of monies provided by taxpayers could be controversial. Not all companies, industries, or countries would be seen by the public as appropriate places to invest these funds. In short, the question of investing trust fund assets in securities other than U.S. Treasury bonds is one that would deserve close and careful consideration of all the possible ramifications.

Allowing the civil service retirement trust fund to invest in private-sector securities also would have implications for the federal budget. Currently, the trust fund is credited by the Treasury with agency contributions on behalf of covered employees, and it receives revenue in the form of employee contributions. Agency contributions are intra-governmental transfers, and have no effect on the size of the government's annual budget deficit or surplus. Employee contributions, however, are revenues of the U.S. government. As it now operates, the only outlays of the trust fund are payments to annuitants and relatively minor outlays for administrative expenses. If the trust fund were to purchase private assets such as corporate stocks and bonds rather than U.S. Treasury bonds, there would be an immediate outlay of funds. This outlay by the trust fund would be paid for in part by employee contributions that would be diverted from the general fund of the Treasury. The remainder of the purchase, financed by agency contributions, would replace an intra-governmental transfer with a direct outlay of federal funds.

Because the Treasury would no longer receive employee contributions toward CSRS and FERS as revenue, it would have to borrow an equal amount from the public. Consequently, without an offsetting reduction in outlays elsewhere in the budget or an increase in revenues other sources, the net effect of these transactions would be an increase in the government's budget deficit (or a decrease in the budget surplus). If the budget accounting period extended over a long enough time, these transactions would cancel one another out because the long-term effect would merely move some outlays from the future, where they would have occurred as payments to annuitants, to the present, where they would occur partly as outlays to purchase assets and partly as a reduction in revenues that currently go to the general fund of the Treasury.

APPENDIX. LEGISLATIVE PROPOSALS IN THE 112TH CONGRESS

Several pieces of legislation in the 112th Congress proposed changes to the benefits and financing of the federal employee retirement system. For instance, P.L. 112-96 (i.e., the H.R. 3630 conference report), enacted on February 22, 2012, made a number of changes to FERS. In addition, the House-passed version of H.R. 3630, H.R. 3813, the House Rules Committee print of H.R. 7, H.R. 5652, H.R. 6684, and H.R. 6688 included proposals to increase employee contributions and make other comprehensives changes to retirement benefits for certain federal employees. This legislation is summarized below. Additionally, federal retirement recommendations from the President's Budget Proposal for FY2013 are also described.

P.L. 112-96, Title V of the Middle Class Tax Relief and Job Creation Act of 2012

Title V, Sections 5001-5003 of P.L. 112-96, the Middle Class Tax Relief and Job Creation Act of 2012, contained provisions related to federal employee retirement contributions and benefits. P.L. 112-96 (i.e., the H.R. 3630 conference report) was passed in the House and the Senate on February 17, 2012, and signed into law on February 22, 2012. P.L. 112-96 increased the

FERS employee contributions by 2.3% for FERS employees hired (or rehired with less than five years of FERS service) after December 31, 2012.[25] Under P.L. 112-96, the FERS employee contribution rate for most newly hired/rehired FERS employees is 3.1% (rather than 0.8% for FERS employees first hired before 2013). The new employee contribution rate for Members of Congress and congressional staff is also 3.1% (rather than 1.3% for Members first elected before 2013). For newly hired (rehired with less than five years of service) FERS employees after December 31, 2012, who are law enforcement officers, firefighters, air traffic controllers, or nuclear waste handlers, the FERS employee contribution rate is 3.6% under P.L. 112-96 (rather than 1.3% for these FERS employees hired before 2013).[26] FERS agency contributions were decreased in proportion to the FERS employee contribution increases for employees first hired in 2013 or later.

P.L. 112-96 also made changes in the FERS benefit accrual rates for Members of Congress and congressional staff hired (or rehired with less than five years of service) after December 31, 2012. This law set the benefit accrual rate (used in the FERS pension amount calculation) for new Members of Congress and new congressional staff at the same level as for most FERS employees. Prior to enactment of P.L. 112-96, all Members of Congress and all congressional staff covered by FERS had a benefit accrual rate of 1.7% per year for the first 20 years of service and 1.0% for any years of service after 20 years. Under P.L. 112-96, Members and congressional staff first elected or hired in 2013 or later are treated like regular FERS employees for the purposes of the FERS benefit accrual rate: 1.0% per year of service, or, if an employee has at least 20 years of service and works until at least the age of 62, the benefit accrual rate is 1.1% per year of service.

H.R. 3630 (as passed in the House), Title V, Subtitle E of the Middle Class Tax Relief and Job Creation Act of 2011

On December 9, 2011, Representative Camp introduced, H.R. 3630, the Middle Class Tax Relief and Job Creation Act of 2011. This version of H.R. 3630 was passed by the House on December 13, 2011. Among other provisions, the House-passed version of H.R. 3630 contained a number of proposals related to federal employee retirement benefits. Some of these federal retirement provisions would have impacted current federal employees covered by CSRS and FERS, whereas other provisions would have been effective for newly hired FERS (or rehired with less than five years of FERS service) employees after December 31, 2012.

The House-passed version of H.R. 3630 would have increased retirement contributions for current Members of Congress and current federal employees covered by CSRS and FERS by an additional 0.5% per year over calendar years 2013, 2014, and 2015. Beginning in calendar year 2015, the CSRS and FERS employee contribution would, therefore, have been 1.5% higher than under current law. (These increased contributions for current federal civilian employees would also have applied in the same way for current employees covered by the Foreign Service Retirement System, the Central Intelligence Agency Retirement and Disability System, and the Tennessee Valley Authority retirement pension plan.)

This version of H.R. 3630 would also have eliminated the FERS supplement for employees separating from service under FERS after December 31, 2012, with the following exception: the FERS supplement would have been preserved for any FERS employee subject to a mandatory retirement age (law enforcement officers [LEOs], firefighters, air traffic controllers, etc.).

Finally, the House-passed version of H.R. 3630 would have made a number of changes to the retirement benefits of FERS employees hired (or rehired with less than five years of FERS service) after December 31, 2012; i.e., to (1) increase the FERS employee contribution rates for regular FERS employees to 4.0% of pay (the FERS employee contribution rate for Members of Congress, congressional staff, LEOs, air traffic controllers, nuclear materials couriers, customs and border patrol agents, and other categories similar to LEOs [i.e., LEOs/etc.] would have been 4.5%); (2) change the measure of pay used to calculate the FERS annuity from the current law three highest, consecutive years of base salary to be the five highest, consecutive years of base salary ("high-5"); and (3) reduce the benefit accrual rate by 0.3% for regular FERS employees with less than 20 years of service; Members of Congress, congressional staff, and LEOs/etc. with less than 20 years of service; and LEOs/etc. with more than 20 years of service.

H.R. 3813, Securing Annuities for Federal Employees Act of 2012

Representative Ross introduced H.R. 3813 on January 24, 2012. H.R. 3813 proposed many of the same changes to federal employee retirement benefits as in the House-passed version of H.R. 3630. For instance, H.R. 3813 would also have eliminated the FERS supplement for individuals separating from service after December 31, 2012, except if the individual was an LEO/etc. subject to mandatory retirement age. Like the House-passed version of H.R. 3630, H.R. 3813 would have increased CSRS and FERS employee contributions for current employees by 1.5% over three calendar years.[27] In addition, for FERS employees hired (or rehired with less than five years of FERS service) after December 31, 2012, H.R. 3813 would also have increased the FERS employee contribution to be 4.0% of pay for regular FERS employees and 4.5% of pay for certain special categories of FERS employees: Members of Congress, congressional staff, and LEOs/etc. Finally, like the House-passed version of H.R. 3630, H.R. 3813 would have changed the measure of pay used to calculate the FERS annuity for FERS employees hired (or rehired with less than five years of FERS service) after December 31, 2012, to be based on high-5 pay instead of high-3 pay.

H.R. 3813 proposed slightly different changes in the FERS benefit accrual rates for FERS employees hired (or rehired with less than five years of FERS service) after December 31, 2012, in comparison with the House-passed version of H.R. 3630. H.R. 3813 would also have reduced the benefit accrual rate by 0.3% for regular FERS employees with less than 20 years of service; Members of Congress, congressional staff, and LEOs/etc. with less than 20 years of service; and LEOs/etc. with more than 20 years of service. However, unlike the House-passed version of H.R. 3630, H.R. 3813 would also have reduced by 0.3% the benefit accrual rate for Members of Congress and congressional staff with more than 20 years of service.

Finally, H.R. 3813 contained a provision—not found in the House-passed version of H.R. 3630— that would have allowed TSP participants to deposit any accumulated annual leave into their TSP accounts, subject to current annual TSP contributions limits.[28]

H.R. 7, Title XVI, Securing Annuities of Federal Employees Act of 2012

Sections 16001 through 16006 of Title XVI (the Securing Annuities of Federal Employees Act of 2012) of the House Rules Committee print of H.R. 7 contained the identical federal retirement provisions as found in H.R. 3813.[29]

H.R. 5652, Title V of the Sequester Replacement Reconciliation Act of 2012

Title V of H.R. 5652, the Sequester Replacement Reconciliation Act of 2012, contained several provisions related to federal retirement benefits. First, H.R. 5652 proposed to increase the federal retirement contributions of current CSRS and FERS employees. Phased in over five years— FY2013 through FY2017—these employee contribution increases included an additional

- 5.0% of pay over current law for current, regular CSRS and FERS employees as well as CSRS and FERS LEOs/etc.;
- 7.5% of pay over current law for current, congressional staff under FERS; and
- 8.5% of pay over current law for current, congressional staff under CSRS and current Members of Congress under CSRS and FERS.

In addition, H.R. 5652 would have ended the FERS annuity supplement for new FERS employees hired after December 31, 2012. Finally, H.R. 5652 would have allowed TSP participants to contribute lump sum payments of any unused annual leave to their TSP accounts, subject to current law TSP contribution limits.

H.R. 5652 was introduced in the House on May 9, 2012, by Representative Ryan. H.R. 5652 passed the House on May 10, 2012.

H.R. 6684, Title V of the Spending Reduction Act of 2012

Representative Cantor introduced H.R. 6684 on December 19, 2012. H.R. 6684 passed the House on December 20, 2012. Title V of H.R. 6684, the Spending Reduction Act of 2012, contained the identical federal retirement provisions as found in H.R. 5652.

H.R. 6688, Title I, Subtitle E, of the Averting the Fiscal Cliff Act of 2012

Representative Jordan introduced H.R. 6688 on December 19, 2012. Subtitle E of Title I of H.R. 6688, the Averting the Fiscal Cliff Act of 2012, contained the identical federal retirement provisions found in H.R. 5652 and H.R. 6684.

President's Budget Proposal FY2013

The President's Budget Proposal for FY2013 contained some recommendations related to federal retirement benefits and financing. This proposal recommended increased CSRS and FERS employee contributions for current federal workers, but by a lower amount than the House-passed version of H.R. 3630, H.R. 3813, the House Rules Committee print of H.R. 7, H.R. 5652, H.R. 6684, and H.R. 6688. The President's Budget Proposal for FY2013 recommended increasing current employee contributions by 0.4% in each of three calendar years—2013, 2014, and 2015— for a cumulative increase of 1.2% of pay over current contributions.

This proposal also recommended eliminating the FERS annuity supplement for new employees. The President's Budget Proposal for FY2013 did not make any further recommendations related to FERS benefit changes.

End Notes

[1] The actuarial equivalent of a life annuity is a lump-sum payment that could purchase an annuity of equal value, assuming a certain interest rate and life expectancy.

[2] The open season held from July through December 1998 was authorized by P.L. 105-61, enacted on October 10, 1997.

[3] This report describes basic retirement benefits for federal employees under CSRS and FERS. Both programs also provide for disability retirement, benefits for surviving dependents, and benefits for former spouses. These benefits are described in three other CRS reports: CRS Report RS22838, Disability Retirement for Federal Employees; CRS Report RS21029, Survivor Benefits for Families of Civilian Federal Employees and Retirees; and CRS Report RS22856, Retirement and Survivor Annuities for Former Spouses of Federal Employees.

[4] U.S. Government Accountability Office, Federal Pensions: Thrift Savings Plan Has Key Role in Retirement Benefits, HEHS-96-1, October 1995.

[5] This calculation is based on nominal or "current dollars" rather than indexed or "constant dollars."

[6] For additional details on FERS accrual rate changes made by P.L. 112-96, see U.S. Office of Personnel Management, Benefits Administration Letter, 12-104, October 3, 2012, available at http://www.opm.gov/retire/pubs/bals/2012/12- 104.pdf.

[7] For estimates of the replacement rates under FERS, see CRS Report RL30387, Federal Employees' Retirement System: The Role of the Thrift Savings Plan, by Katelin P. Isaacs.

[8] Under both CSRS and FERS, automatic COLAs are paid out beginning in January each year, based on the percentage increase in the CPI-W for the most recent third quarter (July-

September) compared to the third quarter in the last year a COLA was determined. In 1994, 1995, and 1996 COLAs for civil service annuitants were delayed from January until April as a means of achieving budgetary savings. In 2010 and 2011, there were no automatic COLAs for civil service annuitants. In 2013, the automatic COLA for both CSRS and FERS is 1.7%. See CRS Report 94-834, Cost-of-Living Adjustments for Federal Civil Service Annuities, by Katelin P. Isaacs for a complete history of COLAs under CSRS and FERS.

[9] See 26 U.S.C. §402(g). Prior to 2006, employee contributions were limited to the lesser of a specific percentage of pay or the amount permissible under I.R.C. §402(g). The Consolidated Appropriations Act of 2000 (P.L. 106-554) eliminated the percentage-of-pay limitations on contributions to the TSP, effective in 2006.

[10] The "S" and "I" funds were added in 2001 in accordance with the Thrift Savings Plan Act of 1996 (P.L. 104-208).

[11] Statement of Gary A. Amelio, former executive director of the Federal Retirement Thrift Investment Board before the Senate Subcommittee on Securities and Investment, June 14, 2005.

[12] An annuity is a contract between the individual and an insurance company that pays a monthly income in exchange for an initial premium. The monthly income that a given premium will purchase depends on both on the estimated rate of return from the investment and actuarial estimates of the annuitant's remaining life expectancy.

[13] Former federal employees are eligible for Medicare at the age of 65, regardless of whether they were covered by CSRS or FERS. Workers in both programs pay the Hospital Insurance (HI) payroll tax of 1.45% on all salary and wages.

[14] See also CRS Report RL30631, Retirement Benefits for Members of Congress, by Katelin P. Isaacs.

[15] In general, state and local governments do not face this risk either; however, they are more like private businesses in that they have in some cases defaulted on their public debts.

[16] As is explained later in this report, a large balance in the civil service retirement trust fund does not by itself make it easier to pay these benefits when they come due because the trust fund invests exclusively in U.S. Treasury securities.

[17] A pension plan's normal cost is the level percentage of pay that, invested today at a particular real rate of interest, will be sufficient to fully finance the retirement benefits under the plan.

[18] Two other elements of a pension plan's dynamic normal cost are increases in benefits that result from (1) new or expanded benefits and (2) newly covered groups of workers.

[19] The actuarial present value of benefits is based on their dynamic normal cost, including future COLAs.

[20] Civil Service Retirement and Disability Fund, Annual Report of the Board of Actuaries, Civil Service Retirement and Disability Fund, Fiscal Year Ended September 30, 2010, p. 17.

[21] Federal trust funds represent budget authority. Only revenues and outlays affect the size of the annual budget surplus or deficit. The excess revenues that result in a trust fund surplus therefore reduce the government's deficit (or increase its surplus) and the outlays for retiree and survivor benefits either reduce the government's budget surplus or increase the budget deficit. However, the exchange of cash for bonds (or vice versa) between the trust fund and the Treasury does not affect the deficit because it is an exchange that occurs entirely within the government.

[22] U.S. Office of Management and Budget, Budget of the United States Government, Fiscal Year 2010: Analytical Perspectives, 2009, p. 345.

[23] Ibid.

[24] The Railroad Retirement and Survivors' Improvement Act of 2001 (P.L. 107-90) authorizes the Railroad Retirement Trust Fund to acquire corporate stocks, bonds, and other assets to fund railroad retirement benefits. According to the Congressional Budget Office, "such an action has no clear precedent and raises questions about how the federal government might behave as an investor in private enterprises." (Congressional Budget Office, The Budget and Economic Outlook: Fiscal Years 2003-2012, January 2002, p. 88.)

[25] These increased employee contributions for new civilian employees also apply in the same way for new employees covered by the Foreign Service Retirement System and the Central Intelligence Agency Retirement and Disability System.

[26] Under P.L. 112-96, FERS agency contributions are reduced by the amount of the increased employee contributions.

[27] As in the House-passed version of H.R. 3630, these contributions for current federal civilian employees would also have applied in the same way for current employees covered by the Foreign Service Retirement System, the Central Intelligence Agency Retirement and Disability System, and the Tennessee Valley Authority retirement pension plan.

[28] This TSP provision was added to H.R. 3813 as part of an amendment in the nature of a substitute, which was offered by Rep. Ross on February 6, 2012.

[29] See House Rules Committee Print 112-4, February 8, 2012, available online here: http://docs.house.gov/ billsthisweek/20120213/CPRT-112-HPRT-RU00-HR7RCP.pdf.

In: Retirement Savings and Security
Editor: Linda A. Eisterhold

ISBN: 978-1-62948-132-6

Chapter 6

FEDERAL EMPLOYEES' RETIREMENT SYSTEM: THE ROLE OF THE THRIFT SAVINGS PLAN*

Katelin P. Isaacs

SUMMARY

Federal employees participate in one of two retirement systems. The Civil Service Retirement System (CSRS) was established in 1920 and covers only employees hired before 1984. Participants in the CSRS do not pay Social Security payroll taxes and they do not earn Social Security benefits. For a worker retiring after 30 years of federal service, a CSRS annuity will be equal to 56.25% of the average of his or her highest three consecutive years of basic pay.

The Social Security Amendments of 1983 (P.L. 98-21) required federal employees hired after 1983 to participate in Social Security. Because the CSRS was not designed to coordinate with Social Security, Congress directed the development of a new retirement plan for federal workers hired after 1983. The result was the Federal Employees' Retirement System (FERS) Act of 1986 (P.L. 99-335). The FERS has three elements: (1) Social Security, (2) the FERS basic retirement annuity and FERS supplement, and (3) the Thrift Savings Plan (TSP).

---

* This is an edited, reformatted and augmented version of a Congressional Research Service publication, CRS Report for Congress RL30387, from www.crs.gov, prepared for Members and Committees of Congress, dated March 8, 2013.

The amount of the FERS basic retirement annuity is determined by three factors: (1) the salary base, (2) the accrual rate, and (3) years of service. The salary base is the average of the worker's highest three consecutive years of pay. Under FERS, the benefit accrual rate is 1.0% per year of service, or 1.1% for workers retiring at the age of 62 or later with 20 or more years of service. A worker with 30 years of service retiring at the age of 62 will receive a FERS pension equal to 33% of the average of his or her highest three consecutive years of pay, or about 32% of final annual salary.

The TSP is a defined contribution retirement plan similar to the 401(k) plans provided by many employers in the private sector. The income that a retired worker receives from the TSP will depend on the balance in his or her account. In 2013, employees covered by FERS or CSRS can contribute up to $17,500 to the TSP. Employees aged 50 or older can contribute an additional $5,500. Contributions of up to 5% of pay made by workers under FERS are matched by the federal government. Workers covered by CSRS can contribute to the TSP, but they receive no matching contributions.

The TSP is a key element of the FERS, especially for workers at the upper ranges of the federal pay scale. The Social Security benefit formula is designed to replace a greater share of income for low-wage workers than for high-wage workers. The FERS basic annuity will replace about 32% of final salary for an employee retiring at the age of 62 with 30 years of service. Higher-wage federal workers need to contribute a greater percentage of pay to the TSP to reach the same level of income replacement as lower-paid workers can achieve from just the FERS retirement annuity and Social Security. At an annual rate of return of 6.0%, income from the TSP can replace about 33% of final pay for a federal employee who contributes 10% of pay over 30 years.

INTRODUCTION

Federal employees participate in one of two retirement systems. The Civil Service Retirement System (CSRS) was established in 1920 and covers only employees hired before 1984. Participants in the CSRS do not pay Social Security payroll taxes and they do not earn Social Security benefits. For a worker retiring after 30 years of federal service, a CSRS annuity will be equal to 56.25% of the average of his or her highest three consecutive years of basic pay.

Because the Social Security trust funds needed additional cash contributions to remain solvent, the Social Security Amendments of 1983 (P.L. 98-21) required federal employees hired after 1983 to participate in

Social Security. To coordinate federal pension benefits with Social Security, Congress directed the development of a new retirement system for federal employees hired after 1983. The result was the Federal Employees' Retirement System (FERS) Act of 1986 (P.L. 99- 335).

The FERS consists of three elements:

- Social Security,
- the FERS basic retirement annuity and the FERS supplement, and
- the Thrift Savings Plan (TSP).

All federal employees initially hired into federal employment on or after January 1, 1984, are enrolled in the FERS, as are employees who voluntarily switched from CSRS to FERS during "open seasons" held in 1987 and 1998.[1] Of 2,831,000 federal civilian and Postal Service employees enrolled in these federal retirement plans as of September 30, 2010, 2,458,000 (87%) were participating in the FERS and 373,000 (13%) were under the CSRS.[2]

THE FERS BASIC RETIREMENT ANNUITY

Retirement Age and Service Requirements

Federal employees are fully vested in the FERS basic retirement annuity after five years of service. The earliest age at which a worker can retire under FERS was 55 for workers born before 1948. The minimum retirement age (MRA) under FERS began to increase in 2003 for workers born in 1948, and it eventually will reach the age of 57 for those born in 1970 or later (see *Table 1*). In 2012, a worker who has completed at least 30 years of service can retire with an immediate, unreduced annuity at the age of 56. An employee with 20 or more years of service can retire with an immediate, unreduced annuity at the age of 60, and an employee with at least five years of service can retire with an immediate annuity at the age of 62.[3]

Under FERS, employees (or former employees) who have completed 10 or more years of government service can elect to receive a reduced retirement annuity at the minimum retirement age. For those who choose this option, their annuities are permanently reduced by 5% multiplied by the number of years between 62 and the individual's age at the time the annuity begins. For example, an employee who retires at 56 years old with fewer than 30 years of service would have his or her annuity reduced by 30% below the amount that would have been paid if the individual were aged 62 or older at retirement.

Table 1. Minimum Retirement Age under FERS

Year of Birth	Minimum Retirement Age
1947 or earlier	55 years
1948	55 years, 2 months
1949	55 years, 4 months
1950	55 years, 6 months
1951	55 years, 8 months
1952	55 years, 10 months
1953 to 1964	56 years
1965	56 years, 2 months
1966	56 years, 4 months
1967	56 years, 6 months
1968	56 years, 8 months
1969	56 years, 10 months
1970 or later	57 years

Source: 5 U.S.C. §8412,

Of the 39,337 federal employees covered by CSRS who retired under normal, voluntary rules in FY2011, 42% were between the ages of 55 and 59. They had an average of 34.8 years of federal service.[4] Thirty percent of federal workers who took normal retirement under CSRS in FY2011 were aged 62 or older.

The average age of all federal workers covered by CSRS who retired in FY2010 under normal, voluntary retirements was 60.7 years. Their average length of federal service was 35.5 years. Because relatively few employees hired before 1984 elected to switch to FERS, individuals who have been retiring under FERS have tended to be those who joined or rejoined the federal work force relatively late in their careers. In FY2011, 27,006 federal employees retired with immediate annuities under FERS. Their average age was 63.5 years, and their average length of service in the federal government was 20.9 years.[5]

The average length of service for workers retiring under FERS will rise over time as the proportion of federal employees who spent their entire careers under FERS continues to increase.

Calculating the FERS Basic Retirement Annuity

The FERS basic retirement annuity is a defined benefit (DB) pension. The amount of the pension benefit is determined by multiplying three factors—the employee's number of years of service, the annual benefit accrual rate, and the salary base—as is shown in the following formula:

pension amount = *years of service* x *accrual rate* x *salary base*

Salary Base

In both CSRS and FERS, the salary base is the average of the employee's three highest consecutive years of basic pay, sometimes called "high-three pay."[6]

Accrual Rate

The annual benefit accrual rate is the percentage of the salary base that a worker earns in pension benefits for each year of service. Under FERS, retirement benefits accrue at the rate of 1.0% per year. A worker with 30 years of service will have accrued a pension benefit equal to 30% of the FERS salary base.[7] Employees with 20 or more years of federal service who retire at the age of 62 or later are credited with a benefit accrual rate of 1.1% for each year of service. For example, a worker under FERS who retires at 61 years old with 29 years of service would receive a FERS annuity equal to 29% of his or her high-three average pay. Delaying retirement by one year would increase the annuity to 33% of high-three average pay because the benefit accrual rate would be 1.1% for each year of service rather than 1.0% per year of service.

Under CSRS, employees accrue pension benefits at rates that increase with length of service. The CSRS benefit accrual rate is 1.5% for each of the first 5 years of service; 1.75% for the 6th through 10th years of service; and 2.0% for each year of service after the 10th year.[8] This results in a retirement annuity equal to 56.25% of high-three average pay for a worker who retires with 30 years of service.

Social Security, and the "FERS Supplement"

Congress intended the FERS to be a complete retirement package consisting of Social Security, the FERS annuity, and the Thrift Savings Plan. Because Social Security retirement benefits cannot begin before the age of 62, Congress included in the FERS a temporary supplement for federal workers who retire before the age of 62. The FERS supplement is equal to the portion of the Social Security benefit to which the worker will be entitled at the age of 62 that is attributable to his or years of federal employment under FERS. The FERS supplement is paid until age 62 to workers who retire at the minimum retirement age (currently 56) or older with at least 30 years of service, or at age 60 with at least 20 years of service. The FERS supplement terminates at the age of 62, regardless of whether the individual applies for Social Security retired worker benefits at that time.

Cost-of-Living Adjustments

Cost-of-living adjustments (COLAs) protect the purchasing power of retirement benefits from being eroded by inflation. COLAs increase the *nominal* amount of retirement income, but they do not increase its *real* value. COLAs have been in effect since 1962 for CSRS, and since the inception of FERS.

Retirement benefits paid under CSRS are fully indexed for inflation, as measured by the Consumer Price Index for Wage and Salary Workers (CPI-W).[9] The FERS basic annuity is fully price-indexed only if the annual rate of inflation is 2% or less. FERS benefits are partially indexed if inflation is in excess of 2%. If the CPI-W increases by 2% or less, the FERS monthly benefit is increased by the annual percentage increase in the CPI-W. If the CPI-W increases by 2% to 3%, the increase in the FERS annuity is limited to 2%. If the CPI-W increases by more than 3%, the increase in the FERS annuity is equal to the rise in the CPI-W minus one percentage point. Under FERS, COLAs are provided only to retirees who are aged 62 or older, annuitants under age 62 who retired because of a disability, and survivor annuitants.

The Thrift Savings Plan

The Thrift Savings Plan is a defined contribution (DC) retirement plan similar to the 401(k) plans provided by many employers in the private sector.[10] Newly hired federal employees who participated in a 401(k) plan can, if they choose, roll over their 401(k) account balances into the TSP. Workers who leave the federal government for jobs in other sectors of the economy can leave their money in the TSP—where it will continue to accrue interest, dividends, and capital gains according to the performance of the funds in which they have chosen to invest—or they can roll over their TSP funds on a tax-deferred basis into another tax-qualified retirement savings account such as an IRA or a 401(k) plan. All TSP participants are immediately and fully vested in their contributions to the plan, federal matching contributions, and any growth in the value of their investment from interest, dividends, and capital gains. Participants are fully vested in the 1% agency automatic contributions to the TSP after three years (two years for congressional employees and executive-branch political appointees).

P.L. 106-361 (October 27, 2000) allows "rollover distributions" into the TSP from other tax-qualified retirement savings plans, such as those authorized for private-sector firms under Section 401(k) of the tax code and for non-profit organizations under I.R.C. Section 403(b). This law also allows employees to begin making tax-deferred contributions to the TSP immediately upon becoming employed by the federal government. P.L. 106-398 (October 30, 2000) allows uniformed military personnel on active duty or in the ready reserve to participate in the TSP under the same terms and conditions as civilian federal employees, but without matching contributions.[11]

P.L. 111-31 (June 22, 2009) provides for newly hired federal employees to be enrolled automatically in the TSP at a default contribution rate of 3% of pay. Default contributions are invested in the "G" fund (government security fund) of the TSP. Participants can elect a different contribution rate and select a different investment fund or funds, or they can elect not to contribute to the TSP. P.L. 111-31 also eliminates a previous waiting period for employees under FERS to be eligible to receive agency automatic (1%) and agency matching contributions.

Employee and Agency Contributions

Federal agencies contribute an amount equal to 1% of basic pay to the TSP for each employee under FERS, whether or not the employee chooses to contribute anything to the plan. In 2013, employees can contribute up to $17,500 to the TSP.[12] Employees aged 50 and older can contribute an additional $5,500. These employee contributions may be made on a pre-tax basis, in which case neither the contributions nor investment earnings that accrue to the plan are taxed until the money is withdrawn. Alternatively, P.L. 111-31 authorized a qualified Roth contribution option to the TSP. Under a Roth contribution option, employee salary deferrals into a retirement plan are made with after-tax income. Qualified distributions from the Roth TSP plan option—generally, distributions taken five or more years after the participant's first Roth contribution and after he or she has reached the age of 591/2—are tax-free.

In addition, contributions of up to 5% of pay made by employees under FERS are matched by the federal government according to the schedule shown in *Table 2.* Federal workers covered by CSRS also may contribute to the TSP, but they receive no matching contributions from their employing agencies.

Table 2. Government Matching Rate on TSP Contributions by FERS Participants (as a percentage of salary)

Employee[a]	Government	Total
0.0	1.0	1.0
1.0	2.0	3.0
2.0	3.0	5.0
3.0	4.0	7.0
4.0	4.5	8.5
5.0 or more	5.0	10.0

Source: 5 U.S.C. §8432.

[a] Subject to a maximum of $17,500 in 2013 under I.R.C. §402(g).

Maximum Allowable Thrift Savings Plan Contribution

Prior to July 1, 2001, employees under FERS could contribute no more than the lesser of 10% of pay or the maximum tax-deferred contribution permissible under section 402(g) of the Internal Revenue Code. P.L. 106-554 (December 21, 2000) increased the maximum allowable employee contribution to the TSP by one percentage point each year for five years. Beginning in July 2001, employees in the FERS were allowed to contribute up to 11% of pay to the TSP, and employees in the CSRS were allowed to contribute up to 6% of pay to the TSP. The maximum permissible contribution rose by one percentage point each year until reaching 15% for FERS and 10% for CSRS in 2005.

The percentage-of-pay limits on contributions to the TSP were eliminated beginning in 2006. Employee contributions to the TSP are now subject only to the limits applicable under IRC Section 402(g). This limit is $17,500 in 2013. Employees who will be aged 50 or older at any time in 2013 can make additional "catch-up" contributions of up to $5,500.

Penalty on Early Withdrawals

With certain exceptions, I.R.C. Section 72(t) imposes a 10% additional tax on distributions from all qualified plans, including the TSP, unless the individual is over the age of 591,4, dies, or becomes disabled.[13] This additional tax does not apply to early distributions if they are paid:

1. after the plan participant has reached age 591,4;
2. to a beneficiary after the death of the participant;
3. because the participant has become disabled;
4. to an alternate payee under a qualified domestic relations order (QDRO);
5. to an employee who has separated from service under an early retirement arrangement after reaching age 55;
6. as dividends paid from an Employee Stock Ownership Plan (ESOP);
7. through an IRS levy to collect back taxes owed by the plan participant;
8. to pay medical expenses of the plan participant, a spouse, or dependent, but only to the extent that they exceed 7.5% of adjusted gross income;
9. as part of a series of substantially equal periodic payments (SEPPs) over the life of the participant or the joint lives of the participant and beneficiary; or,
10. to a reservist who is ordered to active duty for more than 179 days.

A participant in the TSP must begin taking distributions from the TSP no later than April of the year after the year in which the participant attains the age of 701,4, unless the participant is still employed by the government. These distributions must be included in the participant's taxable income for the year. The requirement to begin taking distributions after the age of 701,4 does not apply to qualified Roth contributions, because Roth contributions are made with after-tax income.

Participant Loans

Participants may borrow from their TSP accounts. General purpose loans must be repaid within five years. Residential loans taken for the purpose of purchasing a primary residence must be repaid within 15 years. Participant loans may be taken only from participant contributions and attributable earnings and cannot exceed the lesser of one-half of the participant's vested account balance or $50,000.[14]

The interest rate for TSP loans is the "G Fund" interest rate at the time the loan agreement is issued by the plan's record keeper. The rate is fixed at this level for the life of each loan. Interest earned on loans is allocated to the participant account upon repayment. Participants whose loans are in default have until the end of the following calendar quarter to pay the overdue amount. If not repaid by that time, the loan plus accrued interest is treated as a taxable distribution to the plan participant, which may be subject to the 10% penalty on retirement plan distributions made before the age of 591,4. If the participant leaves federal service, the balance of the loan must be repaid in full or the loan will be treated as a taxable distribution.

Age-based Withdrawals and Hardship Withdrawals

In general, participants cannot withdraw money from the TSP until they separate from federal employment. Distributions while the participant is still employed by the federal government are permitted only if the individual is experiencing a financial hardship or has reached age 591,4. Participants who are over the age of 591,4 and are still employed by the federal government can take a single age-based withdrawal from the TSP. The participant must include the withdrawal in his or her taxable income for the year unless the withdrawal is deposited into an IRA or other tax-qualified retirement plan within 60 days.[15]

A participant can take an in-service withdrawal from the TSP if he or she is experiencing a financial hardship. Hardship withdrawals must be included in the participant's taxable income and they may be subject to an additional 10% tax if the participant is under 591,4 years old. Only the participant's contributions and earnings on those contributions can be withdrawn and the amount of the withdrawal is limited to the amount of his or her financial need. A participant is prohibited from contributing to the TSP for six months after the date on which he or she receives a hardship withdrawal.

To qualify for a hardship withdrawal, the participant's financial need must arise from one or more of the following:

- negative monthly cash flow;
- medical expenses that are not covered by insurance;
- personal casualty losses that are not covered by insurance; or
- legal expenses arising from separation or divorce.

TSP Investment Options

The contribution that the TSP will make to a federal employee's retirement income depends on the value of the account at retirement. The value of the account in turn depends on the worker's salary during his or her federal service, the percentage of salary contributed to the TSP, the number of years over which investment earnings accrued to these contributions, and the performance of the funds into which the employee directed the contributions. Currently, participants in the TSP can deposit their contributions into one or more of five funds:

- The "C" fund invests in a stock market index fund that replicates the Standard and Poor's 500 Index of 500 large- to medium-sized U.S. companies.
- The "F" fund invests in bonds in the same proportion as they are represented by the Barclays Capital U.S. Aggregate Bond Index.
- The "G" fund invests in U.S. government securities and pays interest equal to the average rate of return on government securities with maturities of four years or more.
- The "S" fund invests in a stock index fund that tracks the Dow Jones U.S. Completion Total Stock Market Index.
- The "I" fund invests in a stock index fund that replicates the Morgan Stanley Capital International EAFE (Europe, Australasia, Far East) Index.[16]

In 2005, the TSP introduced "Lifecycle Funds." The Lifecycle Funds are invested in various combinations of the five existing TSP funds. The allocation of contributions among the five core TSP funds is based on the year that the participant expects to begin withdrawing money from the TSP.

As the participant approaches retirement, the proportion of contributions invested in the C, I, and S funds—which invest in stocks—is reduced. The proportion invested in the G and F funds— which invest in bonds—is increased. This helps to protect participants who are nearing retirement from investment losses that would occur from a sharp decline in equity prices. The TSP L funds consist of the L2020, L2030, L2040, and L2050 funds and the L Income Fund.

Historical rates of return for the five core TSP funds are shown in Table 3.

Table 3. Annual Rates of Return for Thrift Savings Plan Funds

Year	G Fund	C Fund	F Fund	S Fund[a]	I Fund[a]
1988	8.8%	11.8%	3.6%	20.5%	26.1%
1989	8.8%	31.0%	13.9%	23.9%	10.0%
1990	8.9%	-3.2%	8.0%	-13.6%	-23.6%
1991	8.1%	30.8%	15.7%	43.5%	12.2%
1992	7.2%	7.7%	7.2%	11.9%	-12.2%
1993	6.1%	10.1%	9.5%	14.6%	32.7%
1994	7.2%	1.3%	-3.0%	-2.7%	7.8%
1995	7.0%	37.4%	18.3%	33.5%	11.3%
1996	6.8%	22.8%	3.7%	17.2%	6.1%
1997	6.8%	33.2%	9.6%	25.7%	1.5%
1998	5.7%	28.4%	8.7%	8.6%	20.1%
1999	6.0%	21.0%	-0.8%	35.5%	26.7%
2000	6.4%	-9.1%	11.7%	-15.8%	-14.2%
2001	5.4%	-11.9%	8.6%	-2.2%	-15.4%
2002	5.0%	-22.1%	10.3%	-18.1%	-16.0%
2003	4.1%	28.5%	4.1%	42.9%	37.9%
2004	4.3%	10.8%	4.3%	18.0%	20.0%
2005	4.5%	5.0%	2.4%	10.5%	13.6%
2006	4.9%	15.8%	4.4%	15.3%	26.3%
2007	4.9%	5.5%	7.1%	5.5%	11.4%
2008	3.8%	-37.0%	5.5%	-38.3%	-42.4%
2009	3.0%	26.7%	6.0%	34.9%	30.0%
2010	2.8%	15.1%	6.7%	29.1%	7.9%
2011	2.5%	2.1%	7.9%	-3.4%	-11.8%
Average Return, 1988-2011	5.8%	10.9%	7.2%	12.4%	6.9%

Source: Federal Retirement Thrift Investment Board. Returns are net of TSP expenses.
Note: "Average Return" is the average annual rate of return over the 1988-2011 period.
[a] Actual rates of return for S and I Funds since May 2000. Rates of return for Wilshire 4500 Index and the EAFE Index, respectively, before May 2000.

TSP Withdrawal Options

At retirement, an employee can withdraw funds from the TSP immediately or at a later date. There are four ways that an employee can withdraw funds from the TSP:

- as a life annuity,[17]
- in a single lump-sum payment,

- in a series of monthly payments, either for a fixed number of months or in a fixed dollar amount, until the account is depleted, or
- partly as a lump sum, and partly as an annuity or series of payments.[18]

TSP Participation Rates

As of November 2012, there were 4.6 million active and retired participants in the TSP, including both current and former civilian employees and members of the armed services. Among civilian federal employees who were enrolled in FERS, 86% of those who were eligible to participate in the TSP were making payroll contributions. Among employees enrolled in the CSRS, 63% were contributing to the TSP. The average TSP account balance in November 2012 was $89,311 among FERS participants and $89,839 among CSRS participants.

As of September 2012, assets invested in the TSP totaled $325.7 billion. The "G" fund held assets of $136.6 billion; the "C" fund held assets of $78.7 billion; and the "F" fund held assets of $25.4 billion. The "S" fund held assets of $25.1 billion and the "I" fund held assets of $16.2 billion. The new "L" funds—which invest in the other five TSP funds—held assets of $43.7 billion.

As a share of TSP assets, the "G" fund held 43% of the total, the "C" fund held 25%, the "F" fund held 8%, the "S" fund held 8%, the "I" fund held 5%, and the "L" funds held 14% of the total assets in the TSP. The share of total TSP assets held in each fund reflects the historical rates of return among the funds, the distribution of employer and employee contributions among the funds, and transfers of account balances among the funds by participating employees.[19]

Illustrations of the TSP's Role in Providing Retirement Income

Using a series of simplifying assumptions, the following tables illustrate the role of the TSP in assuring an adequate income during retirement for federal employees enrolled in the FERS. Each table shows the annual salary in the year before retirement for four employees: one at the GS-4 level, one at GS-8, one at GS-12, and one at GS-15. The salaries shown are the estimated pay at step 8 of the pay grades in the year 2042 (*Table 4* and *Table 5*) or 2032

(*Table 6* and *Table 7*), assuming that future federal salary increases 3.9% per year.[20] The salary amounts are expressed in their 2013 dollar equivalents, based on the Social Security Actuary's estimated future inflation rate of 2.8% per year. The tables show the estimated replacement rates during the first year of retirement for the annual income provided by converting an employee's TSP account into a level, single-life annuity.[21]

Within each of the four tables, two factors are varied: pay grade and the employee contribution to the TSP. Final salaries and retirement income replacement rates are shown for each of four illustrative pay grades. The replacement rate is shown for employees who make no contribution to the TSP, and thus receive only the agency automatic 1% contribution; for workers who contribute 5% of pay, and therefore receive a 5% contribution from their employing agencies; and for workers who contribute 10% of pay, which results in the same 5% agency contribution as would a 5% employee contribution.

Across the four tables, two factors are varied: the assumed rate of return on contributions to the TSP and the employees' number of years of service at retirement. The results shown in *Table 4* and *Table 6* are based on a constant, nominal rate of return on investment of 6.0% per year. In *Table 5* and *Table 7*, the results are based on a constant, nominal rate of return of 8.0% per year.[22] Because the rate of inflation is assumed in these estimates to be 2.8% per year, the real rate of return on investment is 3.1% in *Table 4* and *Table 6*, whereas in *Table 5* and *Table 7* the real rate of return on investment is 5.1% per year.[23] In *Table 4* and *Table 5*, the replacement rates have been estimated for a federal employee who retires on December 31, 2042, at the age of 62 after 30 years of service under FERS. In *Table 6* and *Table 7*, the replacement rates have been estimated for an employee who retires on December 31, 2032, at the age of 62 after 20 years of service under FERS.

The results presented in each of the following tables assume that the employee contributed the same percentage of pay to the TSP each year over the length of his or her entire career. The tables illustrate the effects of career-long employee contribution rates of 0%, 5%, and 10%. *Table 4* and *Table 5* show the replacement rates after a 30-year career, assuming nominal rates of return on investment of 6.0% per year and 8.0% per year, respectively. Obviously, actual rates of return on an employee's TSP account will vary from year to year, and over 30 years an employee could achieve average rates of return that are higher or lower than the results shown here. Moreover, many employees begin their careers contributing little or nothing to the TSP and gradually increase their contributions as their incomes increase, and as they become more aware of the need to save for retirement. Consequently, these examples should be regarded as illustrations only.

TSP Estimated Replacement Rates for a 30-Year Employee

The proportion of pre-retirement income that will be replaced by converting the employee's TSP account into a retirement annuity will depend on the individual's age, the balance in the account, and the interest rate at which the account balance is converted to an annuity. The account balance at retirement depends on the percentage of pay that the employee contributed throughout his or her career, the rate of return earned by the funds in which these contributions were invested, and the length of time over which contributions to the TSP were in the fund earning interest, dividends, and capital gains. For any given account balance, an older individual will receive a larger annuity than a younger person. Likewise, a higher annuity interest rate will provide a larger annuity. The annuity interest rate is determined by the prevailing long-term interest rates in the nation's credit markets.[24]

Employees enrolled in the FERS have an amount equal to 1% of pay contributed to the Thrift Savings Plan by their employing agencies, even if the employee makes no voluntary contributions to the TSP. This amount is not deducted from employee pay. It is paid by the employing agency from sums appropriated to it by Congress for salaries and related expenses. Assuming a nominal annual investment return of 6.0%, an employee who retires after 30 years of federal employment will be able to replace only about 2% of final salary from his or her TSP account if he or she never makes a voluntary contribution to the plan. (See *Table 4*.) Assuming an 8.0% rate of return, the TSP would replace about 3% of pay for a worker who makes no voluntary contributions. (See *Table 5*.)

By contributing 5% of pay, however, the TSP replacement rate can be boosted substantially. Even assuming a nominal rate of return on investment of 6.0%, annual employee contributions of 5% of pay to the TSP would boost the replacement rate to 22% after a 30-year career.

The impact on replacement rates of the first 5% of employee contributions is especially large because each additional percentage of pay contributed by the employee brings matching contributions from the employer. The first 3% of pay contributed by the employee is matched dollar-for-dollar by the employing agency, and the next 2% of pay is matched by the employer at the rate of 50 cents on the dollar.

Table 4. Illustration of TSP Annuity Replacement Rates under FERS for an Employee Retiring in 2042 at Age 62 After 30 Years of Service (Assuming an annual nominal rate of return on TSP of 6.0%)

	GS-4	GS-8	GS-12	GS-15
Final salary in 2013 dollars:	$47,001	$72,139	$115,550	$190,998
TSP Contribution Rates	Percentage of pre-tax final salary replaced:			
TSP monthly annuity with only 1% agency automatic contribution	2%	2%	2%	2%
TSP monthly annuity with 5% from employee and 5% agency match	22%	22%	22%	22%
TSP monthly annuity with 10% from employee and 5% from agency	33%	33%	33%	33%

Source: Estimates prepared by the Congressional Research Service.

Notes: Estimates of income from the TSP are based on a level, single-life annuity at the January 2013 annuity interest rate of 1.750%. Other simplifying assumptions used in illustration calculations: 3.9% salary growth per year; 2.8% inflation per year; a constant TSP contribution as a percentage of salary made by the employee per year; and a constant annual nominal rate of return on TSP account (6.0% for Table 4).

Table 5. Illustration of TSP Annuity Replacement Rates under FERS for an Employee Retiring in 2042 at Age 62 After 30 Years of Service (Assuming an annual nominal rate of return on TSP of 8.0%)

	GS-4	GS-8	GS-12	GS-15
Final salary in 2013 dollars:	$47,001	$72,139	$115,550	$190,998
TSP Contribution Rates	Percentage of pre-tax final salary replaced:			
TSP monthly annuity with only 1% agency automatic contribution	3%	3%	3%	3%
TSP monthly annuity with 5% from employee and 5% agency match	30%	30%	30%	30%
TSP monthly annuity with 10% from employee and 5% from agency	45%	45%	45%	45%

Source: Estimates prepared by the Congressional Research Service.

Notes: Estimates of income from the TSP are based on a level, single-life annuity at the January 2013 annuity interest rate of 1.750%. Other simplifying assumptions used in illustration calculations: 3.9% salary growth per year; 2.8% inflation per year; a constant TSP contribution as a percentage of salary made by the employee per year; and a constant annual nominal rate of return on TSP account (8.0% for Table 5).

Higher investment returns would result in a higher replacement rate. For an employee who contributes 5% of pay over a 30-year career, an 8.0% annual rate of return on investment would result in a TSP account balance that, when converted to a retirement annuity would replace 30% of final salary. (See *Table 5*.)

Employee contributions above 5% of pay are not matched by the employing agency, but they still have a substantial impact on replacement rates. Assuming a 6.0% annual rate of return, a 10% employee contribution to the TSP over a 30-year career would result in a replacement rate from the TSP of approximately 33% of final pay. (See *Table 4.)* Assuming a rate of return on investment of 8.0%, employees who contribute 10% of pay over a 30-year career can replace about 45% of their final pay from the TSP. (See *Table 5*.)

TSP Estimated Replacement Rates for a 20-Year Employee

Table 6 and Table 7 show the estimated TSP replacement rates for an employee who retires at age 62 after 20 years of service under FERS. For employees who make no voluntary contributions to the TSP, the replacement rates are negligible. For an employee with 20 years of service who makes no contributions to the TSP, the agency automatic 1% contribution would replace about 1% of final pay based on a 6.0% annual rate of return. (See Table 6.) Assuming an 8.0% annual investment return, the agency automatic contribution would replace only 2% of pay for an employee retiring after 20 years of service. (See Table 7.)

The estimates displayed in Table 6 and Table 7 also show that a worker who participates in the TSP only during the 20 years immediately preceding retirement will achieve a much lower income replacement rate than an employee who participates for 30 years. Table 6 shows that an employee contributing 5% of pay and earning a 6% annual rate of return would be able to replace about 13% of final pay from his or her TSP account. This is 8 percentage points lower than the 22% replacement rate achieved by an employee who contributes 5% of pay over 30 years and earns a 6% annual return. Contributing 10% of pay over 20 years at an annual investment return of 6.0% would raise the employee's replacement rate to 23%; however, this is 10 percentage points below the 33% replacement rate achieved by an employee who contributes 10% of pay over a 30-year period, assuming a 6.0% rate of return.

Table 6. Illustration of TSP Annuity Replacement Rates for FERS-Covered Employee Retiring in 2032 at Age 62 After 20 Years of Service (Assuming an annual nominal rate of return on investment in TSP = 6.0%)

	GS-4	GS-8	GS-12	GS-15
Final salary in 2013 dollars:	$42,256	$64,855	$103,883	$171,713
TSP Contribution Rates	Percentage of pre-tax final salary replaced:			
TSP monthly annuity with only 1% agency automatic contribution	1%	1%	1%	1%
TSP monthly annuity with 5% from employee and 5% from agency	13%	13%	13%	13%
TSP monthly annuity with 10% from employee and 5% from agency	19%	19%	19%	19%

Source: Estimates prepared by the Congressional Research Service.

Notes: Estimates of income from the TSP are based on a level, single-life annuity at the January 2013 annuity interest rate of 1.750%. Other simplifying assumptions used in illustration calculations: 3.9% salary growth per year; 2.8% inflation per year; a constant TSP contribution as a percentage of salary made by the employee per year; and a constant annual nominal rate of return on TSP account (6.0% for Table 6).

At an 8.0% annual rate of return, an employee contributing 5% of pay each year can achieve a replacement rate of 23% from the TSP. (See Table 7.)

Table 7. Illustration of TSP Annuity Replacement Rates for FERS-Covered Employee Retiring in 2032 at Age 62 After 20 Years of Service (Assuming an annual nominal rate of return on investment in TSP = 8.0%)

	GS-4	GS-8	GS-12	GS-15
Final salary in 2013 dollars:	$42,256	$64,855	$103,883	$171,713
TSP Contribution Rates	Percentage of pre-tax final salary replaced:			
TSP monthly annuity with only 1% agency automatic contribution	2%	2%	2%	2%
TSP monthly annuity with 5% from employee and 5% agency match	15%	15%	15%	15%

	GS-4	GS-8	GS-12	GS-15
TSP monthly annuity with 10% from employee and 5% from agency	23%	23%	23%	23%

Source: Estimates prepared by the Congressional Research Service.

Notes: Estimates of income from the TSP are based on a level, single-life annuity at the January 2013 annuity interest rate of 1.750%. Other simplifying assumptions used in illustration calculations: 3.9% salary growth per year; 2.8% inflation per year; a constant TSP contribution as a percentage of salary made by the employee per year; and a constant annual nominal rate of return on TSP account (8.0% for Table 7).

Additional Income Replacement from Social Security and the FERS Annuity

The TSP was designed to supplement retirement income from the FERS annuity as well as Social Security. For a federal employee who begins his or her career in 2013 and retires at age 62 after 30 years of service, the FERS basic annuity will provide first-year retirement income equal to about 32% of the worker's final annual salary.[25] For a worker who begins his or her career in 2013 and retires at age 62 with 20 years of service, the basic FERS retirement annuity would replace about 21% of final earnings, regardless of the GS-level from which he or she retires.[26] In both of these cases, the dollar amount of the annuity will be higher for higher-paid employees, but the replacement rate will be approximately the same, regardless of the employee's final salary level.

The replacement rate for Social Security benefits, however, declines as a worker's income increases. The percentage of earnings replaced by Social Security is greater for low-wage workers than for high-wage workers.[27] During their years as federal employees covered by FERS, individuals are covered by Social Security. But it may also be the case that the career histories of these federal employees include additional non-federal, Social-Security-covered employment.[28]

The Social Security Administration (SSA) estimates that for individuals who retire at age 65 in 2012, Social Security benefits would replace about 41% of career-average earnings for a "scaled medium earnings" hypothetical worker, who has career-average earnings of $40,702. This earnings profile is similar to a GS-4 federal employee. For a "scaled high earnings" hypothetical worker retiring at age 65 in 2012, who has career-average earnings of $65,124 and could be compared with a GS-8 federal employee, Social Security benefits would replace about 34% of career-average earnings. Finally, GS-12 and GS-15 employees could be compared with a "steady maximum earnings" hypothetical worker (with career-average earnings of $94,006) for whom Social Security benefits would replace about 27% for retirement at 65 in 2012, as estimated by SSA.[29]

Workers Who Leave Federal Employment Before Reaching Retirement Age

For employees who switch jobs one or more times over the course of their careers, a defined contribution retirement plan such as the TSP has an advantage over the traditional defined benefit pension in that the value of the accrued benefit can continue to increase until the employee reaches retirement age. All that is required for this to occur is for the employee to refrain from spending any lump-sum distributions that he or she may receive before retiring and for the accrued benefit to remain invested in a tax-deferred retirement account that achieves a total rate of return before retirement that is greater than the rate of inflation.

Employees who have become vested in a traditional defined benefit pension—including the FERS basic annuity—are legally entitled to the benefit they have earned upon reaching the plan's normal retirement age even if at that time they no longer work for the employer where they earned the pension. In most defined benefit pension plans, including FERS, the annuity is based on the employee's actual earnings during their period of employment with the firm. These salary amounts are not adjusted for inflation between the time the employee leaves the firm and the date of retirement. For example, consider an employee who leaves the federal government for another employer at age 40 after 10 years of service in 1991. If this individual's highest three consecutive years of earnings averaged $50,000, he or she would be entitled to an annuity of $5,000 per year beginning at age 62.[30] The worker in this example would be eligible to begin receiving the $5,000 annuity at age 62 in 2013, 22 years after leaving the federal government. If inflation were to average 3.0% per year over those 22 years, the retiree's first-year annuity of $5,000 would be worth only about $2,600 in 2013 dollars.[31]

In contrast to the example just cited, money held in a defined contribution plan like the TSP can continue to grow throughout an individual's working life, regardless of how often he or she changes jobs. If the employee in the example above had contributed 10% of pay to the TSP each year and the contributions had earned an average rate of return of 6%, the account would have reached a value of approximately $81,000 after 10 years in 1991.[32] If the departing employee were to leave this money invested in the TSP or transfer it to another tax-deferred retirement account, this sum would continue to grow until the employee withdrew the funds.[33] Assuming that the funds earned an annual return of 6.0%, the total would increase to $291,887 by the time he or she reaches the age of 62 in 2013, 22 years after leaving the federal government. At current interest rates, this would be sufficient to purchase an annuity that would pay the retiree about $17,553 per year ($1,462 per month) for the rest of his or her life.[34]

THE THRIFT SAVINGS PLAN ENHANCEMENT ACT OF 2009

P.L. 111-31, the Family Smoking Prevention and Tobacco Control Act, was signed into law by President Barack Obama on June 22, 2009. P.L. 111-31 contains the Thrift Savings Plan Enhancement Act as Title I of Division B of the bill. As enacted, P.L. 111-31:

- provides for newly hired federal employees to be enrolled automatically in the Thrift Savings Plan (TSP) at a default contribution rate of 3% of pay;
- requires the Federal Retirement Thrift Investment Board to establish within the TSP a qualified Roth contribution program that provides for after-tax contributions and tax-free distributions;
- gives the Federal Retirement Thrift Investment Board authority to allow TSP participants to invest in mutual funds in addition to the five investment funds now included in the TSP;
- requires the Thrift Board to submit to Congress an annual report that includes demographic information about TSP participants and fund managers;
- requires participants to sign an acknowledgement of risk if they invest contributions in any investment option other than government securities;
- grants the executive director of the TSP authority to issue subpoenas under certain circumstances;

- allows funds held in an individual's TSP account to be subject to court orders with respect to payment of restitution to victims of certain crimes;
- requires the Secretary of Defense to report to Congress the estimated cost of an agency match on contributions to the TSP by members of the uniformed services; and
- allows the surviving spouse of a deceased TSP participant to maintain the decedent's account with the TSP.

CONCLUSION

The Thrift Savings Plan plays a pivotal role in helping federal workers achieve adequate retirement income. Employees enrolled in the FERS who do not make voluntary contributions to the TSP, and thus receive only the 1% agency automatic contribution, will be able to replace only 1% to 3% of final annual salary from the TSP at retirement. Most workers in the lower and middle ranges of the federal salary scale will be able to achieve the 70% salary replacement recommended by many pension analysts from the benefits paid by Social Security and the FERS basic retirement annuity, but this is not so for higher-wage federal workers. Federal employees at all income levels can significantly boost their retirement income by contributing to the TSP, and such contributions are essential in order for those in the upper third of the federal pay scale to achieve a level of income that will allow them to maintain their pre-retirement standard of living.

APPENDIX. ADMINISTRATION OF THE THRIFT SAVINGS PLAN

The Thrift Savings Plan is administered by an independent government agency, the Federal Retirement Thrift Investment Board, which is charged in statute with operating the Thrift Plan prudently and solely in the interest of the participants and their beneficiaries.[35] The assets of the Thrift Plan are maintained in the Thrift Savings Fund, which invests the assets in accordance with participant instructions in five investment funds authorized by Congress to be included in the plan. The Thrift Board currently contracts with BlackRock Institutional Trust Company to manage the index funds in which the F, C, S, and I Fund assets are invested. The contracts for each fund are open to competitive bids by qualified investment managers every three to five years.

The costs of administering the TSP are paid from the assets of the thrift fund. Administrative costs of the TSP in 2011 were 2.5 basis points (one basis point is 1/100th of 1 percent, or 0.01%), or about 25 cents for each $1,000 invested.[36]

Participant Accounts

The Thrift Plan maintains individual accounts for each participant. Participant accounts are credited with the participant's contributions and agency contributions, and are charged for withdrawals. The value of the participant's account reflects the number of shares and the daily share prices of the funds in which the account is invested. Administrative expenses are a component of the share price calculation. The benefit to which a participant is entitled is the participant's vested account. Thrift Plan participants can receive account-balance information and conduct transactions by automated telephone service or on the Thrift Plan's website.[37]

The Federal Retirement Thrift Investment Board

The Federal Retirement Thrift Investment Board was established by the FERS Act of 1986.[38] The board is responsible for developing the investment policies of the Thrift Plan and overseeing the management of the plan, which is under the day-to-day direction of an Executive Director appointed by the board.

Three of the five members of the board—including the chairman—are appointed by the President. The President chooses a fourth member of the board in consultation with the Speaker of the House and the House minority leader and a fifth member in consultation with the majority and minority leaders of the Senate. Members of the board serve four-year terms and all nominations are subject to Senate confirmation. The law requires that all nominees to the board must be individuals with "substantial experience and expertise in the management of financial investments and pension benefit plans."[39]

Communication and Education

The Thrift Board communicates with plan participants to help them better understand the investment choices, benefits, and administration of the TSP. Employing agencies distribute information, including the Summary of the Thrift Savings Plan for Federal Employees, which provides a comprehensive description of the Plan, as well as booklets describing the loan program, withdrawal programs, and annuity options under the plan. Investment information also is provided through the TSP Fund Sheet and the Managing Your Account leaflets which are available on the TSP website. The Thrift Board also issues a quarterly newsletter, *TSP Highlights*. Participants can obtain their account balances from the website, request contribution allocations and interfund transfers or, in some cases, loans and withdrawals. The website also provides various calculators that can be used as retirement planning tools.

A TSP video is available that explains the basics of the TSP. TSP Bulletins are issued regularly to inform agency personnel and payroll specialists of current operating procedures. The ThriftLine, the Board's toll-free automated voice response system, provides both general plan and account-specific information.

The authorizing legislation that established the Thrift Board defines the board's authority and responsibilities. It provides for substantial independence of the board from political pressures.

Authority

The Thrift Board has the authority to

- appoint the Executive Director of the Thrift Plan;
- remove the Executive Director for cause (requires four votes);
- establish investment policies for the Thrift Plan;
- instruct the Director to take whatever actions the Board deems appropriate to carry out the policies it establishes; and
- submit to the Congress legislative proposals relating to its responsibilities under federal law.

Independence

Members of the board are nominated by the President and confirmed by the Senate, but once confirmed they cannot be removed from their four-year terms without good cause. The selection and nomination process are designed to assure that members of the board are individuals who are supported by the President and Congress. They serve in times of good behavior, rather than at the pleasure of the President or Congress, assuring that they can carry out the responsibilities of their positions without removal from office. The Federal Retirement Thrift Investment Board receives no appropriations from Congress. Administrative expenses are paid through agency-automatic contributions forfeited by employees who leave federal service before they have vested and charges against participant accounts.

Responsibility

The law requires that the members of the board shall discharge their responsibilities solely in the interest of participants and beneficiaries. In practice, this means that the investment policies and management practices of the fund are evaluated by the board exclusively in reference to the efficient and prudent management of the fund's assets. This exclusive responsibility serves to further insulate the board from pressures to adopt investment policies or management practices that might not be in the long-term interest of preserving and increasing the security and investment performance of the fund's assets.

Oversight

To assure that the members of the Thrift Board remain aware of the interests and concerns of Thrift Plan participants and beneficiaries, the authorizing legislation established the Employee Thrift Advisory Council. This 14-member council is appointed by the chairman of the Thrift Board and must include representatives of federal employee and Postal Service labor organizations, managerial employees, supervisory employees, female employees, senior executives, and annuitants. All fiduciaries of the plan, including members of the Thrift Board, are required by law to be bonded.[40] The Secretary of Labor is authorized by law to investigate any suspected breach of duty by a fiduciary of the plan. The financial statements of the Thrift Board are audited regularly by an independent accounting firm. Congressional oversight of the Thrift Plan is performed by the House Committee on Oversight and Government Reform and the Senate Committee on Homeland Security and Governmental Affairs.

End Notes

[1] Relatively few employees who were covered by CSRS chose to switch to FERS. Only about 5% of eligible employees switched in 1987, and fewer than 2% switched in 1998.

[2] U.S. Office of Personnel Management, Annual Report of the Board of Actuaries, Civil Service Retirement and Disability Fund, Report for the Fiscal Year Ended September 30, 2011.

[3] Members of Congress and congressional staff, federal law enforcement officers, firefighters, air traffic controllers, and nuclear materials couriers can retire with an immediate, unreduced annuity at the age of 50 after 20 years of service or at any age after 25 years of service.

[4] "Normal, voluntary" retirements exclude those occurring due to disability, involuntary and voluntary retirements resulting from reductions in force, and mandatory early retirement for federal law-enforcement officers, firefighters, and air traffic controllers.

[5] All data cited in this paragraph come from U.S. Office of Personnel Management, "Statistical Abstracts Fiscal Year 2011, Federal Employee Benefits Programs."

[6] This calculation is based on nominal (current) dollars rather than indexed (constant) dollars.

[7] Under FERS, Members of Congress first elected prior to 2013, congressional staff first hired prior to 2013, and certain public safety workers accrue benefits at the rate of 1.7% per year for the first 20 years of service and 1.0% per year for service over 20 years. These rates yield a pension equal to 34% of the FERS salary base after 20 years of service and 44% after 30 years of service, provided that both the age and length of service requirements for retirement with a full FERS annuity have been met.

[8] Under CSRS, initial benefits are capped at 80% of high-3 average salary. Members of Congress and congressional staff accrue benefits at the rate of 2.5% for each year of service. This yields an annuity equal to 75% of the CSRS salary base after 30 years of service. Certain public safety workers accrue benefits at 2.5% per year for up to 20 years of service and 2.0% per year for service beyond 20 years.

[9] Under both CSRS and FERS, COLAs are paid out beginning in January each year, based on the percentage increase in the CPI-W for the third calendar quarter (July-Sept.) of the most recent year compared with the average CPI-W for the third calendar quarter of the last year a COLA was determined. In 1994, 1995, and 1996, COLAs for civil service annuitants were delayed from January until April to achieve budgetary savings. There was no automatic COLA for civil service annuitants in 2010 or 2011. In 2013, the automatic COLA for CSRS and FERS is 1.7%. For more details on COLAs for CSRS and FERS annuitants, see CRS Report 94-834, Cost-of-Living Adjustments for Federal Civil Service Annuities, by Katelin P. Isaacs.

[10] "401(k)" refers to the section of the Internal Revenue Code that authorizes deferral of income taxes until the time of withdrawal for contributions to certain kinds of savings plans and for the interest and dividends on those contributions.

[11] Members of the uniformed services are eligible for matching contributions only in some cases. Matching contributions are permitted only for personnel in critical occupational specialties, and they must agree to re-enlist for six years to be eligible for the agency contribution. The FY2006 National Defense Authorization Act expanded the authority for agency contributions to include the duration of the initial enlistment of enlisted personnel.

[12] Maximum annual salary deferrals are set in law at I.R.C. Section 402(g).

[13] For more information, see CRS Report RL31770, Individual Retirement Accounts and 401(k) Plans: Early Withdrawals and Required Distributions, by John J. Topoleski.

[14] More information on TSP loans is available at https://www.tsp.gov/PDF/formspubs/tspbk04.pdf.

[15] More information on in-service withdrawals from the TSP is available at http://www.tsp.gov/forms/tspbk12.pdf.

[16] The "S" and "I" funds were added in 2001 in accordance with the Thrift Savings Plan Act of 1996 (P.L. 104-208).

[17] A life annuity is a contract between the individual and an insurance company, in which the individual exchanges a lump sum for a guaranteed stream of monthly payment for the rest of his or her life, and often for the lifetime of a surviving spouse. The insurance company invests the lump sum and uses the earnings of the investment as well as the principal to make the payments to the annuitant, which are based both on the estimated rate of return from the investment and actuarial estimates of the annuitant's remaining life expectancy. TSP annuities are issued by MetLife.

[18] The annuity or series of payments must begin at the time the lump sum is paid.

[19] TSP totals for fund percentages exceed 100% due to rounding.

[20] This salary growth assumption comes from the U.S. Social Security Administration's "The 2012 Annual Report of the Board of Trustees of the Federal Old-Age and Survivors Insurance and Federal Disability Trust Funds;" Table V. B1 (available online: http://www.ssa.gov/oact/tr/2012/lr5b1.html). This assumption—and the ensuing illustrations of FERS replacement rates—does not take into consideration the recent "pay freeze" for federal workers. This pay freeze, as authorized by the Continuing Appropriations and Surface Transportation Extensions Act, 2011 (P.L. 111-322; signed December 22, 2010), suspended statutory pay adjustments (under section 5343(a) of title 5, U.S. Code) for the period between January 1, 2011, and December 31, 2012. P.L. 112-175 extended this pay freeze until April 7, 2013. For more information on pay for federal workers, including the process by which pay adjustments are made, see CRS Report RL34463, Federal White-Collar Pay: FY2009 and FY2010 Salary Adjustments, by Barbara L. Schwemle.

[21] A "single-life annuity" pays benefits until the annuitant dies. A "joint and survivor annuity" pays a smaller monthly benefit, but guarantees continued payment until the death of the annuitant or the annuitant's spouse, whichever comes later. A "level annuity" pays a fixed monthly benefit year after year. A "graded annuity" pays a smaller initial monthly benefit, but the benefit is increased by a fixed percentage (often 3%) as a means of preserving the real value of the benefit against the effects of inflation.

[22] See Table 3 for actual historical rates of return for TSP. For the purpose of simplification, constant rates of return for TSP—either 6.0% per year or 8.0% per year—are assumed in this report's illustrative calculations.

[23] The real rates of return are derived as follows: 1.06/1.028 = 1.031 and 1.08/1.028 = 1.051.

[24] The January 2013 annuity interest rate of 1.750% is used to calculate the TSP replacement rates in this report.

[25] Estimate prepared by the Congressional Research Service, assuming (1) federal salary at step 8 of pay grades in the year 2042; (2) future, average federal salary increases of 3.9% per year; and (3) average inflation rate of 2.8% per year. This estimate uses the same assumptions as the estimates in Tables 4 and 5.

[26] Estimate prepared by the Congressional Research Service, assuming (1) federal salary at step 8 of pay grades in the year 2032; (2) future, average federal salary increases of 3.9% per year; and (3) average inflation rate of 2.8% per year. This estimate uses the same assumptions as the estimates in Tables 6 and 7.

[27] Social Security is intended to replace a relatively higher percentage of career-average pay for low-wage workers than for high-wage workers in part because Congress recognized when designing the program that low-wage workers are less able to save for retirement.

[28] To qualify for a retired worker Social Security benefit, an individual must accumulate at least 40 quarters of covered employment, or 10 years of Social Security-covered employment (among other requirements). These Social Security benefits are based on the average of a worker's highest 35 years of earnings. Federal employees, including employees covered by FERS, may qualify for Social Security benefits based on a lifetime earnings and employment history that includes more than federal service.

[29] SSA estimates taken from Table V.C7 of 2012 Annual Report of the Board of Trustees of the Federal Old-Age and Survivors Insurance and Disability Insurance Trust Funds, April 23, 2012, at http://www.socialsecurity.gov/OACT/TR/ 2012. For additional details on earnings patterns, see SSA Actuarial Note Number 2011.3 at http://www.socialsecurity.gov/OACT/NOTES/ran3/an2011-3.html.

[30] FERS employees accrue benefits each year equal to 1.0% of the average of their high-3 pay. An employee with five or more years of service can receive a full annuity at age 62.

[31] Once payment of a FERS annuity begins, it is protected from inflation by annual cost-of-living adjustments—but only partially and only for retirees age 62 and older. See CRS Report 94-834, Cost-of-Living Adjustments for Federal Civil Service Annuities, by Katelin P. Isaacs.

[32] Based on contributing 10% of pay (plus 5% employer match) from a starting salary of $32,000 and ending salary of $52,000 to an account earning 6.0% compounded annually.

[33] Departing employees who have not reached age 55 can leave their TSP accounts intact, in which case they will continue to accrue interest, dividends, and capital gains until the individual withdraws the money. They also can "roll over" their TSP accounts into another tax-qualified retirement account such as an Individual Retirement Account (IRA) or another employer's 401(k). Alternatively, a departing employee can withdraw his or her funds from the TSP without rolling them over into another account, in which case both regular income taxes and a 10% tax penalty will apply.

[34] Based on a level, single-life annuity at an interest rate of 1.750% (January 2013).

[35] See 5 U.S.C. §8472(h).

[36] TSP expense ratio data are available at TSP.gov https://www.tsp.gov/investmentfunds/fundsoverview/ expenseRatio.shtml.

[37] The URL of the Thrift Savings Plan website is http://www.tsp.gov.

[38] See 5 U.S.C. §8472.

[39] See 5 U.S.C. §8472(d).

[40] A "fiduciary" is a person in a position of trust with regard to the property of another. A "bond" is form of insurance against the potential malfeasance of a plan fiduciary.

In: Retirement Savings and Security
Editor: Linda A. Eisterhold

ISBN: 978-1-62948-132-6

Chapter 7

RETIREMENT SECURITY: ANNUITIES WITH GUARANTEED LIFETIME WITHDRAWALS HAVE BOTH BENEFITS AND RISKS, BUT REGULATION VARIES ACROSS STATES*

United States Government Accountability Office

ABBREVIATIONS

CDA	contingent deferred annuities
FINRA	Financial Industry Regulatory Authority
IRA	individual retirement account
NAIC	National Association of Insurance Commissioners
NASD	National Association of Securities Dealers
NOLHGA	National Organization for life and Health Guaranty Associations
SEC	Securities and Exchange Commission
VA	variable annuities
VA/GLWB	variable annuities with guaranteed lifetime withdrawal benefits

---

* This is an edited, reformatted and augmented version of The United States Government Accountability Office publication, Report to Congressional Requesters, GAO-13-75, dated December 2012.

WHY GAO DID THIS STUDY

As older Americans retire, they may face rising health care costs, inflation, and the risk of outliving their assets. Those entering retirement today typically face greater responsibility for managing their retirement savings than those who retired in the past. Lifetime income products can help older Americans ensure they have income throughout their retirement. VA/GLWBs and CDAs, two such products, may provide unique benefits to consumers. According to industry participants, while annuities with GLWBs have been sold for a number of years, CDAs are relatively new and are not widely available. GAO was asked to review issues relating to these financial products. This report (1) compares the features of VA/GLWBs and CDAs and examines potential benefits and risks to consumers and potential risks to insurers, and (2) examines the regulation of these products and the extent to which regulations address risks to consumers. GAO analyzed insurance company product information, proposed and final rules and regulations, and studies and data related to retirement and product sales. GAO also interviewed federal and state regulators and selected insurers, consumer advocates, and industry organizations.

GAO provided a draft of this report to NAIC and SEC. Both provided technical comments, which have been addressed in the report, as appropriate.

WHAT GAO FOUND

Annuities with guaranteed lifetime withdrawals can help older Americans ensure they do not outlive their assets, but do present some risks to consumers. Two such products, variable annuities with guaranteed lifetime withdrawal benefits (VA/GLWB) and contingent deferred annuities (CDA), share a number of features but have some important structural differences. For example, both provide consumers with access to investment assets and the guarantee of lifetime income, but while VA/GLWB assets are held in a separate account of the insurer for the benefit of the annuity purchaser, the assets covered by a CDA are generally held in an investment account owned by the CDA purchaser. Consumers can benefit from these products by having a steady stream of income regardless of how their investment assets perform or how long they live, while at the same time maintaining access to their assets for unexpected or other expenses. VA/GLWBs and CDAs are complex products that present some risks to consumers and require them to make multiple important decisions. For example, consumers might purchase an unsuitable product or make withdrawal decisions that could negatively affect their potential benefits. Several insurers and regulators GAO spoke to said it was important for consumers to obtain professional financial advice before purchasing these products and making key decisions. These products can also create risks for insurers which, if not addressed, could ultimately affect insurers' ability to provide promised benefits to consumers.

VA/GLWBs are considered to be both securities and insurance products, and are therefore covered by both federal securities regulations and state insurance regulations. For CDAs, the National Association of Insurance Commissioners committee responsible for life insurance and annuities products has determined CDAs to be life insurance products subject to state law and regulation for annuities. According to SEC officials, existing CDAs have been registered as securities with SEC, and therefore are covered by both federal securities laws and regulations, and state insurance regulations. At the state level, NAIC has developed state disclosure and suitability regulations for annuity products. However, states differ on the extent to which they have adopted these annuity regulations, and some do not have protections at all. As a result, consumers in states that have adopted different regulations may benefit from different levels of protection. NAIC and state regulators told GAO that they are currently reviewing the regulations of CDAs. In March 2012, NAIC began reviewing existing annuity regulations to determine whether any changes are needed to address the unique product design features of CDAs, including potential modifications to annuity disclosure and suitability standards. It is also reviewing what kinds of capital and reserving requirements may be needed to help insurers manage product risk. In addition, NAIC and the National Organization of Life and Health Guaranty Associations are each working to determine whether state insurance guaranty funds, which protect consumers in the event insurers become insolvent, cover CDA products. Both agree that each state will have to reach its own conclusion about whether their particular state guaranty fund laws allow for CDA coverage. Until these regulatory issues are resolved, consumers may not be fully protected.

December 10, 2012

The Honorable Herb Kohl
Chairman

Special Committee on Aging
United States Senate

The Honorable George Miller
Ranking Member
Committee on Education and the Workforce
House of Representatives

Longevity risk, or the potential for outliving one's financial resources in retirement, is a critical issue for today's older Americans. Life expectancy for many older Americans grew significantly from 1980 to 2010, and today's retirees may face a greater number of years than earlier generations for which they will require income.

They also face the risks of inflation and rising health care costs. Because of a decrease in defined benefit retirement plans that guarantee retirees a certain level of income for life, workers entering retirement today also typically have more responsibility for managing their retirement savings than previous retirees and must make difficult investment and withdrawal decisions.

Recent market turbulence has also sparked questions about retirement account values and longevity risk, and many Americans already retire without sufficient savings to sustain them throughout a lengthy retirement. For example, a recent study showed that only 42 percent of those surveyed had calculated how much in savings they would need for retirement, and the percentage of Americans saving for retirement had declined by 9 percent from 2009 to 2012.[1]

Products with guaranteed lifetime withdrawals, such as variable annuities with a guaranteed lifetime withdrawal benefits rider (VA/GLWB) and contingent deferred annuities (CDA) can potentially help older Americans plan for retirement and address longevity and market risks by providing guaranteed income even after retirement assets are depleted. However, some industry participants suggest that VA/GLWBs and CDAs are complex products which involve potential risks for both consumers and insurers.

In response to questions you have raised about annuities with guaranteed lifetime withdrawals, this report:

- compares the features of VA/GLWBs and CDAs, and examines the potential benefits and risks to consumers and potential risks to insurers of these products; and

- examines the regulation of these products and the extent to which regulation addresses any identified risks to consumers.

To compare the features of VA/GLWBs and CDAs, we analyzed specific insurance company products to obtain information on how the products function, including how investment gains and losses are treated, how withdrawal amounts are determined, and what happens when a consumer's investment account is depleted. We also interviewed insurance company officials to verify our understanding of their products and VA/GLWBs and CDAs in general.

To identify potential benefits and risks to consumers, we analyzed the product information we obtained and also interviewed insurers, consumer advocates, and state insurance regulators. To understand the potential risks these products pose to insurers and how they manage these risks, we also interviewed NAIC officials and reviewed information from insurers and stakeholder groups.

We also obtained data from industry organizations on the sale of annuity products with guaranteed lifetime withdrawals. We discussed the sources and reliability of the data with officials from these organizations and found the data sufficiently reliable for the purposes of this report.

To determine how VA/GLWBs and CDAs are regulated and the extent to which regulation addresses identified concerns, we identified regulations and processes used by federal and state regulators, as well as any proposed regulations, and compared them with the risks to consumers that we identified as part of the work under the previous objective. We reviewed model laws developed by NAIC, specific state regulations, and SEC and FINRA rules. We also interviewed NAIC, state, SEC and FINRA officials to determine how VA/GLWBs and CDAs are regulated. We also interviewed other stakeholder groups, such as consumer advocates and industry organizations, to gain their perspective on issues related to regulation of lifetime income products considered in our review. Appendix I contains additional information on our scope and methodology.

We conducted this performance audit from February 2012 to November 2012 in accordance with generally accepted government auditing standards. Those standards require that we plan and perform the audit to obtain sufficient, appropriate evidence to provide a reasonable basis for our findings and conclusions based on our audit objectives. We believe that the evidence obtained provides a reasonable basis for our findings and conclusions based on our audit objectives.

Background

Annuities

An annuity is an insurance agreement or contract that comes in a number of different forms and can help individuals accumulate money for retirement through tax-deferred savings, provide them with monthly income that can be guaranteed to last for as long as they live, or both. A variable annuity is an insurance contract in which a consumer makes payments that are held in a separate account of the insurer. While the insurance company is the owner of the separate account assets, the assets are held for the benefit of consumers. In return, the insurer agrees to make periodic payments beginning immediately or at some future date. The purchaser's payments can be directed into a range of investment options, typically mutual funds, which the insurer makes available in a separate account for the benefit of consumers. Purchasers may withdraw assets from their contracts at any time prior to annuitizing—that is, to convert the account into some form of lifetime payments.

VA/GLWBs protect consumers against outliving their retirement assets and the effects that market losses on those assets can have on lifetime income by allowing them to withdraw a certain percentage each year until death. If the market performs well, the consumer may receive larger withdrawals, but if the market performs poorly, the consumer still receives the set withdrawal amount.

VA/GLWB sales have grown in recent years. Data from LIMRA show that from 2008 to 2011, the number of VA/GLWB contracts in force rose from 1.5 million to 2.8 million and that average annual sales were around $58 billion.[2] During that same period, total VA/GLWB assets held in insurers' accounts increased from $133 billion to $323 billion. According to the Insured Retirement Institute, states with the highest sales of variable annuities in 2010 were California, New York, Florida, Texas, Pennsylvania, and New Jersey.[3] In addition, LIMRA data on the demographics of VA/GLWB consumers show that in 2010 the average age of the consumer purchasing a VA/GLWB was 61 and the average age at first withdrawal was 68. Typically, the average annual withdrawal has been around $5,500. Also according to LIMRA, the average amount of a VA/GLWB contract sale from 2007 through 2010 was around $106,000.

Like a GLWB rider, a CDA is an insurance contract that provides guaranteed lifetime income payments if a consumer's investment account is exhausted, whether through withdrawals or poor market performance. In this case, the investment account contains the "covered assets"— typically mutual funds or managed accounts. However, the insurance company does not have ownership of the assets underlying the CDA, which are typically held in brokerage or investment advisory accounts owned by the CDA purchaser. Similar to a VA/GWLB, a CDA contract defines how much a consumer is able to withdraw—for example, 5 percent of the benefit base annually. Even if the value of the covered assets drops to zero, the insurance company has guaranteed the 5 percent withdrawal benefit (based on the benefit base value when lifetime withdrawals began) and continues making the annual payments to the consumer. Whether or not a policyholder receives payment from the insurance company selling the CDA is contingent upon the covered assets dropping to zero. On the basis of the products we reviewed, fees on CDAs are calculated as a set percentage of the investment assets or benefit base per year. These fees do not include any fees the consumer might pay related to the underlying investment that is covered by the CDA. Such investment management fees are paid to the investment company, not the insurer.

Regulation

State insurance regulators are responsible for overseeing insurance products, while SEC and FINRA are responsible for the oversight of securities. Federal and state regulators consider variable annuities to be both insurance and securities products, and GLWB riders that are attached to variable annuities to be an additional insurance benefit. The National Association of Insurance Commissioners committee responsible for life insurance and annuities products has determined CDAs to be life insurance products subject to state law and regulation for annuities. According to SEC officials, existing CDAs have been registered as securities with SEC, and therefore are covered by both federal securities laws and regulations, and state insurance regulations.

Insurance is unique among financial services in the United States in that it is largely regulated by the states. State insurance regulators are responsible for enforcing state insurance laws and regulations, including those covering the licensing of agents, reviewing insurance products (including variable annuities) and their rates, and examining insurers' financial solvency and market conduct. State regulators typically perform financial solvency examinations every 3 to 5 years, and they generally undertake market conduct examinations in response to specific consumer complaints or regulatory concerns.[4] State regulators also monitor the resolution of consumer complaints against insurers. State insurance laws focus on solvency, market regulation, and consumer protection. In addition to state insurance regulators, NAIC—a voluntary association of the heads of insurance departments from the 50 states, the District of Columbia, and five U.S. territories—plays a role in insurance regulation. While NAIC is not a regulator, it provides guidance and services designed to more efficiently coordinate interactions between insurers and state regulators. These services include providing detailed insurance data to help regulators understand insurance sales and practices; maintaining a range of databases useful to regulators; and coordinating regulatory efforts by providing guidance, model laws and regulations, and information-sharing tools.

Federal securities laws and SEC rules govern the securities industry in the United States. SEC's mission is to protect investors; maintain fair, orderly, and efficient markets; and facilitate capital formation. SEC oversees key participants in the securities markets, including securities exchanges, securities brokers and dealers, investment advisers, and mutual funds. The Securities Act of 1933 (1933 Act) regulates public offerings of securities, requiring that issuers register securities with SEC and provide certain disclosures, including a prospectus, to investors at the time of sale.5 Investors may rely on broker-dealers and investment advisers for information or advice about securities, including insurance products such as VA/GLWBs and CDAs. Money managers, investment counselors, and financial planners who, for compensation, engage in the business of providing advice to others about securities, including asset allocation advice, are subject to the antifraud provisions of the Investment Advisers Act of 1940.6 Large investment advisers, those with $100 million or more of assets under management, generally are subject to SEC registration and regulation under the Investment Advisers Act and accompanying rules. Investment advisers with assets under management of less than $100 million generally are regulated by the states.7 Securities, including annuities that are securities, are subject to registration and disclosure requirements under the 1933 Act, and large investment advisers providing advice about securities must be registered with SEC. Broker-dealers that are engaged in the business of buying and selling securities generally are subject to broker-dealer regulation at the federal and state levels. FINRA is the largest regulator of securities firms doing business with the public in the United States. All registered securities broker-dealers who do business with the public must be members of FINRA and their personnel must be licensed with FINRA. FINRA oversees almost 4,500 brokerage firms and approximately 630,000 registered securities representatives.

Features of VA/GLWBs and CDAs May Benefit Consumers but also Pose Risks to Consumers and Insurers

VA/GLWBs and CDAs share a number of features, but they also have some important structural differences. For example, both provide consumers with access to investment assets and the guarantee of lifetime income, but while VA/GLWB assets are held in a separate account of the insurer for the benefit of the annuity purchaser, the assets covered by a CDA are generally held in an investment account owned by the CDA purchaser. In part because of their shared features, these products can provide similar benefits to consumers. Yet as complex instruments that require consumers to make multiple important decisions, they also present certain risks to consumers. VA/GLWBs and CDAs may also involve risks for insurers, who must manage these risks in order to make promised payments to consumers.

VA/GLWBs and CDAs Share Some Features

VA/GLWBs and CDAs share a number of product features. In general, both allow consumers to take lifetime withdrawals from their assets at a rate that the insurance company guarantees even if such withdrawals and investment losses deplete the consumer's assets. VA/GLWBs and CDAs generally have three distinct phases of ownership: an accumulation phase, a withdrawal phase, and an insured phase (see fig. 1).[8]

Accumulation Phase

The accumulation phase begins when a consumer purchases a VA/GLWB or CDA contract.[9] The initial premium paid under a VA contract with a GLWB rider or the value of assets covered by a CDA contract establishes the initial withdrawal value, or benefit base, on which the amount of lifetime withdrawals are based.10 This benefit base is not a cash value that can be withdrawn, but rather is the amount to which lifetime withdrawal percentages will be applied during the withdrawal phase.

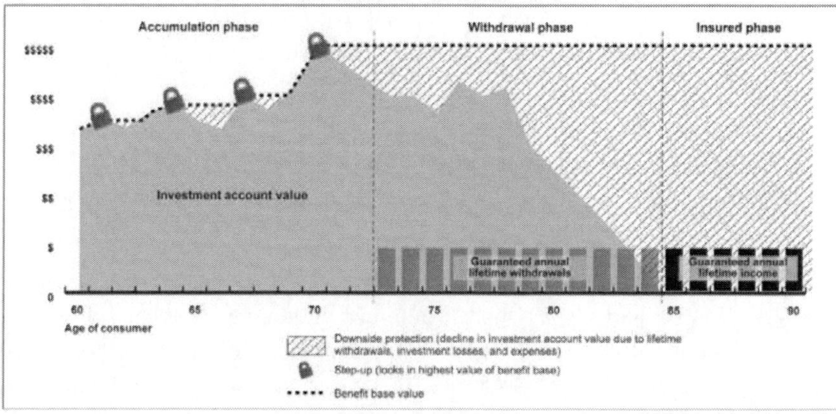

Source: GAO analysis of VA/GLWB and CDA product information provided by insurers.

Note: This figure is a hypothetical illustration of the phases and features of a VA/GLWB or CDA and may not represent the actual results of any product we reviewed. The actual results for each consumer will depend on the particular product's features and costs, as well as factors such as the amount invested, the consumer's age when the guarantee was purchased, the actual return on investments, the timing and amount of withdrawals, and how long the consumer lives.

Figure 1. Accumulation, Withdrawal, and Insured Phases of a VA/GLWB or CDA.

The investment account value, on the other hand, represents the total value of the consumer's investments, which is increased by investment gains and decreased by fees, withdrawals, and any investment losses.11 During this phase the consumer decides how to allocate investment assets among various options, including funds made available by an insurance company for investment under its VA/GLWB products and funds that an insurance company has agreed to cover under its CDA products.12 Also during this phase, the insurance company monitors each consumer's account value and automatically adjusts the benefit base periodically should investment gains increase the value of this account. This feature, which exists for the VA/GLWBs and CDAs we reviewed, is referred to as a step-up or ratchet.13 Once a consumer's benefit base is stepped up, it cannot later decline because of investment losses that reduce the consumer's investment account value.

Some VA/GLWBs have an additional feature that guarantees that, no matter how the investments perform, the benefit base will grow each year by a set percentage. This guaranteed percentage, alternatively referred to as a roll-up rate, growth credit, or bonus, is added to the benefit base, as adjusted for any prior step-ups. For example, some of the VA/GLWBs we reviewed included annual roll-up rates that ranged from 5 to 7 percent. The amount of the roll-up rate and the frequency, duration, and manner of calculation can affect the value of a consumer's benefit base and thus the amount that can be taken as lifetime withdrawals. While such features can increase a consumer's benefit base on which lifetime withdrawals are determined, annuities with higher roll-up rates can have higher fees.

Withdrawal Phase

The withdrawal phase starts when a consumer begins taking annual lifetime withdrawals. The maximum amount of lifetime withdrawals that a consumer can take each year (without incurring a reduction in their benefit base) is calculated as a percentage of the consumer's benefit base at the time of the first lifetime withdrawal. The VA/GLWBs and CDAs we reviewed had withdrawal percentages for a single life that ranged from 3 percent to over 8 percent of the benefit base, and the percentages were generally lower for younger consumers and higher for older consumers.[14] Some products also have a joint life option where, if the consumer dies, the guarantee of lifetime income passes to their spouse. When such an option is elected, withdrawal amounts are typically one-half a percent less than they would be otherwise.[15]

Step-ups, like those during the accumulation phase, can increase the benefit base after lifetime withdrawals have begun, increasing the amount of annual lifetime withdrawals. Typically, the insurance company will increase the benefit base if a consumer's account value, net of withdrawals and fees, has increased above this amount. After a step-up during the withdrawal phase, the base and the lifetime maximum withdrawals cannot decline because of investment losses that reduce the consumer's account value. Step-ups that occur after lifetime withdrawals begin allow consumers to benefit from investment gains that can offset the effects of inflation.[16]

Insured Phase

A consumer enters the insured phase only if their investment account value has been reduced to zero as a result of lifetime withdrawals; investment losses; or any expenses, fees, or other charges. In such cases, the consumer's benefit base on which lifetime withdrawals are determined (the amount to which the withdrawal percentage is applied) remains unchanged but the consumer's investment account value, which was the source for the funds previously withdrawn, is zero. Consequently, the funds needed to continue paying the same level of benefits to the consumer (and spouse, if a joint life option is elected) would then come from the insurance company's own assets, and consumers receive payments from the insurance company that are equal to their prior lifetime withdrawal amount. Once the insurance company begins paying the agreed-upon withdrawal payment, the fees that the consumer had been paying for that protection would cease, as would any investment management and other fees paid for other benefits. Once the insured phase begins, all rights and benefits under a VA/GLWB or CDA contract, except those related to continuing benefits, terminate.[17] In addition, all lifetime withdrawal benefits will continue to be paid to the consumer on the established schedule and generally cannot be changed.

Structural Differences Exist between VA/GLWBs and CDAs

Although VA/GLWBs and CDAs have some common features and function in similar ways, the contractual, product, and cost structures differ in terms of where the underlying investment assets are held and what benefits are offered, and the amount of fees charged for those benefits. With variable annuity contracts, including those with GLWB riders, consumers can direct premium payments into a range of investment options, typically mutual funds made available by and held in a separate account of the insurance company. The mutual funds may be managed by outside advisers, but the insurance company holds these assets for the benefit of consumers. By comparison, the investment assets covered by a CDA are held by the consumer in his or her own brokerage or investment advisory account and invested in investment funds, such as mutual funds, that the insurance company has agreed to cover under a CDA. The investment assets are not owned—nominally or otherwise—by the insurance company issuing the guarantee. Like the investment options available under a VA/GLWB, the investment assets covered by a CDA may or may not be managed by the insurance company or an affiliate. In this way, consumers can accumulate retirement assets in a personal account, such as an individual retirement account (IRA), and obtain lifetime withdrawal guarantees without having to transfer those assets to an insurance company.

Further, the base variable annuity contracts to which GLWB riders are attached provide additional benefits not available under CDAs. For example, a VA/GLWB contract permits the consumer to annuitize an account balance in the future and receive benefit payments from the insurance company for life at rates set forth in the annuity contract.[18] Also, with a VA/GLWB, if a consumer dies before annuitizing the account balance or taking lifetime withdrawals, the death benefit payable to beneficiaries is typically the greater of the sum of premiums paid or the investment account value.[19] The additional VA/GLWB benefits come with additional costs, however. For example, in addition to the guarantee fee, variable annuity contracts with death benefits entail additional fees to cover the cost to the insurer. For the CDAs we reviewed, the assets covered by the CDA could not be annuitized in the future. The assets would first have to be sold and the proceeds used to purchase a separate annuity. In addition, unlike a variable annuity contract, a CDA does not have a death benefit.[20]

VA/GLWBs and CDAs Can Provide Consumers with Similar Benefits

Similar to other annuity products, VA/GLWBs and CDAs can provide consumers with the benefit of a guaranteed stream of income for life. That is, for a fee, they can ensure that consumers receive a minimum annual payment until they die, regardless of how long they live or how their investment assets might perform. These products may also lock investment gains into the benefit base on which future lifetime withdrawals are determined and, in the case of variable annuities, also offer other potentially beneficial features such as death benefits, which pass on certain guaranteed amounts to a spouse or other beneficiaries. Further, VA/GLWBs and CDAs typically offer consumers the ability to invest their assets in a variety of investment funds.

A unique benefit of these products is that they allow consumers to receive income guarantees while still maintaining ownership of and access to their funds during the accumulation and withdrawal phases. With traditional annuity products, in order to receive lifetime income consumers must transfer assets to the insurer, who holds them in their own general account and uses them to fund an annuity (they are annuitized). Consequently, once these assets are annuitized the consumer does not have access to these assets. With VA/GLWBs and CDAs, however, the consumers' assets are not annuitized. As a result, consumers can withdraw any or all of their funds at any time. This can benefit consumers should they need funds for unexpected uses, such as medical or other expenses.

One benefit specific to CDAs is that the guarantee of lifetime withdrawals can, in certain cases, be applied to existing investment assets. That is, consumers who have existing investment assets may be able to purchase a

CDA to cover those assets, if an insurer agrees to cover those assets under a CDA. If the same consumers wanted to use those assets to obtain a guaranteed stream of income through a traditional annuity, they would have to first sell the investment assets and then use the proceeds to purchase the annuity.

Consumers Face Risks When Purchasing and Withdrawing Funds from VA/GLWBs and CDAs

Several insurers and regulators we spoke with said that VA/GLWBs and CDAs are complex products, and emphasized the importance of obtaining professional financial advice before purchasing these products and making key decisions.

Consumers that purchase VA/GLWBs and CDAs can face risks similar to those they may face with the purchase of other financial products. These risks include purchasing an unsuitable product, paying too much, making withdrawal decisions that decrease benefits, and having an insurer become insolvent before benefits are received.

First, consumers face the risk of purchasing an unsuitable product if they do not understand how a particular product functions and meets their own needs, including how much might be appropriate to invest in a particular product. Insurers with whom we spoke said that VA/GLWBs and CDAs are generally attractive to middle-income consumers who want more control and flexibility over the investments they are relying on to provide retirement income.

In addition, one insurer with whom we spoke said that consumers investing in such products have generally had around $500,000 in retirement savings and invested around 20 percent of that amount.

Second, consumers may face the risk of being unable to determine if they are obtaining the best price for similar benefits provided by different insurers. Several insurers and regulators told us that because of the uniqueness of VA/GLWB and CDA products, it would be difficult to compare one insurer's product to that of another insurer. For example, products can function in slightly different ways, have different combinations of features, and charge different amounts for the guarantees. As a result, consumers would find it difficult to take a price quoted to them from one insurer for a specific product with specific features, then compare that to a product from another insurer to determine if they could receive similar benefits at a lower price.

Third, VA/GLWBs and CDAs pose a risk that certain decisions by consumers in withdrawing their assets, such as the timing and size of the withdrawals, could affect them negatively. For example, these decisions can reduce or even eliminate guaranteed benefits and result in additional fees that further reduce their assets. The investment assets underlying VA/GLWB and CDA guarantees are typically available for withdrawal before guaranteed lifetime withdrawals begin, but taking withdrawals too early or above certain thresholds can result in financial penalties and deplete assets, as the following examples illustrate,

- Variable annuities are frequently sold without any up front sales charges but impose contingent deferred sales charges, or "surrender" charges, on withdrawals taken during the early years of the contract (for example, the first 7 years) that are above a "free" withdrawal limit.[21] Surrender charges on variable annuities are expressed as a series of percentages that decline over time and are applied to annual withdrawals that are typically greater than either accumulated earnings or 10 percent of premiums paid.[22] Because CDAs split insurance and investment elements of the guarantee, there are no surrender charges on the CDA contract. However, a surrender charge may apply when a consumer sells shares of mutual funds covered by the CDA contract.[23] In addition to sales charges, income taxes and an additional 10 percent penalty tax on withdrawals taken before age 591/2 may apply.[24]
- With some VA/GLWB products, taking withdrawals of any amount after reaching a minimum age can trigger the beginning of lifetime withdrawals (at a specified percentage) and stop all future roll-ups of the benefit base.[25] In addition, a consumer who takes withdrawals sooner than initially planned can experience a permanent reduction of the lifetime withdrawal amount. For example, for one of the products we reviewed a withdrawal at age 64 triggers the establishment of a 4 percent lifetime withdrawal percentage, but waiting for a year would raise the percentage to 5 percent. Further, starting lifetime withdrawals during a downturn in the market can have a negative effect on lifetime income because the investment account balance will be that much lower than the benefit base, making the possibility of a step-up, and a possible increase in the withdrawal percentage and amount, less likely.

- The age at which lifetime withdrawals begin can have an impact on the value of other benefits and guarantees. For example, withdrawals and the related charges can reduce the cash value and death benefits under a variable annuity contract, leaving fewer assets available for surviving spouses and other beneficiaries. On the other hand, waiting too long to withdraw benefits can result in not living long enough to benefit from the product's guarantees or receiving enough income to offset the amount of fees paid. For example, a person who first purchases a VA/GLWB or CDA at age 60 and waits until age 85 to begin taking lifetime withdrawals will be able to take a higher amount, but likely for a shorter period of time. Further, the purchaser will have paid fees for 25 years to protect against outliving his assets, a possibility that becomes less likely over time.

In addition to deciding when to begin taking lifetime withdrawals, consumers need to decide how much to withdraw and need to be aware of certain product features when doing so. For example, lifetime withdrawals above the maximum annual amount specified in the withdrawal guarantee are permitted and are referred to as "excess withdrawals." However, such withdrawals typically reduce the benefit base to which withdrawal percentages are applied, thus reducing future annual withdrawal amounts. Further, guarantee fees and other charges are typically not counted as withdrawals for purposes of calculating the maximum for a given year, but some VA/GLWB and CDA products we reviewed counted certain fees and charges or those above a certain threshold toward the annual lifetime withdrawal maximum.

Finally, as with the purchase of any long-term insurance product, consumers can face some level of risk that by the time the consumer needs the benefit promised by the insurer, the insurer may not be able to provide it. However, insurers and insurance regulators take a number of steps to ensure that insurers remain financially solvent. In addition, in the event of an insurer's insolvency, state insurance guaranty funds can help pay consumers what was promised by insurers, up to any coverage limits of those guaranty funds. According to officials from the National Organization for Life and Health Guaranty Associations (NOLHGA), while promises made under GLWBs, which are distinct from the investment portion of a variable annuity, are generally covered by state guaranty funds, such certainty does not exist with respect to CDAs. As a result, a risk exists that if an insurer who sold a CDA became insolvent, consumers owning those CDAs might not collect any promised benefits.

Insurers Must Also Manage Risks Associated with VA/GLWBs and CDAs

As with the sale of life insurance products in general, insurers must manage the financial risks associated with VA/GLWBs and CDAs in order to ensure their ability to make promised payments and, depending on the amount of such products they sell, their financial solvency. Risks to insurers can arise when investment returns, interest rates, consumer longevity, and consumer behavior are different from what they expected. While a number of insurers and NAIC officials said that VA/GLWBs and CDAs do not pose undue risk to insurers, as we noted, at least one major insurer has decided not to sell CDAs because of the potential risk involved, and another insurer told us that they do not sell VA/GLWBs because they do not fit with the company's risk profile.

Insurance company officials with whom we spoke told us that in designing their products they consider not only the features that will help to meet consumer needs, but also the company's own appetite for certain risks, the methods for managing those risks, and the price charged for the products' guarantees. According to insurers with whom we spoke, ways in which insurers can use product design to help manage their risk can include the following.

- Establishing the minimum age at which consumers can begin taking withdrawals and the extent to which consumers can benefit from growth in the investments protected by the guarantee.
- Specifying which investments consumers may have covered by the products' guarantees. For example, one CDA product we reviewed limited a consumer's investments in equity funds to no more than 80 percent of the consumer's total investment account value. Another insurer that sells CDAs told us that they were only willing to cover index funds for major, highly traded indices, such as the Standard and Poor's 500.[26]
- Determining the formulas used to rebalance consumers' investments into and out of fixed-income funds to mitigate some of the financial risks associated with providing lifetime withdrawal guarantees.[27] Prospectuses for these VA/GLWB products disclose that the automatic rebalancing feature may limit the consumer's participation in future market gains and, therefore, the potential for future increases in their annual lifetime income.

Insurers will also price their products to ensure they have sufficient revenue and capital to pay for the expenses they expect to incur related to the products they sell. That is, they will charge more for products that they deem to be more risky or on which they expect to incur greater costs. With respect to VA/GLWBs and CDAs, for example, insurers may charge higher fees for products with features that can result in a higher guaranteed benefit base. Insurers also use hedging programs to help further manage the investment risks of the assets underlying the VA/GLWB and CDA. Hedging involves buying financial instruments, such as options, to offset the potential loss on an investment.

To the extent that product design and hedging is not sufficient, insurers can also manage financial risks by modifying their products after they have been purchased by consumers to the extent permitted by their contracts, their prior disclosure, and applicable law. For the VA/GLWB and CDA products we reviewed, insurers sometimes reserve certain rights, such as the right to determine which investment funds will be covered by a GLWB rider or CDA guarantee and the conditions surrounding the allocation of a consumer's investment assets, change the frequency and amount of a guarantee fee, or reject additional contributions or transfers. Some insurers have recently raised fees on VA/GLWB guarantees or stopped accepting additional contributions to existing contracts in response to changing market conditions. Insurers generally cannot change the roll-up, step-up, or withdrawal rates for existing contract holders, but can make these changes prospectively for new customers.

Federal and State Oversight Varies by Type of Product and Is Currently under Industry Review

Federal disclosure and suitability regulations apply to the offer, recommendation, and sale of securities products such as variable annuities, including variable annuities with GLWB riders. While it has long been accepted that variable annuities constitute securities under the federal laws, because CDAs are a relatively new product, analysis under the federal securities law is less developed. However, SEC officials have said that CDAs currently being offered in the retail market are being registered as securities and are therefore covered by federal securities law and state insurance regulations. In addition, NAIC has developed annuity disclosure and suitability regulations for use at the state level, but state adoption and protection levels vary, so CDA consumers may not be uniformly protected. Further, questions about the adequacy of existing annuity regulation and the applicability of state insurance guaranty funds for CDA consumers if insurers become insolvent have prompted industry oversight reviews, which were ongoing as of October 2012.

Federal Disclosure and Suitability Regulations Apply to Registered Annuity Products

Federal disclosure and suitability regulations apply to the offer, recommendation, and sale of securities products such as variable annuities, including variable annuities with GLWB riders. These requirements aim to inform consumers about products and ensure that the products themselves are reasonably appropriate for consumers before they are purchased. As previously noted, while it has long been accepted that variable annuities constitute securities under federal law, CDAs are a relatively new product and analysis under the federal securities law is less developed.[28] To our knowledge, no court has addressed the securities law treatment of CDAs, and SEC has not provided written guidance with respect to the status of CDAs under the federal securities laws. However, according to SEC officials, existing CDAs have been registered under the Securities Act of 1933, absent specific exemptions from registration such as the exemption for contracts sold to certain types of tax-qualified retirement plans, and are therefore covered by federal securities law and state insurance regulations.

The 1933 Act generally requires issuers of securities that are offered to the public to register them with SEC and make certain disclosures through a prospectus that has been filed with SEC. The 1940 Act generally requires investment companies, including separate accounts that fund variable annuities, to be registered under the Act. Pursuant to these requirements, SEC has issued rules and standards for prospectuses offering registered variable annuities. The purpose of these requirements is to ensure that investors receive descriptive information on basic product features, fees, benefits, and risks that can help inform their investment decisions.[29] Disclosures made through prospectuses filed with SEC under the federal securities laws are subject to the anti-fraud provisions of the 1933 Act, which prohibit material misrepresentations or omissions and provide a general anti-fraud remedy for purchasers and sellers of securities.[30]

Since variable annuities, including those with guaranteed benefits, are securities, they must be offered and sold through registered broker-dealers. On the basis of anti-fraud provisions of the federal securities laws and FINRA rules, broker-dealers are required to deal fairly with their customers and only recommend securities to an investor that are appropriate for the investor based on his or her individual facts and circumstances. The suitability obligation is part of a broker-dealer's duty of fair dealing.[31] SEC and FINRA rules also require communications used with investors to promote the offer and sale of variable annuities to be fair and balanced, not misleading, and to include certain disclosures regarding the risks and fees associated with these products. These rules include the following:

- FINRA Rule 2090, which requires broker-dealers to ask about and retain essential information on each customer ("Know Your Customer") and concerning the authority of each person acting on behalf of the customer.
- FINRA Rule 2111, which requires broker-dealers to have a reasonable basis to believe that a recommended securities transaction or investment strategy is suitable for the customer based on information obtained through reasonable diligence of the broker-dealer or its associated person to ascertain the customer's investment profile. This profile includes, but is not limited to the customer's other investments, financial situation and needs, tax status, investment objectives, investment experience, investment time horizon, liquidity needs, risk tolerance, and any other information the customer may disclose to the broker-dealer or associated person in connection with the recommendation.
- National Association of Securities Dealers (NASD) Rule 2210, which regulates broker-dealers' communications with the public and applies to, among other things, variable annuity advertisements. Broker-dealers must file retail communications concerning variable annuities with FINRA and respond to comments provided by FINRA staff on such communications.[32]
- FINRA Rule 2330, specific to deferred variable annuities, which governs member broker-dealers' compliance and supervisory responsibilities with respect to the recommendation of the initial purchase or exchange of deferred variable annuities, and initial subaccount allocations.

These requirements apply to the recommendation and sale of variable annuity products, including those with guaranteed lifetime withdrawal benefits. According to SEC officials, issuers of CDAs have been registering offerings of their CDA products with SEC, and SEC is reviewing the disclosures associated with these products. While we did not observe and were not told of any such instances, if CDAs were sold without being registered as securities, SEC could take action if it determined that securities laws were being violated. If it were determined that federal securities laws did not apply to CDA offerings, relevant state regulations would still apply. In addition, FINRA officials said that they regulate member broker-dealers that offer variable annuity products, including variable annuities with GLWB riders. If a broker-dealer offers a CDA that is registered under the federal securities laws, FINRA also regulates the sale of such a CDA. If state insurance law issues arise in connection with a firm's sale of a CDA, FINRA staff may refer these issues to relevant state insurance regulators.

NAIC Has Developed Annuity Disclosure and Suitability Regulations, but State Adoption and Protection Levels Vary

The NAIC committee responsible for life insurance and annuities issues considers CDAs to be insurance products and has developed annuity disclosure and suitability model regulations for use by state insurance regulators. NAIC has developed these model disclosure and suitability regulations for annuity products in collaboration with consumer advocates and industry experts. However, unlike federal standards that are consistently applied to variable annuities regardless of where consumers live, state adoption of these model regulations varies, so protections may be stronger in some states than in others. In 2011, NAIC developed a model disclosure regulation for annuity products that serves several functions for consumers and insurers, including:

- helping ensure that consumers understand annuity products by explaining basic features, benefits, and fees;
- suggesting that annuity products with guaranteed income or benefit provisions are intended to be longer-term investment products;
- providing guidance for insurers when they choose to develop product illustrations intended to help consumers better understand how a particular annuity product works. In particular, the guidance provides

illustration formats and specifies what kinds of illustration disclosures must be made when an insurer chooses to develop them; and

- requiring that annuity customers be provided or referred to NAIC's Annuity Buyer's Guide that also contains general product information and provides answers to basic questions about risks and investing that consumers can use to decide whether these products are right for them.

In addition to its model disclosure regulation, NAIC developed a model suitability regulation in 2003 to help ensure that insurers consider the financial needs and objectives of consumers and that these needs are appropriately addressed at the time annuity sales or exchanges occur. More specifically, the model suitability regulation requires insurers and insurance agents to inquire about consumers' suitability information and ensure that they have reasonable grounds to believe that annuity products would benefit consumers before recommending purchases or exchanges.[33] In 2006, NAIC revised the model regulation to expand its scope to consumers of all ages, and in 2010 the model regulation was again revised to further strengthen a number of annuity suitability protections. Among other changes, the 2010 revision requires insurers to

- be responsible for compliance with the model regulation whether or not they contract suitability functions out to a third party;
- maintain procedures for reviewing each investment recommendation made to consumers and helping ensure that the product is suitable for the particular purchaser and that the purchaser understands the annuity product recommended;
- ensure that insurance agents, or producers, complete general annuity training before selling annuity products; and
- provide product-specific annuity training and training materials to the agent or producer before an agent or producer can solicit the sale of a product.

In addition to these changes, NAIC adopted the revised the model regulation to set standards and procedures for suitable annuity recommendations and to require insurers to establish a system to supervise recommendations so that the insurance needs and financial objectives of consumers are appropriately addressed. The revised NAIC model regulation includes a "safe harbor" provision that is intended to prevent duplicative suitability standards from being applied to sales of annuities through FINRA member broker-dealers. Annuity sales made in compliance with FINRA requirements are deemed to comply with the suitability requirements outlined in NAIC's model regulation. Violations of state law developed from the model regulation can result in remedies for consumers and penalties for insurers and agents. Under the model regulation, state insurance commissioners can require reasonably appropriate corrective action for violations that have harmed consumers.

NAIC information shows that, as of October 2012, state adoption of NAIC's disclosure and suitability regulations varied significantly, meaning that consumers in some states may not be protected as well as those in other states.[34] According to NAIC, many states have adopted some form of annuity disclosure regulation, although some states and the District of Columbia do not have disclosure protections in place. As of October 2012, officials are working to determine which states had adopted the revised model disclosure regulation.[35] In terms of the suitability model regulation, 19 states plus the District of Columbia have adopted NAIC's most recent model regulation that incorporates the added protections noted above, and another 29 states have adopted other suitability protections for annuity consumers. The remaining 2 states do not have suitability regulations in place. According to NAIC officials, model disclosure and suitability standards are not required as part of NAIC's accreditation program. Figure 2 summarizes the state adoption of suitability regulations.

Whether or not states have adopted NAIC disclosure and suitability regulation is important for CDA consumers. Unlike federal regulations that apply to the sale of VA/GLWBs nationwide, disclosure and suitability regulations for CDAs may depend on the actions of individual states and the extent to which they have implemented these protections. According to NAIC, regulatory action by states can time to occur and depends on legislative cycles and the political environment of states. As the information in figure 2 shows, consumers across states are subject to different suitability protection and in some cases to no protection at all.[36]

The different regulatory approaches among the sample of seven states we reviewed also show the variation in regulation of CDAs across states. Although most states in our sample have not specifically approved CDA sales, most have adopted some form of disclosure and suitability regulation for annuity products. Among these seven states, three have adopted NAIC's model disclosure regulation and three have adopted NAIC's most recent suitability regulation.

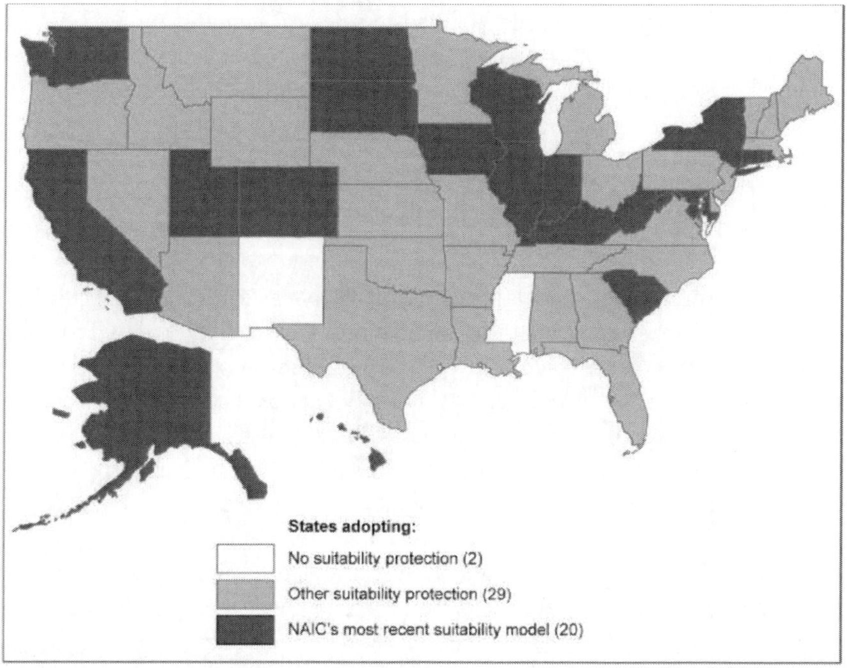

Source: GAO aanalysis of NAIC data Mapnfo.

Figure 2. State Adoption of Suitability Regulations as of October 2012.

For the states that allow CDA sales, the consumer protections found in the model regulations are critical. Of the two states that allow CDA sales—Iowa and Ohio—both have adopted NAIC's model disclosure regulation, but only Iowa has adopted its most recent model suitability regulation. Ohio, according to NAIC information, has passed a previous version of NAIC's model suitability regulation, and therefore has not adopted added protections found in the revised model regulation as outlined above.

Consumers in states that have not adopted NAIC's model regulations may not be benefitting from available disclosure and suitability protections. More specifically, states that have not adopted the most recent model suitability regulations may not be extending to consumers protections developed through NAIC's 2010 suitability revision.

Table 1 shows the variation in the disclosure and suitability protections across our seven sample states.

Table 1. CDA Consumer Regulations in Sample States, as of October 2012

Sample state	CDA sales approved	Model disclosure regulation adopted	Other disclosure protection adopted	Most recent model suitability regulation adopted	Other suitability protection adopted
California				X	
Florida			X		X
Iowa	X	X			
New Jersey			X		
New York			X		
Ohio		X			X
Utah[a]		X		X	

Sources: GAO and NAIC.

Note: According to NAIC, "other disclosure protection" and "other suitability protection" used in this table include but are not limited to adopting earlier versions of the NAIC model regulation, or legislation or regulation derived from other sources such as bulletins and administrative rulings.

[a] State insurance officials with whom we spoke from Utah were unsure whether CDAs had been sold there because Utah is a "file and use" state that does not require state review of insurance products before they are sold. However, Utah officials said that they did not believe that CDAs were being sold in their state.

Regulatory Uncertainty and Concerns about CDA Regulation Have Prompted Industry Oversight Reviews

Some industry participants suggest state insurance regulation and existing actuarial guidance may adequately address risks to insurers offering CDAs and to consumers. Others said that CDAs may pose solvency risks for both because insurers offer consumers an income guarantee but do not maintain the assets on which the guarantees are made. One major insurer has said that CDAs pose significant enough pricing and reserving challenges that it does not offer CDAs.

In addition, two consumer advocates with whom we spoke highlighted the solvency risks CDAs pose for insurers. One advocate suggested that reasonable and appropriate insurer reserving and capital requirements do not currently exist for CDAs and that considerable NAIC and state regulatory work would be needed to develop them.

The same advocate said selling CDA products before key issues concerning the regulatory framework are finalized might expose consumers to risks that might result from an insurer's potential insolvency. The advocate concluded that the potential for insurers to increase the marketing and sale of CDAs, given the growing needs of retirees, makes having consumer and insurer protections in place important.

Potential risks to CDA consumers and insurers have prompted industry oversight reviews of these products and their regulation. Although NAIC has determined that CDAs are a life insurance product, it is working with state regulators, insurers, and consumer advocates through its CDA Working Group, formed in March 2012, to build greater consensus around the classification of CDAs and to determine whether any adjustments to state regulation might be appropriate. In particular, NAIC is evaluating the adequacy of existing state annuity laws and regulations for CDA sales, including those on insurer solvency such as capital adequacy and reserve requirements.

According to NAIC officials, both NAIC and state insurance regulators recognize the complexity of CDA products for consumers and are also working to revise disclosure and suitability practices where appropriate.

Another industry review by the NOHLGA, NAIC, and state insurance regulators aims to address whether CDA consumers are protected by state insurance guaranty funds in the event of an insurer's insolvency. According to NOLHGA officials, variable annuities are not covered by guaranty funds because they are indistinguishable from equity products. That is, they are not supported by assets in an insurer's general account, but by specific assets in separate accounts dedicated to the particular fund or funds chosen for the variable annuity.

However, the officials said that guaranteed lifetime withdrawal benefits, which are now part of most variable annuity contracts, are distinct from the equity portion of a variable annuity and are generally covered by state guaranty funds.

The officials said that while CDAs would also appear to have an equity portion and a guarantee portion, they have a committee studying the extent to which CDAs might be covered by state guaranty funds. Officials noted that even when the committee has reached a determination on guaranty fund protections, each state will have to reach its own conclusion about whether their particular guaranty fund laws allow for CDA coverage.

AGENCY COMMENTS

We provided a draft of the report to SEC and NAIC and relevant excerpts to FINRA. Each provided technical comments that were incorporated as appropriate.

Alicia Puente Cackley
Director
Financial Markets and Community Investment

APPENDIX I: OBJECTIVES, SCOPE, AND METHODOLOGY

To compare the features of variable annuities with guaranteed lifetime withdrawal benefits (VA/GLWB) and contingent deferred annuities (CDA), we analyzed specific insurance company products to obtain information on how the products function, including how investment gains and losses are treated, how withdrawal amounts are determined, and what happens when a consumer's investment account is depleted. We also interviewed insurance company officials to verify our understanding of their products, and VA/GLWBs and CDAs in general. We judgmentally selected the companies based on criteria that included their market share of variable annuity sales and their decisions to sell or not to sell CDAs. To identify potential benefits and risks to consumers, we analyzed the product information we obtained and also interviewed insurers, consumer advocates, and state insurance regulators. To understand the potential risks these products pose to insurers and how they manage these risks, we also interviewed NAIC officials and reviewed information from insurers and stakeholder groups. We also obtained data from industry organizations on the sale of annuity products with guaranteed lifetime withdrawals. We discussed the sources and reliability of the data with officials from these organizations and found the data sufficiently reliable for the purposes of this report.

To determine how VA/GLWBs and CDAs are regulated and the extent to which regulation addresses identified concerns, we identified regulations and processes used by federal and state regulators, as well as any proposed regulations, and compared them with the risks to consumers that we identified as part of the work under the previous objective. Our review of state regulation included model laws developed by the National Association of Insurance

Commissioners (NAIC), specific state regulations, and Securities and Exchange Commission (SEC) and Financial Industry Regulatory Authority (FINRA) rules. We selected the sample of states for our analysis based on the volume of sales of VA/GLWBs and CDAs in the state, whether the state allowed the sale of CDAs, and the state's population. We interviewed NAIC, state, SEC, and FINRA officials to determine how VA/GLWBs and CDAs are regulated. We also interviewed other stakeholder groups, such as consumer advocates and industry organizations, to gain their perspective on issues related to regulation of lifetime income products considered in our review.

We conducted this performance audit from February 2012 to November 2012 in accordance with generally accepted government auditing standards. Those standards require that we plan and perform the audit to obtain sufficient, appropriate evidence to provide a reasonable basis for our findings and conclusions based on our audit objectives. We believe that the evidence obtained provides a reasonable basis for our findings and conclusions based on our audit objectives.

End Notes

[1] The Employee Benefits Retirement Institute and Matthew Greenwald and Associates, 2012 Retirement Confidence Survey (Washington, D.C.: March 2012).

[2] LIMRA is a financial research firm that provides consulting and research services to its over 850 member financial services firms.

[3] The Insured Retirement Institute is a trade association that provides research and information to its members, including financial firms and advisors.

[4] State regulators periodically perform financial examinations of insurance companies to investigate their accounting methods, procedures, and financial statement presentation. Market conduct exams by state regulators help ensure fair and reasonable insurance prices, products, and trade practices to protect consumers.

[5] Securities Act of 1933, 48 Stat. 74 (1933) (codified as amended at 15 U.S.C. §§ 77a et seq.).

[6] Investment Advisers Act of 1940, 54 Stat. 847 (1940) (codified as amended at 15 U.S.C. §§ 80b-1 et seq.).

[7] The Investment Advisers Act of 1940 was amended by the Dodd-Frank Wall Street Reform and Consumer Protection Act (Dodd-Frank) to provide that midsized investment advisers, those managing assets between $25 million and $100 million, generally be exempt from federal registration requirements and subject to state regulation. Small investment advisers managing assets under $25 million were already exempt from federal registration requirements under the Investment Advisers Act prior to Dodd-Frank.

[8] One insurance company whose products we reviewed referred to the insured phase as the "settlement phase." The American Council of Life Insurers and the Insured Retirement Institute refer to it as the "annuity payments phase."

[9] The VA/GLWBs we reviewed are allowed to be added either when annuity contracts are first purchased, on a contract's first anniversary, or anytime after the contract's issue date subject to availability and the consumer's eligibility. The CDAs we reviewed can be purchased when eligible investment funds are purchased. While some products we reviewed had no minimum eligibility age for purchasing the VA/GLWB or CDA, others had established minimums that ranged from ages 35 to 50. According to LIMRA, consumers initially purchase VA/GLWB contracts at about age 61.

[10] The minimum initial premium or investment in the VA/GLWBs and CDAs we reviewed ranged from no minimum to $100,000 with maximums that ranged from $500,000 to $5 million. According to LIMRA, the average initial premium paid for a variable annuity with a GLWB rider is about $100,000.

[11] The investment account value may be greater or less than the benefit base.

[12] The number of investment options available under the VA/GLWBs and CDAs we reviewed ranged from 1 to over 100 different funds.

[13] The VA/GLWBs and CDAs we reviewed stepped up benefit base values to either the highest daily, monthly, or annual account value. For example, on each contract anniversary an insurer may compare the benefit base to the account value at the end of each of the past 12 months and step up the benefit base to the highest of those 12 values. A more frequent step-up may increase the chances of locking in investment gains, but the level of these gains, and thus the value of a more frequent step-up, may be affected by the nature of the funds and any investment limitations, restrictions, and nondiscretionary asset reallocation formulas used by the insurance company to manage market risks and volatility.

[14] Two products we reviewed (one VA/GLWB and a CDA) set withdrawal rates based on a combination of age and the 10-year Treasury bond yield at the time of the owner's first withdrawal. The older the owner and the higher the 10-year bond yield results, the higher the withdrawal rates.

[15] The joint life withdrawal rates for one of the VA/GLWB products we reviewed were the same as for a single life, except that the withdrawal percentage was based on the younger of the two lives. Another VA/GLWB product we reviewed, whose withdrawal rates were based on the 10-year Treasury bond yield, set the joint life withdrawal rates at 90 percent of the single life rates.

[16] The withdrawal percentages for some VA/GLWB and CDA products we reviewed can increase when an owner enters a new age band preceding a step-up of the benefit base. VA/GLWB and CDA products that base the withdrawal percentage on the 10-year Treasury bond yield and recalculate the owner's withdrawal amount based on the current bond yield potentially provide a more direct connection between increases in future withdrawal amounts and long-term inflation to the extent that 10-year Treasury bond yields vary with inflation or inflationary expectations.

[17] For example, the right to make additional contributions and receive the benefit of future step-ups in the withdrawal amount would no longer be available to an owner once the account is depleted.

[18] Guaranteed lifetime withdrawal benefits terminate upon annuitization of the base contract's account value. Further, the VA/GLWBs we reviewed had maximum annuity commencement ages of either 91 or 95. At those ages, annuitants are typically required to annuitize their remaining account balance or take a lump sum distribution. For all but one of the products we reviewed, in cases where an owner starts taking lifetime withdrawals and later reaches the maximum annuity commencement age, the lifetime withdrawal payments cease and the annuity payments would be calculated as the greater of the lifetime

withdrawal amount or the annuity amount for the selected payment option under the contract.

[19] To illustrate, if an owner who paid $200,000 in premiums had investments that had declined in value to $190,000 at the time of their death, and had not annuitized their account balance or begun taking lifetime withdrawals, the insurance company would pay the owner's beneficiaries $200,000.

[20] For the VA/GLWB and CDA products we reviewed, if the consumer elects a joint life withdrawal option, upon their death during the accumulation phase surviving spouses typically could elect to continue the guarantee and maintain the benefit base.

[21] A "free" withdrawal limit is an amount below which consumers may take withdrawals without penalty.

[22] The period during which surrender charges are assessed typically varies from 3-7 years according to the variable annuity share class. For example, some variable annuities we reviewed had 7-year surrender charge periods with first-year surrender charges of between 7 and 8.5 percent that declined to 0 percent over 7 years. The free withdrawal limit for the annuities of this type that we reviewed was either 10 percent of premiums paid or the greater of either accumulated earnings or 10 percent of premiums paid.

[23] Surrender charges are a form of sales charges that are levied on annuities and mutual funds and are used to pay commission expenses.

[24] Some of the products we reviewed established age 591/2 as the minimum age when guaranteed lifetime withdrawals could begin. Withdrawals made earlier than the minimum age may reduce the benefit base on which lifetime withdrawals are calculated.

[25] Owners of the VA/GLWB and CDA products we reviewed that did not have a roll-up feature could not trigger the lifetime withdrawal percentage merely by taking withdrawals but had to affirmatively elect to take lifetime withdrawals before they became effective.

[26] The Standard and Poor's 500 is an index of 500 U.S. company stocks from various industries that meet certain criteria for inclusion in the index, including a market capitalization in excess of $4 billion.

[27] There are various factors that determine the amount and timing of transfers, including the difference between an owner's account value and benefit base. Insurance company officials told us that owners who invest more aggressively can expect more frequent rebalancing than those who invest more conservatively.

[28] See SEC v. United Benefit Life Ins. Co., 387 U.S. 202 (1967); SEC v. Variable Annuity Life Ins. Co., 359 U.S. 65 (1959) (variable annuities are securities).

[29] SEC Form N-4, the form used to register variable annuities with the SEC, is filed under the Investment Company Act of 1940 and the Securities Act of 1933 and subject to review by SEC staff. Part A of the form, the product prospectus, must present clearly written information about the contract and its costs, including information about annuity payments and death benefits. Part B includes information about premiums and underwriters, as well as insurance company and separate account financial statements. Part C contains information about directors and officers of the insurance company and indemnification, and a representation regarding contract fees.

[30] See §17 of the Securities Act of 1933 (15 U.S.C. §77q); §10(b) of the Securities Exchange Act of 1934 (15 U.S.C. 78j(b)).

[31] SEC staff has recommended consideration of rulemakings that would apply a fiduciary standard to both broker-dealers and investment advisers no less stringent than that applied currently to investment advisers. The SEC staff also identified certain areas where laws and regulations that apply to broker-dealers and investment advisers differ, and recommended

the Commission consider whether these areas should be harmonized for the benefit of retail investors. SEC Staff Study on Investment Advisers and Broker-Dealers As Required By Section 913 of the Dodd-Frank Wall Street Reform and Consumer Protection Act (2011), (Washington, D.C. January, 2011).

[32] FINRA, which formed in 2007, is in the process of converting the older NASD rules into its own rule book. Some rules have not yet been converted, and therefore retain the NASD label. FINRA rule 2210 replaces NASD Rule 2210 effective February 4, 2013.

[33] According to NAIC's model regulation, suitability information refers to information that is reasonably appropriate to determine the suitability of an annuity recommendation for a consumer, including the following: age, annual income, financial situation and needs, financial experience and objectives, intended use of the annuity, financial time horizon, existing assets, liquidity needs, liquid net worth, risk tolerance, and tax status.

[34] According to NAIC officials, NAIC has not collected nationwide data on which states allow the sale of CDA sales, so we were unable to determine which states allow CDA sales but have not adopted disclosure and suitability regulations.

[35] According to NAIC officials, "other suitability protection" includes but is not limited to adopting earlier versions of the NAIC model suitability regulation, or developing legislation or regulations derived from other sources such as bulletins and administrative rulings. For the purpose of this study, we reviewed NAIC's model disclosure and suitability regulations, but did not review states' other disclosure or suitability protections.

[36] In prior work that was designed to provide insights for the development of a federal financial services regulatory framework, we highlighted the importance of, among other things, providing consistent consumer protections for similar financial products and services. See GAO, Financial Regulation: A Framework for Crafting and Assessing Proposals to Modernize the Outdated U.S. Financial Regulatory System, GAO-09-216 (Washington, D.C.: Jan. 8, 2009). In a report looking at regulation of the insurance industry, a function carried out by the states, we pointed out the importance of state regulation supporting the goals of this framework. See GAO, Insurance Reciprocity and Uniformity: NAIC and State Regulators Have Made Progress in Producer Licensing, Product Approval, and Market Conduct Regulation, but Challenges Remain, GAO-09-372 (Washington, D.C.: Apr. 6, 2009).

INDEX

A

B

C

D

E

F

G

N

O

P

T

U

V

W

Y